american exorcism

American
Exorcism

Expelling Demons in
the Land of Plenty

MICHAEL W. CUNEO

Doubleday
New York   London   Toronto
Sydney   Auckland

PUBLISHED BY DOUBLEDAY
a division of Random House, Inc.
1540 Broadway, New York, New York 10036

DOUBLEDAY and the portrayal of an anchor with a dolphin
are trademarks of Doubleday, a division of Random House, Inc.

Library of Congress Cataloging-in-Publication Data

Cuneo, Michael W.
American exorcism / Michael W. Cuneo. — 1st ed.
p. cm.
Includes bibliographical references and index.
1. Exorcism — United States. 2. Demoniac possession —
United States. 3. Exorcism — United States — Case studies.
4. Demoniac possession — United States — Case studies.
5. United States — Church history — 20th century. I. Title.
BV873.E8 C86 2001
265'.94'0973 — dc21
00-047439

ISBN 0-385-50176-5

September 2001

First Edition

1 3 5 7 9 10 8 6 4 2

Book design by Jennifer Ann Daddio

TO MARGARET

contents

Acknowledgments   *ix*

Introduction   *xi*

Part One
The Exorcist as Hero

1. The Blatty Factor   *3*
2. Malachi's Hostages   *14*

Part Two
Entrepreneurs of Exorcism

3. Demon-Busters   *27*
4. Demonic Breakdowns   *41*
5. The Priest-Exorcist as Hero—Revisited   *59*

Part Three
charismatic Deliverance ministry

6. Heartland Deliverance 73
7. Pentecostalism Joins the Mainstream 83
8. The Heyday of Charismatic Deliverance 96
9. Discerning Demons 111
10. Exorcism as Therapy 129

Part Four
The rough-and-ready school

11. The Hegewisch Shuffle 167
12. Carolina Blues 182

Part Five
The rise of Evangelical Deliverance

13. Satanic Conspiracies 195
14. On the Front 217

Part Six
roman catholic Exorcism

15. A Day at the Office 239
16. Official, Unofficial, Quasi-Official 257

Conclusion 270
Notes 283
Index 303

acknowledgments

I carried out part of the research for this book with the help of research grants from Fordham University and the Society for the Scientific Study of Religion. I did much of the writing during a thoroughly enjoyable semester as a visiting professor in the Department of Religious Studies at the University of Dayton. I am grateful to Terrence Tilley; Maureen Tilley; James Heft, S.M.; Sandra Yocum Mize; Joe Jacobs; Una Cadegan; and my other Dayton colleagues for their generosity and support. Bill Portier; Marvin Reznikoff; Jeffrey von Arx, S.J.; and Richard Cimino offered me advice and encouragement along the way, and Robert Wuthnow gave me an opportunity to present several of my case studies at his Friday-afternoon religion workshop at Princeton. I would like to thank everyone who agreed to speak with me about exorcism in the United States, and who sometimes invited me to sit in on actual exorcisms. Thanks also to my agent, Susan Gleason, and my editor at Doubleday, Andrew Corbin. Thanks most of all to Rebecca E. Cuneo and Shane D. Cuneo for reading the manuscript in various drafts and offering valuable suggestions for its improvement.

introduction

This is a book about exorcism in contemporary America. On the face of it, this might seem an improbable topic. Demon-expulsion in the land of suburban glitz and high-tech razzmatazz? Could there really be much here worth writing about?

Surprisingly, yes. Over the past several years I have discovered a side of America that I never knew existed. In the course of intensive and far-flung research, I have sat in on dozens of exorcisms—not just Roman Catholic exorcisms but a wide variety of Protestant ones also. I have met with hundreds of people, from various walks of life, who are convinced not only that demons exist but also that they routinely cause trouble in the lives of ordinary women and men.

Standing at the back of an auditorium in suburban Chicago, I have seen several hundred impeccably groomed, middle-class Americans writhing and shrieking and groaning (some simulating masturbation) while attempting to free themselves from demons of sexual perversity. At a drab medical complex on the outskirts of Boston, I have watched an avuncular physician exorcising spirits of guilt and self-hatred from one of his patients. At several conservative Protestant churches in the Midwest, I have observed people retching and cursing and flinging themselves violently to the floor while being delivered of entire squadrons of demons. (On one such occasion I have even been forced to intercede physically on behalf of a minister who was being tossed into the air and bounced off walls while trying to perform an exorcism on a 250-pound accountant.) I have received numerous invitations to undergo exorcism myself, once from two Episcopalians who wanted to shackle me to the support beams of a rural shed so that my demons would depart peaceably. I have observed people at high-toned suburban churches vomiting profusely into trash containers while being purged of their evil spirits. I have heard fabulous accounts (from apparently sincere and lucid people) of gyrating heads, levitating bodies, and navel-licking tongues. I have interviewed psychiatrists charged with the responsibility of evaluating suspected cases of demonic possession for the Roman Catholic Church in the United States. And, not least of all, I have personally encountered more varieties of Catholic exorcism — official Catholic exorcism, bootleg Catholic exorcism, you-name-it Catholic exorcism — than I ever imagined existed.

As unlikely as it may sound, exorcism is alive and well in contemporary America. It's a booming business — operating below radar perhaps, invisible to anyone not specifically on the lookout for it, but booming nevertheless. Untold numbers of Americans, many of them staunchly middle-class, the kind of people you might chat with at the supermarket checkout counter or bump into at the local mall, have undergone exorcisms of one kind or another, and many claim to have come out much the better for it.

It wasn't long ago, however, that almost nothing of this sort was going on in the United States. As recently as the late sixties, exorcism was all but dead and forgotten — a fading ghost long past its prime. It was rarely spoken of and even more rarely assumed to possess any practical significance. By the mid-seventies, however, the ghost had sprung miraculously back to life. Suddenly countless people were convinced that they themselves, or perhaps a loved one, were suffering from demonic affliction; and exorcism was in hot demand.

And what brought this about? A number of factors, but none more important, especially where Catholic exorcism is concerned, than the release of William Peter Blatty's *The Exorcist* and the publication of

Malachi Martin's demon-busting pulp classic *Hostage to the Devil.* As if by alchemy, the dramatic (and seductively grotesque) arrival of demons on the screen and the bestselling page resulted in demons rampaging through the bedrooms and workplaces of Middle America. The pop culture industry cast its spell, so to speak, and an obliging nation fell into line. New exorcism ministries were brought into being to deal with the sudden onslaught of demonism, and older ministries were rejuvenated and found themselves with more business than they could possibly handle.

In subsequent years, moreover, it was much the same story. With its incessant demon-mongering, the popular entertainment industry was sometimes responsible for directly stimulating the exorcism market during the 1980s and 1990s, and sometimes (rather more modestly) for fostering a cultural climate conducive to the performance of exorcisms. One way or another, whenever (and wherever) belief in demons and exorcism cropped up during these years, Hollywood and its accomplices in the culture-capitalism field were almost certain to be somewhere on the scene.

There's something else worth considering at the outset. In a sense the real curiosity isn't that exorcism is practiced in contemporary America, but that it isn't practiced far more widely. It would be difficult, after all, to imagine a better deal. Whatever one's personal problem—depression, anxiety, substance addiction, or even a runaway sexual appetite—there are exorcism ministries available today that will happily claim expertise for dealing with it. With the significant bonus, moreover, that one is not, for the most part, held personally responsible for the problem. Indwelling demons are mainly to blame, and getting rid of them is the key to moral and psychological redemption. Personal engineering through demon-expulsion: a bit messy perhaps, but relatively fast and cheap, and morally exculpatory. A thoroughly American arrangement.

And this is precisely the point. In addition to being influenced by the popular entertainment industry, the practice of exorcism in contemporary America is remarkably well suited to the therapeutic ethos of the prevailing culture. No less than any of the countless New Age nostrums or twelve-step recovery routines on the current scene, exorcism ministries offer their clients endless possibilities for personal transformation—the prospect of a thousand rebirths. With its promises of therapeutic well-being and rapid-fire emotional gratification, exorcism is oddly at home in the shopping-mall culture, the purchase-of-happiness culture, of turn-of-the-century America.

American Exorcism is based on my personal interviews with exorcists and their clients, and my firsthand observation of more than fifty exorcisms. All of the incidents recounted in the book are true. Due to their highly intimate nature, however, I have sometimes disguised real-life identities. The book has two interrelated objectives: to tell the story of real-life exorcism ministries in contemporary America and to investigate the ways in which various cultural forces have helped to inspire and sustain these ministries.

The book is not, I should emphasize, an exhaustive inventory of exorcism in contemporary America. There are entire schools of exorcism—Afro-Caribbean, New Age, Eastern Orthodox—to which I give little more than a passing glance. My primary concern is with exorcism as it's practiced among mainstream, predominantly middle-class Christians—the white-bread sector of American society, as it were. It's not the complete story, but it's more than enough.

The book, I might add, is a cultural commentary—no more, no less. I am concerned simply with assessing the cultural significance of exorcism-related beliefs and practices in the contemporary United States, *not* with passing judgment on their ultimate validity.

As stage-setters, Parts 1 and 2 show how the popular entertainment industry in the United States has helped stimulate the market for exorcism—especially (but not exclusively) Roman Catholic exorcism. Parts 3 through 5 present detailed case studies of exorcism ministries within the religious worlds, respectively, of the charismatic renewal movement, the extreme Protestant right, and Protestant evangelicalism, and they also examine how these ministries have been influenced

by therapeutic trends in the broader culture. Part 6 features case studies of both official and underground exorcisms in contemporary
American Catholicism. A short concluding chapter attempts to make
sense of all this in historical, psychological, and sociological terms.

A brief word, finally, about myself.

I saw *The Exorcist* at a movie theater in Toronto during my late
teens. I was fascinated and titillated and properly horrified, and then
I abruptly forgot all about it. This was purely the stuff of Hollywood
fantasy, I thought. Surely there was nothing in real life even remotely
approximating it. Years later, however—almost two decades later, in
fact—after having taken up a career in the academic study of religion,
I began to hear intriguing rumors. From people I ran into while re-
searching other projects, from an occasional friend or colleague, I
heard that exorcism was actually being practiced in the contemporary
United States, by Protestants as well as Catholics, and on a scale I
could scarcely imagine. For some time I ignored the rumors, but finally I decided to take the plunge.

For more than two years I tracked exorcism ministries across the
country. My research strategy was simple and straightforward: I was
determined to see exorcisms for myself and to speak personally with
the people involved. The results were more than I could have bargained for. No one I am aware of—absolutely no one—has gained
firsthand access to such a rich variety of exorcisms. If demons do in
fact exist, and if they're truly capable of afflicting people, I couldn't
have asked for richer opportunity to see them in action.

Part One

The
Exorcist as
Hero

1.

The Blatty Factor

The past three decades haven't been particularly kind to the Catholic priesthood in America. One would be hard-pressed to find another profession that has fallen harder or further from grace in so short a period of time. To begin with, there was the mad rush for the exits that took place during the late 1960s and early 1970s, as thousands of priests decided that being married, or sexually eligible, or almost anything else, was preferable to sticking it out in religious life. And then, for many of those who did try to stick it out, there was the frantic scramble for relevance. No longer confident in the legitimacy of a strictly priestly vocation, they became priest–social workers or priest-psychologists or priest-politicians—hyphenated men with sometimes conflicting allegiances to two separate worlds. And before long there was also the scandal. Endless scandal. Reports of priests engaging in secret (or not so secret) sexual affairs with female parishioners. Of priests cruising gay bars and adopting gay lifestyles. Priests sexually assaulting altar boys and then trying, sometimes with the connivance of their local bishops, to cover up their crimes. All things considered, the story hasn't been a happy one, and there's little indication matters stand to improve much in the near future.

It isn't easy, in all of this, to spell out what precisely has gone wrong. For starters, one could point to the Second Vatican Council, that great transformative event in the life of the modern Catholic Church that ran from 1962 to 1965. In calling for a détente between Catholicism and the modern world, and in bestowing full ecclesiastical blessing upon such straightforwardly secular pursuits as science and politics, the council made the priestly vocation seem somehow less prestigious and its benefits less clear-cut. What was the point, after all, of enduring the burdens of priestly celibacy and obedience when the secular world was now also acknowledged to be bristling with grace and redemptive possibility? The sexual revolution, which was in full bloom in the years following the council, and the more general cultural volatility of the late 1960s and early 1970s should also be counted as significant factors. In a cultural climate relentlessly hostile to traditional authority and to restraint of virtually any kind, the strictures of the priestly role increasingly came to be seen as not only unreasonable but also as downright bizarre.

As time went on, moreover, the growing volume of negative publicity concerning the priesthood became a significant factor in its own right. Endless talk of the priestly crisis—of defections and despair and dereliction—lowered priestly morale even further and made the ordained ministry seem increasingly less desirable, increasingly less feasible. And throughout all of this, of course, the Vatican steadfastly refused to renew (or to redefine) the priesthood by permitting the ordination of women and married men.

Throughout these tough times, needless to say, there have always been individual priests who have comported themselves with dignity and quietly heroic faith, administering the sacraments, tending the sick, consoling the grief-stricken, and sometimes challenging the pathology-inducing structures of the broader society. For the most part, however, their labors have been overshadowed by the distressed public image of the priestly profession as a whole. The priest as hero? Perhaps in another place and another time the image may have worked, but over the past thirty years in America it has more often been the priest as pious fraud, the priest as philanderer, the priest as yesterday's man—equivocating, beleaguered, and thoroughly redundant.

But not entirely. In American popular culture over the past thirty years or so, there is at least one area, one capacity, in which the Catholic priest has consistently been depicted in nothing less than heroic terms. This is an area, revealingly enough, that most liberal-minded Catholics find utterly distasteful and that the leadership of the American church would just as soon banish from public view. Indeed, it is highly doubtful that anything more than a smattering of priests themselves would care to be associated with it. The area is exorcism, and it is the priest-as-exorcist that has somehow managed, in defiance of all odds, to retain a heroic grip on the popular American imagination.

This clearly isn't the way things were supposed to work out. After the Second Vatican Council, one of the great hopes of Catholic liberals in America, including a good many priests, was that their church would finally succeed in throwing off its medieval trappings and become more fully engaged with the intellectual and cultural life of the modern world. In the newly relevant, streamlined, and culturally respectable Catholicism envisioned by liberals, there was hardly room for belief in the Virgin Mary or the saints, let alone spooky spirits and demons and exorcisms.

What Catholic liberals couldn't have anticipated, however, was the intervention of Hollywood and, more specifically, of a Hollywood-based writer named William Peter Blatty. Blatty's story, by this point, is well known. In August 1949, while still an undergraduate at Georgetown University, he came across an article in the *Washington Post* that described, in mesmerizing detail, an exorcism that had recently been carried out on a fourteen-year-old Mount Rainier boy. For some time prior to the exorcism, the article reported, the unidentified boy had been tormented by a battery of bizarre phenomena: There were scratchings and rappings on his bedroom walls, pieces of fruit and other objects were sent flying in his presence, and his bed mysteriously gyrated across the floor while he tried to sleep. The boy's family had initially sought help from a Protestant minister who was a self-professed student of the paranormal, but as the situation grew increasingly more desperate, they called on the Jesuit communities of Washington, D.C., and St. Louis for emergency assistance. With the Jesuits now on the scene, the boy was subjected to intensive medical and psychiatric examination at two Catholic hospitals and placed under round-the-clock observation. When a natural cure wasn't found for his affliction, however, and the bizarre symptoms threatened to rage completely out of control, it was decided to pursue a more drastic course of action. A Jesuit priest in his fifties was assigned to the case, and over the next several weeks (rotating between Washington and St. Louis) he performed more than twenty exorcisms on the boy. In all but the last of these, according to the *Post* article, "the boy broke into a violent tantrum of screaming, cursing and voicing of Latin phrases—a language he had never studied—whenever the priest reached those climactic points of the 27-page [exorcism] ritual in which he commanded the demon to depart."[1] It was the last of the exorcisms, after two nerve-jangling months, that finally did the trick. Following its completion, the strange symptoms disappeared entirely, and the boy was restored to full health.

Blatty was entranced. As a Jesuit-educated Catholic who had once entertained thoughts of joining the priesthood, he found the theological implications of the *Post* story fascinating. Here was tangible evidence (or so it seemed) of the supernatural at work in the capital city of the world's most advanced industrial nation. If the story were true, it meant that Catholicism still possessed relevance far beyond what almost anyone would have thought possible. As the years passed, moreover, and Blatty settled into a career as a writer, the story retained a hold on his imagination. He occasionally tracked down snatches of information on demonic possession and flirted with the idea of someday writing a novel on the topic. Finally, in 1969, he decided to take the plunge, and under the informal tutelage of Father Thomas Bermingham, a Jesuit priest and longtime friend from Blatty's high school

days in Brooklyn, he undertook a crash course in Catholic demonology.

Blatty wanted his novel to be rooted to an actual instance of demonic possession, and the 1949 Mount Rainier case seemed the most
obvious candidate.

W ith the help of his Jesuit connections he was able to locate the
priest who had presided over the 1949 exorcisms, and their
brief correspondence convinced him that something mind-numbingly
extraordinary truly had taken place in Washington and St. Louis
twenty years earlier. He also managed to obtain a copy of a diary that
had been kept by a second Jesuit who had assisted with the 1949 exorcisms. As a meticulous, blow-by-blow account of the entire two-
month-long procedure, the diary proved absolutely spellbinding. It
told of mysterious inflammations—or "brandings"—that sponta-
neously materialized on the fourteen-year-old boy's skin at various
points throughout the ordeal. The brandings sometimes appeared as
actual words, such as SPITE, and sometimes as pictorial representa-
tions, including (most terrifyingly) a hideous satanic visage. It told of
furniture shaking and crashing in the boy's presence and of one especially memorable incident in which a hospital nightstand levitated rapidly from floor to ceiling.[2] And most important of all, at least from
Blatty's perspective, it also told of the enormous spiritual fortitude that
was consistently demonstrated by the Jesuits entrusted with curing
the boy.

With this background in hand, and his studies in Catholic demonology fairly well advanced, Blatty went to work, and in 1971 he
published *The Exorcist,* his novelistic recasting of the 1949 Mount
Rainier possession case. And what a recasting! In Blatty's heavily fictionalized treatment, the fourteen-year-old working-class boy became
a twelve-year-old girl named Regan whose mother was a flamboyant
and hugely successful actress, the action was moved from the relatively unglamorous precincts of Mount Rainier and St. Louis to a

swanky townhouse in Georgetown, and the two Jesuit priests charged with performing the exorcism were both struck down in the line of duty.[3] And then there were Blatty's rather more lurid flourishes. During her possession spells, Regan spewed prodigious volumes of vomit (the boy in the original case seems to have shown a talent mainly for spitting), she violently masturbated with a crucifix, and, for particularly ghoulish effect, she occasionally rotated her head 180 degrees.

This mixture of fact and fancy, human tragedy and diabolic spectacle, proved immensely appealing, and *The Exorcist* rapidly rose to the top of the bestseller lists. One reason for its appeal, in all likelihood, was Blatty's talent for keeping his readers guessing. Was this really a case of demonic possession, or was Regan suffering instead from some mysterious (but ultimately explainable) psychological affliction? And if it was possession, who was the demon and what was the point of the whole ordeal?

In at least one crucial respect, however, there was no need for guessing. From their first appearance in the novel to their climactic deaths, it was clear that Blatty's two Jesuit exorcists were meant to be regarded, for all their human frailty, as mythically heroic figures. Father Damien Karras, the younger of the two, is a priest-psychiatrist plagued by doubt and misgiving. In his early forties, darkly handsome, and a former Golden Gloves boxer, Karras no longer feels assured of his priestly vocation, and he is guilt-ridden over his failure to provide more generously for his impoverished mother during her dying days. When, out of desperation, Regan's mother, Chris MacNeil, asks him to perform an exorcism on her daughter, Karras is initially nonplussed. As a thoroughly modern priest and Harvard-trained psychiatrist, he finds the very notion of demonic possession hopelessly benighted. As the reader expects all along, however, Karras eventually performs the exorcism anyway, and in the process he is brought into direct conflict with an otherworldly force of leering malevolence. In the battle with Regan's demon, Karras's psychiatric training and professional scruples count for nothing; all that matters, as he soon dis-

covers, is supernatural faith, priestly virtue, and the transcendent authority of his church.

Father Lancaster Merrin, a Jesuit-paleontologist and Karras's senior partner in the exorcism, is even more emphatically heroic in
stature.[4] Merrin is a longtime veteran of demonic trench warfare, and
when the detective who is investigating a possible homicide related to
Regan's possession spots him arriving on the scene, the reader feels an
almost palpable sense of relief and gratitude.

> From the cab stepped a tall old man. Black raincoat and hat
> and a battered valise. He paid the driver, then turned and stood
> motionless, staring at the house. The cab pulled away and rounded
> the corner of Thirty-sixth Street. [Detective] Kinderman quickly
> pulled out to follow. As he turned the corner, he noticed that the
> tall old man hadn't moved, but was standing under street-light
> glow, in mist, like a melancholy traveler frozen in time. The de-
> tective blinked his lights at the taxi.[5]

After quickly assessing the situation, Merrin sets the exorcism in
motion, and during a brief interlude outside Regan's bedroom he lends
Karras valuable insight into the dynamics of demonic possession. For
all of the torment experienced by the direct victim of possession, he
says, it is frequently friends and family and onlookers who are even
more acutely vulnerable. By virtue of their exposure to the grotesque,
sometimes bestial, transformations of the victim, they are at risk of losing faith not only in their own humanity but also in the very possibility of a loving, beneficent God. It is precisely this, Merrin says, the
temptation to doubt and despair, that constitutes the most insidious
component of possession, and all those involved in trying to help the
victim must do everything possible to avoid succumbing to it.[6]

In the end both Merrin and Karras succeed in warding off doubt
and despair—but not without enormous personal cost. Merrin is felled
by a fatal heart attack while valiantly attempting to expel Regan's demon; shortly afterward Karras offers himself to the demon as a sacri-

ficial substitute for Regan, and when the offer is taken, he hurls himself to certain death from Regan's bedroom window.

M elodramatic? Contrived? Heavy-handed? Undoubtedly so, but very rarely in recent decades have priests come across so well. And this was still only a warm-up. In the winter of 1973 *The Exorcist* was released as a movie under the same title, and Blatty's Jesuit exorcists proved every bit as commanding on film as they had in print. Not that this, by any stretch, was the exclusive reason for the movie's spectacular commercial success. With William Friedkin as director, and Blatty himself as producer and screenwriter, *The Exorcist* missed very few opportunities to shock and titillate. The crowds that lined up for hours at the nation's theaters to see it were treated to scenes in which Linda Blair, as the twelve-year-old Regan, sexually mutilates herself with a crucifix, levitates horrifically four feet above her bed, and verbally assails the anguished Karras with such zingers as "Your mother sucks cocks in hell!"

Behind all the grotesquerie and gruesome special effects, however, Blatty's theological message played loud and clear. As much as contemporary men and women might want to deny it, there was still a force of supernatural evil active in the world, and both science and reason were powerless against it. It was only through the transcendent authority of the Catholic Church that such evil could be effectively dealt with, and the special agents of the church in this regard were priest-exorcists. The priest was still potentially a heroic figure, in other words, but heroic first and foremost by virtue of his expressly supernatural faculties. It wasn't because they were men of science that Karras and Merrin were able to wage teeth-clenching battle against Regan's demon. In this primordial conflict between good and evil, professional or secular competency was of absolutely no consequence. Karras and Merrin became full-fledged heroes only when they entered the diabolic pit armed with nothing but faith and love and the mysterious powers conferred on them by priestly ordination.

While hardly an unqualified artistic triumph, *The Exorcist* was easily the most newsworthy film of its day. There were reports of people
fainting and vomiting during Regan's possession spells, there were accusations of blasphemy and obscenity, and, in the secular media especially, there were frequent cries of disgust and indignation. Vincent
Canby of the *Times* complained that the movie "treat[ed] diabolism
with the kind of dumb piety movie makers once lavished on the stories of saints," Jon Landau denounced it in *Rolling Stone* as "nothing
more than a religious porn film, the gaudiest piece of big budget
schlock this side of Cecil B. DeMille," and, in a remarkable display of
pique, *New Yorker* film critic Pauline Kael took American Catholics to
task for not being more offended: "Others can laugh it off as garbage,
but are American Catholics willing to see their faith turned into a horror show? Are they willing to accept *anything* just as long as their
Church comes out in a good light? Aren't those who accept this picture getting their heads screwed on backward?"[7]

American Catholics, in fact, were far from unanimous in their
assessment of *The Exorcist*. The U.S. Catholic Conference's Division
of Film and Broadcasting rated it as morally unobjectionable (with
the caveat that some Catholics might find certain scenes offensive
and confusing), and *Catholic News*, the official newspaper of the
Archdiocese of New York, described it as "a deeply spiritual film" and
applauded its "well-researched authenticity" and its characterization
of Karras and Merrin as "powerful, holy men." On the other side of
the ledger, two reviewers for the Jesuit-run *America* magazine decried
the movie as sordid and sensationalistic, and Father Donald Campion,
the magazine's editor, worried about the effect it might have on the impressionable psyches of the nation's moviegoing public.[8]

Campion, as it turns out, had legitimate cause for worry. In the
months that followed the movie's release, thousands of households
across America seemed to become infested all of a sudden with demonic presences, and Catholic rectories were besieged with calls from
people seeking exorcisms for themselves, for their loved ones, and
sometimes even for their pets. It's unlikely that anyone received more
requests for emergency assistance during this period than Father Tom

Bermingham and a Jesuit colleague named Father William O'Malley, both of whom played minor roles in the movie in addition to receiving screen credit as technical advisers to Blatty and Friedkin.

"Making the movie was strange enough, but the aftermath was completely bizarre," Bermingham told me during a recent interview at Fordham University, where he then lived in semiretirement. "I knew very little about exorcism and demonic possession prior to helping Blatty do research for his book and working on the movie, but when the movie came out, I found myself on the hot seat. People saw my face and my name on the screen, and they assumed I was the answer to their problems. For quite a while dozens of people were trying to contact me every week. And they weren't all Catholics. Some were Jewish, some Protestant, some agnostic, and they all believed that they themselves or someone close to them might be demonically possessed. These were truly desperate people, and I did my best to meet with as many of them as possible and discuss their problems. Of course, I approached these discussions with a great deal of skepticism. Demonic possession is an exceedingly rare phenomenon, and the church has always insisted that great caution be taken in evaluating individual cases. The rite of exorcism, in fact, is the only Catholic rite in which the officiating priest is advised to take an initial stance of incredulity. Rather than assuming possession straightaway and proceeding with an exorcism, the priest is supposed to rule out all other possibilities—from organic disorder to psychological pathology to outright fraud. Simply because someone tells you they're possessed doesn't mean they are; almost always, in fact, this is an indication that they're not. Of all the people who came to me, not one struck me as being genuinely possessed. I arranged psychological counseling for some people, but this was sometimes a big disappointment for them. They assumed, because of my association with the movie, that I'd be able to resolve their various difficulties with an exorcism. The funny thing is, I wouldn't have been able to do this even if they were possessed. I've never even participated in a genuine exorcism, and I certainly don't regard myself as qualified to perform one."[9]

Father William O'Malley has never been personally involved with a real-life exorcism either, but he, too, found himself in almost constant demand following the movie's release. "I was teaching at a Jesuit high school in Rochester at the time, and for a while the phone wouldn't stop ringing," he told me recently in New York City. "In the movie I played Father Bill Dyer, Damien Karras's cutesy and solicitous Jesuit friend, and many people seemed to assume from this that I must be some kind of world-class expert on exorcism. They called looking for an instant fix—pleading with me to expel their own demons, their kids' demons, even their cats' demons. It's not that I rule out the possibility of demonic possession. As the saying goes, 'There are more things in heaven and earth, Horatio, than are dreamt of in your philosophy.' But this movie seems to have set off some really strange vibrations."

Strange or not, the panjandrums of American popular culture certainly weren't about to let these vibrations go to waste, and for several years during the mid- to late seventies exorcism was a topic from which there seemed no escape. It was discussed ad nauseam on the talk-show circuit and in the daily press, and a string of mostly hapless films—including *Devil Times Five*, *The Possessed*, *Good Against Evil*, *Boogeyman*, and the redoubtable *Kung Fu Exorcist*—tried desperately to capitalize on demonism's newfound celebrity. The publishing industry, for its part, was hell-bent on keeping pace, and from 1974 to 1976 more than two dozen new exorcism-related titles—ranging from the deadly serious (*Diabolical Possession and Exorcism*, *The Case Against Possessions and Exorcisms*) to the splashy (*Driving Out the Devils*, *The Devil's Bride*) to the downright trashy (*The Story Behind "The Exorcist,"* *Exorcism: Fact, Not Fiction*)—made their way into the nation's bookstores.[10]

William Peter Blatty had obviously started something. It's unlikely even he knew exactly what it was.

2.

malachi's hostages

Despite all this lavish attention, exorcism's popular celebrity might very well have run its course by the late 1970s were it not for the efforts of a breakaway Jesuit and talented controversialist named Malachi Martin. Much like exorcism itself, Malachi Martin's story has sometimes seemed to defy all earthly logic. Born in County Kerry, Ireland, in 1921, and raised in an intensely Catholic and comfortably middle-class family, Martin joined the Jesuits at the age of eighteen and quickly distinguished himself as one of the order's rising young stars. He studied at Trinity College in Dublin, and then at Louvain, Hebrew University, and Oxford, and in the process earned doctorates in Semitic languages, archaeology, and Oriental history. After pronouncing his final Jesuit vows in 1960, he took a teaching position at the Vatican's Pontifical Biblical Institute and eventually made his way into Pope John XXIII's inner circle of advisers and confidants.

Somewhere along the line, however, something apparently went wrong. In June 1964 Martin resigned his position at the Pontifical Institute, and eight months later he asked to be released from the Society of Jesus. He was granted provisional release in May 1965, and under the terms of an agreement that was approved by Pope Paul

VI on June 30, 1965, he was dispensed from his priestly vows of poverty and obedience (but not, significantly, from the vow of celibacy) and returned to the lay state. Martin left Rome in July 1965, and after a brief sojourn in Paris he moved to New York City, where he drove a cab and worked in an East Side doughnut shop before settling into a new career as a writer of bestselling religious potboilers.

Even today, more than thirty years afterward, there is an aura of mystery surrounding Malachi Martin's abrupt departure from the Jesuits. According to the most popular account (which is also the one usually favored by Martin himself), he felt morally compelled to leave the priesthood in protest over the new, and decidedly more liberal, direction the Catholic Church was taking as a result of the Second Vatican Council. Unfortunately, however, this stricken-soldier-of-conscience version of events hasn't always squared with the facts. Far from being a tormented conservative during his years in Rome, Martin was actually an outspoken theological liberal, and while the council was in full swing, he was closely (and publicly) aligned with such leading liberal lights as Monsignor George Higgins and the eminent American Jesuit John Courtney Murray. There is fairly reliable evidence, moreover, that his sudden shift in careers may have been precipitated by romantic intrigue. In 1964, while teaching theology part-time at Loyola University of Chicago's Rome Center, Martin apparently became intimately involved with the wife of Robert Blair Kaiser, a former Jesuit scholastic from California who was serving as *Time*'s bureau chief in Rome. The romance (if such it was) doesn't seem to have lasted for more than a year or so, but this was precisely the time during which Martin negotiated his break with the Society of Jesus.[1]

None of this, of course, would matter much to the story here if Malachi Martin hadn't gone on to play an immensely important role in keeping the flame of exorcism alive in popular American culture. In 1976, a decade after leaving Rome and with two bestsellers already under his belt, Martin published an astonishing book called *Hostage to the Devil*, which purported, in the words of its subtitle, to document "the possession and exorcism of five living Americans." Up to this point it had been widely assumed that Catholic exorcism was an extraordinarily rare procedure that was undertaken by the church only as a last, desperate resort. (Even William Peter Blatty, for all his resourcefulness, had been forced to dredge up an exorcism that was more than two decades old to use as raw material for his landmark novel.) But now here was Malachi Martin writing as if demonic possession and exorcism were almost everyday occurrences. And, what's more, surprisingly accessible occurrences as well. In addition to being extremely rare, exorcism was supposed to be the most deeply secret and closely guarded of all Catholic rituals, and uncovering the intimate details behind any particular exorcism was, by all accounts, a next-to-impossible task. But not apparently for Malachi Martin. In *Hostage to the Devil* he was the man-behind-the-diabolic-scenes—interviewing victims of possession; reconstructing, in delicious detail, extensive case histories of actual exorcisms; and swapping war stories with real-life priest-practitioners. Somehow, it seemed, Martin had broken the seal of secrecy and gained untrammeled access to hitherto forbidden territory. And—here's the clincher—his readers were expected to take all of this on trust alone. In an unusual author's caveat that appeared on the copyright page of *Hostage to the Devil,* Martin wrote:

> All of the men and women involved in the five cases reported here are known to me personally; they have given their fullest cooperation on the condition that their identities and those of their families and friends not be revealed. This stricture has, of necessity, been extended to the publisher, who has therefore not verified the book's contents other than the author's personal assurance, and the publisher's own verification from independent sources that exorcisms have been and continue to be performed currently in the United States.[2]

Events may have occurred precisely as Malachi Martin describes them in *Hostage,* but his track record hardly inspires confidence. Where the details of his personal life are concerned, as we've seen,

Martin has been notoriously slippery and disingenuous, and the same is no less true of his literary life. In virtually all of his writings since the publication of *Hostage* in 1976, Martin has demonstrated a remarkable talent for fabrication and embellishment—for converting, by literary sleight-of-hand, half-truths and innuendo into immutable facts of history. Over the years, in fact, he has become American Catholicism's foremost connoisseur of conspiracy, and in such heavy-breathing books as *The Final Conclave* (1978), *The Jesuits* (1987), and *The Keys of This Blood* (1990), he has tantalized his readers with tale after tale of betrayal and intrigue. Clandestine deal-making between Roman cardinals and secular heads of state, communistic and Masonic cabals operating within the highest reaches of the Vatican, traitorous Jesuits plotting the overthrow of Catholic tradition—in Malachi Martin's world, the conspiratorial possibilities are endless. And so, too, apparently, are his capacities for acquiring insider's knowledge. Wherever there are top-secret, backroom negotiations involving the very survival of Western civilization and the Catholic Church, Martin is bound to be lurking nearby, capturing every arched eyebrow, every slurred syllable and pregnant pause. Again, some of what Martin reports may in fact be true, or at least partly true, but some as well seems the product of outright fantasy. For the most part his writings occupy a twilight zone where fact bleeds into fiction, history into myth, and where trying to sort out the differences is a tortuous business.[3]

Hostage to the Devil may not be quite as reliable as Malachi Martin would have us believe, but even today it makes for fascinating reading. Marianne, the pseudonymous subject of Martin's first case study, is a graduate student in physics at New York University when she is approached one day in Washington Square Park by a demonic presence who invites her to enter into "a marriage with nothingness." Marianne accepts the invitation, and over the next several years she falls deeper and deeper into a state of moral blankness and sexual debauchery. She repudiates her family and urinates over the parcels of food and clothing they deliver to her apartment, she breaks into paroxysms of disgust whenever brought into contact with holy pictures or other symbolic reminders of her Catholic childhood, and she dedicates herself to finding a sexual partner with whom she can experience anal intercourse "to its fullest extent."

Martin's second subject, a youthful and charismatic ex-priest named Jonathan, follows a rather more cerebral pathway into demonic drudgery. While still a seminarian, Jonathan becomes enamored with the evolutionary theology of the Jesuit paleontologist-philosopher Teilhard de Chardin, and this eventually leads him to a position of radical skepticism. He rejects the transcendent dimension of Catholic doctrine and ritual, and several years after his ordination he abandons Catholicism altogether and starts up a sort of mystical-therapeutic congregation of his own in Lower Manhattan. Jonathan's personal fortunes deteriorate badly following his break with the church, however, and they finally hit rock bottom when he tries to drown the bride at a wedding he is presiding over on the New England seashore.

Carl's fall from grace follows a trajectory roughly similar to Jonathan's. During his childhood Carl discovers that he possesses a marvelous array of psychic gifts, including the powers of telepathy and telekinesis. After graduating college with a degree in physics, he decides to dedicate himself to an intensive investigation of alternative states of consciousness. As the years pass, he builds up an impressive professional résumé and world-class reputation in the field of parapsychology, but his research eventually takes him into dangerous and uncharted territory. Using himself as a human guinea pig, Carl undertakes increasingly bizarre experiments in astral travel and reincarnation, and during one particularly ill-advised experiment in the small Italian village of Aquileia he brings himself to the brink of self-annihilation.

In some respects Martin's fourth case study, which features a San Francisco–based disk jockey named Jamsie, is the spookiest of all. While in his early thirties Jamsie finds himself inexplicably hooked up with a minor demon (or "familiar spirit"), which calls itself Uncle Ponto. In the demonic scheme of things Uncle Ponto is strictly bargain basement: With his comically misshapen head, his slapstick antics, and his groveling demeanor, he usually comes across as some kind of castoff from an old Three Stooges short. Harmless fun is the last thing Ponto is interested in, however, and his pratfalls, cajoling, and incessant harassment eventually twist Jamsie into knots.

And then, finally, there's Rita, a transsexual of Lutheran-Jewish background whose story gives *Hostage* several of its most memorably lurid moments. Following her sex-change operation (which she undergoes as part of a lifelong quest for a state of perfect androgyny), Rita is sexually ravaged by a Church of Satan minister named Father Samson during a Black Mass orgy and then subjected to serial cunnilingus by Father Samson's entire congregation. Although this counts as the most satisfying sexual experience of Rita's life, it paves the way for her eventual enslavement to demonic forces.

Of course, the real heroes of these sordid sagas aren't the victims of possession themselves but rather the priest-exorcists who come to their rescue. And the rescuing, as might be expected, is seldom easy. While in the line of duty, Malachi Martin's exorcists are taunted mercilessly by foul-mouthed demons for their past sexual indiscretions, excoriated for their Catholic faith, and sometimes subjected to piercing physical assault. None of this stops them from persevering until the very end, but they invariably emerge from their ordeals battered and bruised—shell-shocked warriors who have put everything on the line in the service of Catholic faith.

In addition to shocking and dazzling his readers, Malachi Martin is concerned in *Hostage* with spelling out a systematic phenomenology of both possession and exorcism—a sort of stage-by-stage plotting of a typical voyage into and out of living hell. To begin with, there is the *entry,* the point at which an evil spirit gains access to an individual, quite often with his or her tacit consent. This is followed by a stage of *erroneous judgments* on the part of the afflicted individual in matters of vital spiritual importance, and then by a *voluntary yielding of control* to the demonic presence. If the afflicted individual continues to cooperate with the presence, the process may culminate in a stage of *complete* or *perfect* possession. In Rita's case, for example, the demonic point of entry was her desire during adolescence (while she was still physically male) to cultivate fully both the feminine and masculine sides of her personality. This led over time to her denying the spiritual and biological importance of male-female sexual differences, and she succumbed almost entirely to her indwelling demon in the course of undergoing her sex-change (or sex-adjustment) therapy. Following her participation in Father Samson's Black Mass orgy, Rita seemed well on the way to a state of complete possession.

The rite of exorcism itself, according to Martin, is also a process consisting of several more or less distinct stages. At the outset the priest-exorcist is forced to contend with the *pretense,* a baffling (and sometimes protracted) stage in which the demonic presence attempts to disguise its true identity and intentions. The *breakpoint* occurs when the demon abandons subterfuge and begins to speak in its own voice; and during the next stage—what Martin refers to as the *clash*—the exorcist and demon become locked in a harrowing contest of wills for the soul of the possessed. Finally, if everything goes according to plan, the process concludes with the *expulsion* of the demonic presence.[4]

Although *Hostage* wasted little time working its way onto the bestseller lists, its early reviews were by no means uniformly positive. Francine du Plessix Gray pilloried it in the *Times* as "dangerously obscurantist" and "sensationalistic," while Peter Prescott of *Newsweek* wondered how anything so deliciously entertaining could also be so frustratingly opaque. The liberal Catholic weekly *Commonweal* was even harsher in its judgment, suggesting that Martin's tales of "Gothic evil" and "hero-priests on spiritual *kamikaze* mission[s]" were entirely unworthy of serious attention. And writing in *National Review,* Father John Nicola, who had served alongside the Jesuits Thomas Bermingham and William O'Malley as a technical adviser to William Peter Blatty during the filming of *The Exorcist,* sounded a note of cautionary skepticism. For all its claims to privileged insider's knowledge, Nicola observed, *Hostage* was actually far less realistic in its depiction of diabolic possession than was Blatty's movie. The inference here was clear: Were these real exorcisms that Martin was writing about or rather figments of his imagination?[5]

Even today Father Nicola's skepticism isn't easily shrugged off. In addition to his cinematic credentials, Nicola is a longtime student of the demonic, and throughout the 1970s and 1980s he served as a principal investigator for the American Catholic bishops into suspected cases of diabolic possession. In very few of these cases, Nicola told me during a recent interview at his home in Pinehurst, North Carolina, were there sufficient grounds for proceeding with an exorcism. "As you know, the Catholic Church is very cautious concerning these matters," he said. "First of all, we want to try to account for phenomena using natural causality—psychiatry, neurology, parapsychology, and so forth. If we find that we're dealing with something that doesn't seem fully explainable by natural causality, then we might move to a consideration of supernatural causality. But this is very rare. Over a twenty- to twenty-five-year period I was asked by various bishops to examine about twenty cases of alleged possession, and in only two of these were exorcisms actually performed. . . . I'm not saying that Malachi Martin invented his case studies, but if they're true, it means that there were more exorcisms taking place in the United States during the 1970s than I was certainly ever aware of."

And more also, it might be added, than Father Benedict Groeschel was ever aware of. During the 1970s and 1980s Groeschel was widely regarded as one of American Catholicism's foremost experts on the demonic. A Franciscan priest, dedicated student of the paranormal, and holder of a Columbia doctorate in psychology, Groeschel was the man Catholic officials in the New York City area, where he was based, most often turned to whenever they were confronted with strange and apparently inexplicable behavior. By the early eighties, in fact, it was widely rumored that Groeschel was the official exorcist of the Archdiocese of New York and quite possibly the most prolific Catholic exorcist in all of America. The rumors, however, were considerably wide of the mark. As it turns out, there was no official exorcist in the New York Archdiocese (or virtually any other American Catholic diocese, for that matter) during the seventies and eighties, and Father Groeschel was never personally involved with anything that he would regard as a bona fide case of demonic possession. To this day, in fact, he seriously doubts that he has ever been in the vicinity of such a case.

In the summer of 1996 I met with Groeschel for the first time at Trinity Retreat, a center for prayer and reflection he established in 1973 in the upscale Westchester community of Larchmont. With his white beard, gray Franciscan tunic, and sharp wit, he struck an impressive, almost prophetic pose—precisely the sort of man you'd want in your corner when the supernatural chips were down. I asked Groeschel why so many people still believed that he had once served (and perhaps still did serve) as an official exorcist of the Catholic Church.

"These stories have followed me around for years now, and I attribute a lot of it to the administrative incompetence of the New York Archdiocese," he said. "As far as I know, there hadn't been an official exorcist in New York since the end of the Second Vatican Council, but bizarre cases seemingly involving the demonic still cropped up from time to time. The archdiocese didn't really know what to do about them, so they usually referred them to me."

And how were these cases dealt with?

"You know, despite my reputation, I don't regard myself as a full-fledged expert in demonic affairs, and when cases were referred to me"—there were a total of six over the years, he later told me—"I usually sought the help of a laywoman in the archdiocese who possessed a gift for discerning spirits. In her view, and also mine, none of the people I brought to her were victims of possession; none of them, in other words, were in need of formal exorcism. But this doesn't mean that they weren't being afflicted or oppressed in various ways by demonic presences. Demonic oppression is much less serious than full-scale possession, and it can usually be dealt with by what we refer to as a simple prayer of deliverance. The laywoman I was working with was very experienced with deliverance, and the cases we were involved with usually had a happy outcome."

And what did Groeschel make of Malachi Martin's intimately detailed accounts of full-scale possession in *Hostage to the Devil*?

"This is very baffling to me," he said. "Several of the exorcisms that Martin reports were supposed to have taken place in the New York area, and I'd like to think I was in a position to have been informed — or at least to have heard — of any exorcisms in the vicinity. But I heard nothing, and I know of no one who has been able to corroborate Malachi Martin's case studies. I'm not telling you that he faked them, but they certainly are a mystery."

Some weeks later, in an effort to get to the bottom of the mystery, I spent several hours with Malachi Martin in his spacious apartment on Manhattan's Upper East Side. For someone who has earned a lucrative living as a scourge of theological and cultural modernism, Martin seemed remarkably gracious and accommodating — only too eager to please. Small and fine-featured, with a vaguely leprechaunish charm, he spoke of his childhood in Ireland, his years as a Jesuit, and his literary life in New York. He told me that as part of his laicization agreement with Pope Paul VI in 1964, he wasn't permitted to function publicly as a priest, but he still said Mass privately in his apartment every morning ("but only the Tridentine Mass; the new Mass is invalid, an utter travesty of faith").

Martin also told me that he was perplexed, and more than a little annoyed, by the swirl of rumors surrounding his personal life. "Look, I've had three heart operations, recently open-heart surgery, and I'm at the point where I'd like to put some of these stories to rest," he said. "I've been accused of everything; speculation on my life is a veritable cottage industry. I'm a lecher, a wife-stealer, and a spy; I'm secretly married with children; I've sexually abused little girls — it's all nothing but fancy."

And what of the suspicions, I asked, that the exorcisms reported in *Hostage to the Devil* were also nothing but fancy?

"Absolutely nothing that I report in *Hostage* is exaggerated," Martin replied, not seeming in the least fazed. "If truth be told, I actually had personal knowledge of eleven exorcisms when I wrote

Hostage, but I couldn't include all of them because this would have made the book too long. And here's something that I don't mention in the book and that very few people realize: I was personally involved with all of these exorcisms as an assistant, and in three of the cases — which aren't included in the book — I was forced to take over from the exorcist when he wasn't able to carry on because of the ferocity of the diabolic attack against him. You can appreciate that I wouldn't relish doing anything like this again, but — thanks be to God — everything turned out for the best."

But wasn't it odd that these exorcisms were unknown to the Catholic Church's own experts in the field? I asked.

"It is difficult for me to comment on this," Martin said. "The exorcisms were known to me, and they were known to the subjects who were involved with them — and this is enough. I can't violate my obligation of confidentiality to these subjects. And, what's more, I have a drawer filled with privacy agreements that I signed with the subjects' lawyers. I will, however, tell you this: The first exorcism that I participated in took place in Cairo prior to my laicization, and then in 1972 — by this time I was well established in New York — I received a call from a good friend named Father Peter. Let's say that Father Peter was a bit of a maverick priest, and he was performing an exorcism in the Bronx for which he may or may not have had official permission. His assistant had collapsed during the ordeal, he needed my help, and so naturally I went. After this I received other calls from priests requesting my help at exorcisms, and I thought it my duty to do everything I could. Did these exorcisms have the official blessing of the Catholic Church? In my view this is beside the point. When someone is suffering from diabolic possession, you're required as a Christian to do everything you can to help them. Without exception the priests who had taken it upon themselves to perform these exorcisms were the bravest and most selfless men I've ever met. And I'll tell you something else: There were far more exorcisms taking place during these years than the Catholic Church's so-called experts ever realized."[6]

Part Two

Entrepreneurs of Exorcism

3.

Demon-Busters

On this point at least Malachi Martin seems on firm ground: During the 1970s and 1980s there were in fact more exorcisms taking place in the United States than the institutional Catholic Church was fully aware of. The publication of Blatty's novel in 1971, and the release of his film two years later, had stimulated an unprecedented demand for Catholic exorcisms, but the chances of procuring one through official Catholic channels were exceedingly slim. Relatively few bishops believed in the possibility of diabolic possession, and no more than two or three dioceses in the entire country had bona fide priest-exorcists at their disposal.

There was, however, a somewhat greater chance of obtaining an exorcism through unofficial channels. Beginning in the early seventies a small number of maverick priests around the country (including, quite possibly, Malachi Martin's supposed friend Father Peter) attempted to respond to the burgeoning market for Catholic exorcisms by going into business on their own. The great majority of these priests seem to have inhabited the right-wing fringes of American Catholicism. Distressed by the rapid modernization of the church that was taking place after the Second Vatican Council, and especially by the declining fortunes of the traditional priesthood, they derived a

perverse satisfaction from the dramatically increased reports of diabolic possession that had resulted from Blatty's novel and film. Here
was startling evidence, in their view, that demonic evil was still a potent force in the contemporary world, and it was the traditionally
faithful priest—not the priest as man-about-town or the priest as
secular professional—who was uniquely qualified to confront it
head-on.

For the most part the exorcisms performed by these maverick
priests were clandestine, surreptitious affairs, undertaken without the
approval of the institutional Catholic Church and without the rigorous
psychiatric screening that the church required. Anyone who desperately wanted an exorcism, and who succeeded in making contact with
one of these priests, stood a good chance of being taken care of—free
of charge, and usually within just a matter of weeks. The difficult
trick, however, was in making contact: Because these underground
exorcisms weren't openly advertised, and because the priests responsible for performing them generally preferred to conduct their business under the cloak of anonymity, prospective clients usually had no
idea where to turn for help. Despite the efforts of maverick priests
such as Father Peter, in other words, the popular demand for exorcisms that had been incited by Blatty's novel and film (and that was
heightened even further by the publication of *Hostage to the Devil* in
1976) remained mostly unfulfilled.

As the years passed, however, there were several notable efforts at
closing the gap between the demand for exorcisms and their availability. The first of these, quite predictably, arose not from the Catholic
Church itself but rather from the popular entertainment industry—
and, more specifically, from a husband-and-wife team with cheesy
B-movie credentials, named Ed and Lorraine Warren. For more than
two decades before either *The Exorcist* or *Hostage* had even seen the
light of day, the Warrens were significant operators in America's occult underworld. As self-styled psychic sleuths, they toured the country for several months each year, investigating reports of hauntings
and demonic infestation, always on the lookout for the case that might
propel them to broader fame. Their breakthrough finally came in early

1976, when they were invited to investigate some strange phenomena that were apparently taking place in Amityville, Long Island.

On December 18, 1975, George and Kathleen Lutz and their three children had moved into a large colonial house at 112 Ocean Avenue in Amityville—the same house where twenty-four-year-old Ronald DeFeo, just a year earlier, had methodically shot to death his parents and four younger siblings. Less than a month later, however, the Lutzes fled their new home, leaving their belongings behind and insisting that they'd never return. In a series of media interviews the Lutzes claimed that 112 Ocean Avenue had turned out to be a chamber of horrors: During their brief occupancy they were assailed by strange knockings, rancid odors, and precipitous drops in room temperature; by slime oozing through the walls and flies swarming on a bedroom window in the freezing cold; and, most terrifying of all, by ghastly spiritual entities, including one with distinctive porcine features, prowling the property in the dead of night.

This was the stuff of tabloid heaven, and within weeks of the Lutzes' departure, 112 Ocean Avenue was besieged by reporters, curiosity-seekers, and a wide assortment of psychic researchers. The Warrens were among the first on the scene, and after pronouncing the house authentically cursed, they conducted a séance on the premises that was televised on the evening news in the New York metropolitan area. Not all self-described psychics were as convinced as the Warrens, however, and one in particular—a native New Yorker named Stephen Kaplan—embarked on a personal crusade to prove that the entire business was nothing more than an elaborate hoax.[1]

Hoax or not, the show was off and running, and neither the Lutzes nor the Warrens were averse to making the most of it. In 1977 *The Amityville Horror,* a docu-schlock novel written by a New York journalist named Jay Anson, became a monster publishing hit, and two years later Hollywood weighed in with a blockbuster film of the same title, starring James Brolin and Margot Kidder as George and Kathleen Lutz. The Lutzes made a small fortune from the rights to their story and moved to California, and the Warrens suddenly found themselves the hottest property on America's psychic scene. The de-

mand for their investigative services skyrocketed; they were interviewed on national television by Mike Douglas, David Susskind, and
Leonard Nimoy; and their adventures in the occult netherworld were
chronicled in a steamy paperback entitled *The Demonologist*.[2]

In *The Demonologist*, and also in many of their media appearances,
the Warrens painted a lurid picture. Amityville, they insisted, was just
the tip of the iceberg. Beneath its smooth suburban surface, middle-
class America was churning with demonic activity, and thousands of
otherwise ordinary people were trapped in conflicts that neither they
nor virtually anyone else fully understood. Some of these people, such
as the Lutzes, had inadvertently stumbled across demonic forces in
their homes or workplaces, and some had unwittingly brought trouble
upon themselves by experimenting with Ouija boards and other cultic
paraphernalia, but nearly all of them, regardless of circumstance, were
suffering deeply—and suffering alone. The medical profession was almost entirely unreceptive to their plight, their friends and neighbors
were confused and sometimes hostile, and the Roman Catholic
Church—the one institution that clearly should have known better—
very rarely answered their cries for help.

Nevertheless, the Warrens claimed, there was still cause for hope.
Despite the unresponsiveness of the institutional Catholic Church,
there were individual priests willing to perform exorcisms without official church approval, and all that was needed was some reliable way
of bringing these maverick priests into contact with people on the demonic skids. The Warrens themselves were only too happy to help out
in this regard, and by the late seventies the nation's most celebrated
ghostbusters had also become its leading brokers of exorcism-related
services.

The deal here was fairly straightforward. Upon being alerted, either through the media or through their network of informants, of
some particularly arresting case of demonic activity, the Warrens
would offer to conduct a preliminary investigation, free of charge, and
if the case struck them as genuine—and also beyond the range of their
own expertise—they would turn it over to a maverick priest-exorcist
for full treatment. As the years passed, dozens of people availed them-

selves of the Warrens' services, and several of their more notable cases were immortalized in *Ghost Hunters*, a 1989 potboiler that was subtitled, without undue modesty, "True Stories from the World's Most Famous Demonologists."

Cindy McBain, the pseudonymous subject of one of these True Stories, was much like any other teenager in her small New England community, hanging out at the local mall and gossiping over Diet Cokes and grilled cheese sandwiches, until one day she purchased a Ouija board at her neighborhood antique shop. After several weeks of experimenting with the board, the changes set in. Cindy stopped eating and flew into frequent rages, she became depressed and antisocial, her voice took on an unfamiliar and menacing tone, and sounds of sexual ecstasy emanated from her bedroom several times daily. Cindy's alarmed parents took her for psychiatric counseling, but when her condition continued to worsen, they put in an emergency call to the Warrens. Almost immediately the Warrens determined that Cindy had been inhabited by a minor demon as a result of her flirtations with the Ouija board, and they arranged for a visiting priest from Nigeria named Father Michael Elemi to perform an exorcism. Father Elemi carried out his duties courageously, but the exorcism (it seems) wasn't entirely successful. Writing in *Ghost Hunters* several years afterward, the Warrens reported that "Cindy, now a young woman, leads a somewhat normal life—but she is always subject to what her doctor calls 'attacks.' He calls it mental illness. But we know better."[3]

And then there was the Smurl family of West Pittston, Pennsylvania, whose sorry tale, besides being featured in *Ghost Hunters*, was given full-length treatment in a 1988 book, *The Haunted*, that was written by the Warrens with journalist Robert Curran, and also, three years later, in a Fox television movie of the same title. Several years after moving into a turn-of-the-century duplex in the working-class town of West Pittston, Jack and Janet Smurl and their three daughters came to the realization that they weren't alone. Talon marks mysteriously appeared on their bathroom sink and tub, ghoulish apparitions materialized out of thin air and then vanished just as suddenly, and strange poundings echoed throughout the house at all hours. The Warrens arrived on the scene with their infrared cameras and other ghostbusting equipment, and after concluding that the Smurl home was demonically infested, they turned the case over to a Connecticut-based priest-exorcist named Father Robert McKenna. This, however, only seemed to inflame the home's resident demons even further. Over the next several weeks Jack Smurl was raped by a succubus (or female demon), Janet was sexually attacked by an incubus (or male demon) in her bedroom, and their oldest daughter, Dawn, was harassed while taking a shower. The fearless Father McKenna performed two separate exorcisms during this period, without appreciable effect, and then Jack, as recounted by the Warrens and Robert Curran in a passage that hovers undecidedly between Gothic horror and Harlequin Romance, was ravished a second time by a succubus while his wife Janet slept beside him.

> A voluptuous young woman was on top of Jack, riding him in the position of sexual domination. Despite her beauty and the pleasure she was obviously enjoying, her eyes remained a shocking and sickly neon green.
>
> Next to him, Janet slept. Jack knew that she was in a deep psychic sleep.
>
> Despite his prayers, the succubus would not be contained. Still in the form of the beautiful young woman whose alabaster nakedness was only complemented by the reddish glow of the rising sun, the succubus plundered Jack sexually, sinking down and then moving up on him several times.
>
> He exhorted the demon to be gone but he found that he was unable to move or speak.
>
> And the succubus continued, mounting him once more, hair flying wildly, neon green eyes growing larger and more lurid as its mouth ran with the drool of satisfaction.
>
> The curious thing was that for all the movement—and the succubus put on a dazzling show, full of tricks—Jack felt no sexual sensation at all.
>
> He lay there and simply watched the demon perform.

And then it was over.

One moment he had been the pawn of Satan himself, and now he lay covered with a gelatinous, sticky mess, the same stuff the night hag had left on him when it had reached a climax during its first attack.[4]

Despite all this demonical thrusting and heaving, the institutional Catholic Church was highly reluctant to lend the Warrens and Father McKenna a helping hand. From the very beginning, officials of the local Catholic diocese of Scranton seemed only too eager to dismiss the entire business as utter nonsense, and when the diocese's own investigator, a Monsignor Eugene Clark, finally agreed to spend a night at the Smurl house, he observed absolutely nothing out of the ordinary. In their cunning, the household's demons had apparently decided to take the night off. They returned with a vengeance following Monsignor Clark's departure, however, and the Smurls were eventually forced to abandon their home and start anew someplace else.

And so it goes—in case after lubricious case in *Ghost Hunters* and the Warrens' other works, demons arise seemingly out of nowhere, terrorizing their hapless victims at work and at home, fracturing families, causing emotional and carnal distress, and, in at least one spectacular case (which also became the subject of a made-for-television movie), actually going so far as to provoke murder.[5] The Warrens and their roving band of priest-exorcists always do their best to restore a sense of peace to their clients' lives, but at almost every turn they are hampered by the spiritual obtuseness of the broader society—including (most maddening of all) the institutional Catholic Church.

It is tempting, in all of this, to dismiss the Warrens as mere charlatans—occultic scam artists trading off the gullibility of America's book-buying and moviegoing publics. Indeed, when I met with them for the first time in the fall of 1996 at their rural Connecticut home— an unpretentious frame house whose interior exudes an immensely appealing, lived-in warmth — I was half expecting them to let me in on the secret with some subtle nudging and winking. Not only was there no nudging and winking, the Warrens gave every indication of being completely sincere in their beliefs and mission. (To some extent, of course, this apparent sincerity may simply have been a performative necessity, a well-oiled occupational prop, but it also seemed to me to run considerably deeper than this.)

Lorraine Warren, tall and elegant and almost preternaturally charming, told me that she and her husband were just as much in demand today as ever before. "People are contacting us all the time," she said. "There are so many people out there who are suffering, and there's just no way we can answer all of their cries for help. If the Catholic Church would only do something to help these people out, things would be so much easier. . . . You know, Ed and myself are very strong Catholics, and we hate to say anything negative about our church, but the lack of sensitivity of the bishops and most priests to the torments that people are suffering because of demonic affliction is really quite shocking. The Catholic Church has turned its back on the whole problem, and this means that Ed and myself have been far busier than we'd want to be. And, you know, even though we're both in our seventies now, we have no intention of retiring. I certainly don't plan on retiring. I have no idea what I'd do with myself."

After twenty minutes or so, Ed Warren emerged from his basement workshop, where he had been sorting through slides for a lecture he and Lorraine were scheduled to give later the same evening. Thickset and brown-haired, with heavy-lidded eyes and a gruffly pleasant demeanor, Ed gave me a brief rundown of the couple's typical operating procedure. Lorraine, he said, was a gifted clairvoyant and light-trance medium, and in any given setting she was usually able to determine whether or not evil spirits were present. His own responsibilities, Ed told me, were rather more prosaic: In addition to interviewing all of the principals involved in a suspected case of demonic affliction, he sometimes attempted to provoke the evil spirits into revealing themselves by sprinkling holy water and invoking the name of Jesus Christ. Once this was accomplished, he and Lorraine were usually in a position to assess whether the situation was serious enough to warrant bringing in a priest-exorcist for full-scale treatment.

I asked Ed if he could tell me something more about the priest-exorcists with whom he and Lorraine have worked for the past twenty years.

"There have been quite a few, and three in particular, who have helped us out regularly," he said. "I should tell you that we're talking about underground priests here. Some of them aren't really part of the official Catholic Church in the United States any longer, but those who still are have had to be very secretive. If they went to their bishop to get an exorcism sanctioned, they'd be laughed out of the chancery and then shipped out to the boondocks as punishment. . . . The underground priest-exorcists have been tremendously helpful to us, but the bishops and the official church haven't lifted a finger to help. Most bishops even refuse to acknowledge the possibility of demonic possession. And do you want to hear a terrific irony? Once the bishop of Worcester, Massachusetts, phoned us and asked if we could recommend an exorcist. Of course, the Worcester chancery office will deny this. Where the demonic is concerned, Catholic chancery offices deny everything."

Before leaving, I asked the Warrens if I could accompany them on one of their future investigations.

"It might be possible to work something out, but you should know what you'd be getting yourself into," Ed said. "Things can get pretty frightening out in the field. Very few people are able to take the pressure. Just to give you an idea of what's involved, you should come up someday and look over our library of case films. There's one, for example, where Father McKenna is exorcising a farmer in Warren, Massachusetts. During the exorcism the farmer's head splits open, blood spurts out of his eyes, and crosses appear on his body. We have all of this on film. This exorcism was so bad that I actually had a heart attack during it. If a professional demonologist such as myself had a heart attack, what do you think would have happened to you?"

In a field notorious for disguised identities and compulsive secrecy, the Warrens stand practically alone in divulging precise names and dates. During our conversation in the fall of 1996 they gave me the intimate details of several of their more recent cases and also the names of six priest-exorcists (in addition to the aforementioned Father McKenna) who have helped them on various occasions throughout the years. I eventually succeeded in contacting two of these priests by telephone, and under the provision of anonymity, both confirmed that they had in fact performed exorcisms for the Warrens in the past, and had done so without official church approval.

For his part, official church approval is just about the last thing that Father Robert McKenna is concerned with. In addition to playing a starring role in the Smurl case of West Pittston, Pennsylvania, and working with the Warrens on dozens of other cases, McKenna has spent the past twenty years in defiant opposition to virtually every aspect of post-1960s Roman Catholicism. Born in 1927 in Grand Rapids, Michigan, and raised as the third of four children in an intensely Catholic family, McKenna became a Dominican priest at the age of twenty-three, and over the next fifteen years he fashioned a deeply satisfying career for himself in parish ministry. During the late sixties and early seventies, however, as Catholicism in the United States and elsewhere frantically set about renewing (or modernizing) itself in response to the recently completed Second Vatican Council, McKenna saw his world fall almost completely apart. In the name of renewal, cherished devotional practices such as novenas and benedictions were downgraded in importance and sometimes cast aside altogether, the priesthood was stripped of much of its former mystique and prestige, and, most traumatic of all, the age-old Latin (or Tridentine) Mass, which had reigned for centuries as a majestic exemplar of Catholic worship, was replaced by a vernacular and decidedly more streamlined liturgy. Like quite a few other Catholics of his generation, McKenna was horrified by all of these changes, and in late 1973 he joined a breakaway organization called the Orthodox Roman Catholic Movement (ORCM) which had been founded earlier that year by a disaffected priest named Father Francis Fenton for the pur-

pose of resisting the Second Vatican Council and its "blasphemous re-
forms." In 1974, after refusing orders to dissociate himself from
ORCM, McKenna was dismissed from the Dominicans, and ever
since he has been a fixture within what has come to be known as the
underground traditionalist movement of American Catholicism.[6]

In November 1996, several days after my initial meeting with
the Warrens, I visited Father McKenna at his chapel in Monroe,
Connecticut. A tall, white-frame structure, with a simple white cross
adorning its gray-shingled roof, Our Lady of the Rosary Chapel was
built in 1839 and served as a Methodist church for almost a century and
a half before being purchased by ORCM in 1973. The chapel houses a
small parish school (with a current enrollment of forty-two students) in
its basement, and to its immediate left is a large three-story frame house
that doubles as a rectory for Father McKenna and a convent for seven
traditionalist nuns who call themselves the Dominican Sisters of the
Immaculate Heart of Mary. Father McKenna, who is sometimes also
referred to as Bishop McKenna (in the mid-eighties he was conse-
crated a bishop by a traditionalist French prelate named Guérard des
Lauriers), emerged from his rectory wearing a black fedora, tinted
glasses, and a charcoal gray overcoat. Tall and thin, with a gaunt,
deeply lined face and reddish hair, he took me on a brief tour of the
property and then, over lunch at a local diner, spoke with disarming
frankness of his experiences as an exorcist.

"My being an exorcist is like winning the World Series by default,"
he said. "I recognized that there was a huge demand for exorcisms,
and hardly no one else was willing to do them. Most establishment
priests and bishops today don't even believe in the devil. . . . The
Warrens were instrumental in getting me involved. They first came to
me in about 1976—they weren't members of the chapel; they have
stuck with the establishment church—but they couldn't get establishment priests to perform exorcisms. I was happy to help out, and over
the years I've worked on dozens of cases with them."

I asked Father McKenna if he was pleased with the outcome of
most of these cases.

"No, I can't really say that I am pleased," he answered. "You have to understand that the devil and his demons work in various ways, and this means that there are various kinds of exorcism. The first kind involves what we call simple demonic affliction. This is where demons lodge themselves in a house and torment its occupants. And this is where I've had my greatest success. But even here there have been some disappointing failures. You've probably heard of the Smurl case in Pennsylvania. This was a classic case of affliction. I tried to exorcise the house three times, but to no avail. The demons refused to leave. Next there is what we refer to as demonic obsession. With obsession, demons latch themselves on to a person, but without actually taking over the entire personality. I've had a fair amount of success with exorcisms in this area. But it's the third kind of exorcism, the kind that deals with full-scale possession, that is the most challenging, and this is where I've had the least success. With possession, the person is completely taken over by a demon, and so the stakes here are very high. So far I've dealt with fifteen cases of possession, and I would say that I've only been successful in five of these."

Probably the most challenging case of possession he'd ever faced, Father McKenna told me, involved a Jewish-American woman from the New England area named Eileen.

"Eileen was a single, middle-aged woman, and I tried to exorcise her on five separate occasions, three to four hours at a time, but the exorcisms were unsuccessful," he said. "As soon as I'd start exorcising, the devil would rant and rave, threatening to kill me and blaspheming God and the Blessed Virgin and the saints. There were five men restraining her, and she was tied in a chair by sheets, but she got free each time without any difficulty. The Warrens have an audiotape, and you can clearly hear the voice of a man—the devil speaking through Eileen—cursing and blaspheming. A couple of times the Warrens had a doctor friend with them during the exorcisms. He took Eileen's vital signs while she was being exorcised and found that they were perfectly normal. And this was while she was shouting and ranting. But, you see, it was really the devil who was shouting and ranting. Eileen would go completely crazy when I abjured Satan with a crucifix. And once, while I was holding an image of the Blessed Virgin before her, the devil shouted, 'She shouldn't have said yes! She shouldn't have said yes! She shouldn't have said yes!' This was in reference to the Virgin agreeing to be the Mother of Christ at the Annunciation. At other times Eileen would howl like a banshee. I knew God was with me; otherwise it would have been very frightening. Eileen has since converted to the establishment Catholic Church and has moved to the West Coast. She is still possessed, but she isn't institutionalized. She lives by herself, and she holds down a job. I am told that other priests have also tried to exorcise her. Apparently she appealed to the Vatican, but the Pope refused to help her."

After lunch, while driving back to Our Lady of the Rosary Chapel, I asked Father McKenna if his partnership with the Warrens had always run smoothly.

"I appreciate Ed and Lorraine tremendously for the service they have provided, but there is a tension for me working with them," he said. "Three years ago I was performing an exorcism in the chapel on a middle-aged woman. She was small and frail, and she had a heart condition, but it still took several men to restrain her. At one point she was ranting and raving and breaking free of the restraints, and Ed Warren panicked and called the paramedics. They came and took her to the hospital in Bridgeport, and this made the whole exorcism look like a farce. It got lots of publicity in the local papers, which the Warrens didn't seem to mind, but I thought it made us look silly. And this is where the tension comes in. Ed and Lorraine are publicity-seekers, and the last thing I need is this kind of publicity. Their books are sensationalized, and you just can't take it all literally. I don't like to be publicly associated with them. The thing is, I don't think we're always approaching the exorcisms from the same point of view. For me it's very simple: Before the Second Vatican Council possession was extremely rare, but after the council there has been a veritable plague of possessions. I see this as an indictment of Vatican II and the new Mass. Now the devil has a free hand to take over people's lives. Take away the true Mass, and the devil takes over. Vatican II and the new Mass gave an opening to the devil, and the devil has fully seized the opportunity."

———

F ather McKenna was uneasy with the idea of my personally attending an exorcism at Our Lady of the Rosary Chapel, but he agreed to let me watch a videotape of a 1991 performance—the so-called case of the Leopard Man—that he described as one of his greatest triumphs. The eponymous Leopard Man was a working-class New Yorker in his late thirties who had apparently been terrifying his wife and children for more than a decade by getting down on all fours and destroying furniture in their family home. The Warrens had taken him to several other priest-exorcists over the years before finally turning the case over to Father McKenna.

With its languid pacing and grainy texture, the video had a desultory, almost dreamlike feel to it. The Leopard Man, burly and balding and dressed in sweater and jeans, sat nervously near the front of the chapel while Ed Warren and five beefy assistants strapped him into a straitjacket and bound his ankles to the supports of a wooden pew. For several long minutes afterward nothing much seemed to happen, but suddenly, as Father McKenna and a second priest stood at the altar reciting the Litany of Saints, the Leopard Man lurched violently in the pew and struggled to break free of his constraints. Father McKenna sprinkled holy water on him while saying "Be still, Satan! Be still, Satan!" and the assistants forced him back down into a sitting position. Following this outburst the Leopard Man sat calmly, with his wife stroking his shoulder, while the exorcism continued. After twenty minutes or so, Father McKenna approached him and asked how he was feeling. The Leopard Man said, "Fine. The devil isn't here anymore." Ed Warren, looking relieved, added, "It looks like it has left." Father McKenna nodded in agreement and said, "Yes. But for safety's sake, let's proceed with the rest of the exorcism."

Demonic Breakdowns

The Rise of
Deliverance Ministry

The Warrens and underground priests such as Father McKenna were by no means alone during the 1980s and early 1990s in perpetuating the mythos of exorcism within American popular culture. Hollywood's B-movie mill continued to churn out films on the topic, including two thuddingly inept sequels to the Blatty-Friedkin 1974 blockbuster, and demonic possession remained a consistently hot ticket for the pulp publishing industry.[1]

But this wasn't even the half of it. In a fascinating development (which I shall discuss at length in subsequent chapters), demonism and demonic affliction had also, by the early eighties, become leading concerns of a middle-class religious movement commonly called neo-Pentecostalism or the charismatic renewal. Neo-Pentecostalism first arose during the late sixties as a loosely structured movement of mainline Christians, both Protestant and Catholic, who were seeking a more immediate and more dramatic experience of faith than was generally available to them in their local churches. From the beginning the movement was centered upon an ecstatic religious experience known as "baptism in the Holy Spirit," which presumably gave rise to such spiritual gifts, or charisms, as speaking in tongues, prophecy, and miraculous healing, and most of its early adherents fully believed they were engaged in building up new communities of spiritual and apostolic vitality. As the years passed, however, many of the movement's most prominent activists became increasingly convinced that not everything in their midst was sweetness and light. At charismatic prayer meetings people sometimes complained of being tormented by uncontrollable vices and disturbing fantasies, and people seeking help at healing services sometimes exhibited grotesque and otherwise unsettling symptoms. The Holy Spirit may have been in the house, but the hounds (it seemed) were baying at the back door.

In an effort to combat the evil that was apparently lurking among them, neo-Pentecostal communities throughout the country gradually began practicing a form of exorcism that they generally referred to as "deliverance ministry." In the process, exorcism was converted from a rare and forbidding procedure into a kind of suburban home remedy. By the late 1970s and early 1980s, middle-class charismatics were lining up by the dozens to have their personal demons expelled. Demons of lust. Demons of anger. Demons of resentment. Demons of addiction. Exorcism (or deliverance) had suddenly become the cure-all for virtually every middle-class affliction imaginable. And more often than not, its practitioners weren't the hero-priests immortalized by William Peter Blatty and Malachi Martin but rather ordinary laypeople whose chief claim to fame was their presumed "baptism in the Holy Spirit."[2]

M. s c o t t p e c k

Exorcism received another (still more improbable) vote of support during the early eighties—and this time from someone of unquestionably greater claim to fame. In a 1983 book entitled *People of the Lie*, the celebrity psychiatrist and mega-selling author M. Scott Peck dropped a bombshell: Not only was he personally fascinated by the subject of demonic possession, Peck confided, but he had actually encountered the phenomenon firsthand in his own psychotherapeutic practice. As much as the medical establishment might scoff at the notion, he wrote, diabolic evil was an active force in the modern world, and conventional therapeutic techniques were utterly unequipped to deal with it by themselves. The best hope for patients afflicted by such evil was exorcism, he claimed, and the best resource for learning about the peculiar dynamics of exorcism and demonic possession was (of all things) Malachi Martin's *Hostage to the Devil.*

Compared to most earlier endorsements of exorcism, this was a shot completely out of the blue. Unlike Malachi Martin and company, M. Scott Peck had no obvious theological ax to grind, and he certainly didn't need exorcism to launch himself to fame and fortune. In Peck's treatment of the subject, moreover, there were no spinning heads, death-defying stunts, or semen-spattered succubi; at almost every turn, *People of the Lie* was sweetly reasoned and patiently expository — a sort of Oliver Sacks–ian excursion into some strange-yet-true frontier of the human condition. In Peck, a decade after Blatty, exorcism appeared to have finally found its voice of mainstream legitimation.

How exactly M. Scott Peck (of all people) came to such a role is not easy to say. Born in New York City in 1936, and raised on the Upper East Side in a silk-stockinged world of private schools and ingrained privilege, Peck did his undergraduate work at Harvard and Columbia, and in 1959 he enrolled in the medical school of Case Western Reserve University. During his first year at Case Western he married Lily Ho, a native of Singapore, and after obtaining his medical degree he spent almost ten years as an army psychiatrist. In late 1972, following his resignation from the service, Peck set up private psychiatric practice in New Preston, Connecticut, on the shores of Lake Waramaug, and six years later he published a book of spiritual and psychological reflection entitled *The Road Less Traveled.*

Despite stumbling a bit coming out of the gate (just twelve thousand sales in its debut publishing year), *The Road Less Traveled* soon proved an unstoppable force. Thanks in large measure to fervent word-of-mouth advertising, and also to rave reviews in the major media (the

Washington Post called it "not just a book but a spontaneous act of generosity"), *Road* became a gargantuan hit, and by the fall of 1988, after surviving 260 consecutive weeks on the *Times* bestseller list, it threatened to dislodge even the Bible as the inspirational book of choice for mainstream America. Somehow Peck had succeeded in taking the temperature of his mostly middle-class readers, in gauging their hopes and doubts and anxieties, and the coaxingly puritanical moralizing that he served up in *Road* seemed precisely what they had been craving to hear. "Life is difficult" is how the book began, and then it went on to argue that facing up squarely to life's difficulties (and life's sufferings), without resorting to either easy euphemism or cultural escapism, was what constituted the true road to spiritual and mental maturity.[3]

Next to the furry-faced, sweetly blabbering, self-help manuals that crammed the psychology shelves of mall bookstores in those days, this was stern stuff; and five years later, with the publication of *People of the Lie*, Peck cranked up the puritan heat several additional notches. In addition to being difficult, he now argued, life was sometimes fraught with evil. Not just metaphorical evil, or the evil of dead-end chances and broken dreams fretted over by sociologists, but the real flesh-and-blood, grimacing, dastardly sort of evil that the medical professions and social sciences had spent years trying to psychologize and environmentalize into nonexistence. Sometimes, as in the American military, Peck conceded, real evil of this sort could take on a distinctive structural or institutional form, which helped account for atrocities such as My Lai, but just as often it was an individual attribute—a character defect of actual men and women. In almost every case, Peck wrote, evil men and women were severely narcissistic, and they took particular delight in imposing their cruel and spiritually stunted wills upon others more vulnerable than themselves. And more often than not their evil was largely the consequence of critical choices they themselves had made in the course of their adult lives.

Then came the punch line. In addition to its human and institutional dimensions, Peck argued, evil was sometimes also a force straight out of hell. And here, as with so much else in life, seeing was believing. While undertaking preliminary research for *People of the Lie*,

Peck wrote, he was brought into direct contact with two patients who were clearly suffering from advanced forms of diabolic possession. In both cases exorcism presented itself as the only realistic course of treatment, and in both cases the exorcisms proceeded almost exactly as if they had been scripted by Malachi Martin. From the *pretense* to the *expulsion,* virtually everything took place as Martin had depicted it in *Hostage to the Devil*—including (in one case especially) the utterly frightful moment when the diabolic presence fully revealed itself.

"When the demonic finally spoke clearly in one case," Peck wrote, "an expression appeared on the patient's face that could be described only as Satanic."

> It was an incredibly contemptuous grin of utter hostile malevolence. I have spent many hours before a mirror trying to imitate it without the slightest success. I have seen that expression only one other time in my life—for a few fleeting seconds on the face of the other patient, late in the evaluation period. Yet when the demonic finally revealed itself in the exorcism of this other patient, it was with a still more ghastly expression. The patient suddenly resembled a writhing snake of great strength, viciously attempting to bite the [exorcism] team members. More frightening than the writhing body, however, was the face. The eyes were hooded with lazy reptilian torpor—except when the reptile darted out in attack, at which moment the eyes would open wide with blazing hatred. Despite these frequent darting moments, what upset me the most was the extraordinary sense of a fifty-million-year-old heaviness I received from this serpentine being. It caused me to despair of the success of the exorcism. Almost all the team members at both exorcisms were convinced they were at these times in the presence of something absolutely alien and inhuman. The end of each exorcism proper was signaled by the departure of this Presence from the patient and the room.[4]

Given the benefit of this experience, Peck wrote, he was now fully convinced that "the role of exorcist [was] a heroic one." And he was no less convinced that the time had arrived to subject both demonic possession and exorcism to scientific investigation. Possession was an unquestionably real (if relatively rare) phenomenon, Peck claimed, and the only thing preventing medical professionals from taking it seriously was an indefensible bias against the supernatural. At the very least, he wrote, what was needed was intensive interdisciplinary research on exorcism, and also the creation of a national resource center that would be responsible for collecting data on demonic possession and developing standards for diagnosis and treatment.[5]

There wasn't much chance, of course, of any of this coming to pass. To Peck's chagrin, the medical establishment simply ignored *People of the Lie,* while the mainstream media tended to dismiss its discussion of exorcism as nothing more than the slightly loopy rambling of an otherwise talented eccentric.[6] In the years that followed the book's publication, moreover, Peck himself seemed only too happy to shift his attention to other concerns. In 1984 he gave up his psychiatric practice and seriously considered making a run for the American presidency, and later the same year he helped create the Foundation for Community Encouragement, a nonprofit organization designed to instruct community activists in the complex arts of conflict resolution and consensus-building. Peck's experiences with the foundation gave rise to a 1987 book entitled *The Different Drum,* and three years later he published a murder mystery called *A Bed by the Window.* Throughout all of this he kept up an enormously busy schedule as a top-billing lecturer on the New Age conference circuit. From the outside, at least, it appeared that Peck's interest in exorcism had merely been a passing fancy—a momentary blip on his celebrity screen.

Even if this were the case, however, Peck had already done more than enough to earn the lasting gratitude of grassroots supporters of exorcism. With its limpid prose, sublime self-assurance, and psychological suavity, *People of the Lie* had succeeded in giving exorcism its first real jolt of middle-class respectability—in delivering it, if only partially, from the double clutches of celluloid camp and incense-clouded fanaticism. Although the book may not have won many new converts to the exorcism cause, it provided powerful ideological reinforcement for those already convinced of the reality of demonic evil in the modern world.

As it turned out, Peck still hadn't spoken his last word on the subject. In a freewheeling interview published in the March 1991 issue of *Playboy,* he emphatically stood up for everything he had written in *People of the Lie* and indicated that his main regret was that so few people in the psychiatric profession seemed willing to give his views on exorcism a fair hearing.[7]

Given his almost sainted status among many rank-and-file advocates of exorcism in America, I was eager to discuss these and related matters personally with Peck, and in October 1996 (after rather delicate negotiations) I finally succeeded in hooking up with him for a lengthy telephone interview. Over the years Peck has gained a certain reputation for arrogance and abrasiveness, but during the course of our conversation he was unfailingly polite and forthright. He told me that his initial interest in exorcism had been sparked by William Peter Blatty's novel and film, but that it was Malachi Martin, more than anyone else, who had inspired him to undertake actual research on the subject.

"Malachi Martin was my big mentor," he said. "I read *Hostage to the Devil* after reading Blatty and seeing *The Exorcist* movie, and I decided that I must take this stuff seriously. Malachi isn't a psychiatrist, and I wouldn't have written *Hostage* in the same way he did, but for the most part he was right on target. As Malachi clearly indicated in *Hostage,* people who are suffering from demonic possession bear some responsibility for their condition. At some level they have cooperated with demonic evil; they have invited it into their life. In such cases there is always—perhaps at an unconscious level—some kind of sellout to evil. *Hostage to the Devil* dissected this dynamic beautifully, and this is one reason why I still regard the book very favorably."

As time went on, Malachi Martin provided Peck with considerably more than just literary inspiration.

"After reading *Hostage,* I made a special point of contacting Malachi," Peck told me. "I was fascinated by possession, and I wanted to pick his brain. And I must say that I've never met anyone nearly so expert on the subject. We became quite close, and Malachi started re-ferring cases to me. At the time I was still an open-minded skeptic. The first two cases that Malachi brought to me struck me as standard psychopathology, but the third case was the genuine article. I was con-verted, and I eventually became personally involved with the two ex-orcisms that I discuss in *People of the Lie*."

Much more deeply involved, in fact, than readers of *People of the Lie* were led to believe.

"In both of these cases I myself served as the principal exorcist, and Malachi Martin coached me in the role," Peck said. "Both cases involved women, one in her late twenties and the other in her early forties. In the first case I was the exorcist by default. I spent more than four thousand dollars over a two-month period searching the country for an exorcist for this first patient. Malachi wrote to the Catholic bishop of Bridgeport, Connecticut, saying he felt this was genuine possession, but the bishop refused to offer any help. We contacted Benedict Groeschel, a quite famous exorcist in the Catholic diocese of New York, but Groeschel claimed that his bishop wouldn't permit him to cross state lines to perform exorcisms. A prominent Methodist min-ister involved in deliverance ministry also refused to help. Finally Malachi found a Catholic bishop willing to perform the exorcism for me, but I had to tell the bishop—and this was one of the most difficult things I've ever had to do—that he wasn't smart enough in psychol-ogy to carry it off. The bishop was a man of goodwill, however, and he agreed to serve as my assistant. Neither he nor Malachi expressed any misgiving that I wasn't a Catholic, let alone a Catholic priest."

I asked Peck whether his thinking on diabolic possession and ex-orcism had changed much in the years since *People of the Lie*'s publica-tion.

"No, not really," he said. "I still fully believe in the reality of pos-session, but I also believe that it's very rare. The only thing that has changed in my mind is that I used to think that Multiple Personality Disorder and possession were completely different things, different diagnoses. Now, given some of my experiences, it's quite clear to me that both can be operative simultaneously."

Did he still hold out hope, I asked, that possession and exorcism would someday become objects of serious scientific investigation?

"I still hope for this, but the chances of it actually happening in the foreseeable future seem slight," he said. "I used to have high hopes of establishing an institute for the study of exorcism, but only once did I come anywhere close to seeing this realized. About fifteen years ago I thought I might be able to set up such an institute at a large psychiatric center in the South. This place had an in-bed service that was run by secular counselors, and an outpatient service that was manned by religiously trained counselors. These two groups, the secular and the religious, had been at loggerheads for years, but they wound up uniting against me. The secular, scientifically trained counselors insisted that the very notion of satanic possession was ridiculous, and the religious counselors insisted that it was ridiculous to think that possession could be examined by scientific means. In the end my proposal was shot down. . . . For a couple of years I ran a conference on evil, and I've also tried to establish a network of exorcists and sympathetic psychiatrists. But all of my efforts have come to naught. And this has been rather frustrating. While many ordinary Americans seem open to the possibility of diabolic possession, most of the country's intellectual and religious elites—and I must, unfortunately, include the leadership of the American Catholic Church in this—have seemed determined to keep the door shut."

Once again there is a clear-cut pattern to all of this. From the Hollywood hype of William Peter Blatty to the bestselling pieties of Malachi Martin and M. Scott Peck, it was the popular culture industry in America that was chiefly responsible throughout the 1970s and 1980s for promoting interest in exorcism. While the Roman Catholic Church—the religious institution most famously associated with exorcism—remained fastidiously silent on the subject, Hollywood and New York seemed rarely at a loss for words. Exorcism was kept alive, and occasionally made to flourish, as both a consumer product and a theatrical spectacle, and in the process it was assured a secure niche in the nation's religious imagination.

This conjuncture of commercialism and religious ritual, of profits and piety, should come as no surprise. Over the course of the twentieth century the popular culture industry, with its endless run of movies, books, and digital delights, has gained a pervasive influence over the national consciousness. It has become part of the very air that Americans breathe, and, as such, it has attained an enormous capacity for shaping everyday beliefs and behaviors. And this includes, naturally, religious beliefs and behaviors. When Hollywood and its allies put out the Word, somebody's guaranteed to be listening.

This is not to say, of course, that everyone who comes into contact with Blatty or Malachi Martin or the Warrens will be converted to the cause of exorcism. For most people, most of the time, the products of Hollywood and the trade publishing industry are nothing more than diversions, transitory titillations. Given the right conditions, however, they can sometimes amount to considerably more than this. In the case of exorcism, the works of Blatty and Malachi Martin appeared at a time when a significant number of Americans seemed anxious for some evidence, some confirmation, that the supernatural was still a potent force in the modern world. Blatty and Martin succeeded (fictitiously or otherwise) in providing such evidence, and in the process they helped generate both popular interest in diabolic possession and an emergent market for exorcisms. As it happened, there were religious entrepreneurs on the scene who were only too happy to exploit this market to their own theological (and sometimes pecuniary) advantage. In the end it was this convergence of interest, or dialectic, between producers and consumers—performers and audience—that enabled exorcism to survive the hoopla of the early seventies as something more than just a passing fad.

As we shall see in subsequent chapters, the popular culture industry may also play a somewhat less direct role in influencing religious beliefs and behaviors. Within certain sectors of the charismatic renewal movement, for example, exorcism (or deliverance) was already being practiced to a limited extent before the works of Blatty and

Malachi Martin and so forth had even seen the light of day. While these works can't be credited for having actually created a demand for exorcisms among charismatics, they nevertheless succeeded, at the very least, in setting a certain cultural tone, or climate, in which exorcisms could be more readily carried out.

satanic panics

In the years that followed publication of *People of the Lie,* America's backseat romance with exorcism gradually gave way to a full-fledged cultural fascination with satanism. Indeed, the ten-year stretch from 1983 to 1993 seems to have been Satan's decade in America. From California to New York, alarm bells rang out: Satanists, it seemed, were now lurking everywhere, torturing helpless toddlers in day care centers, brainwashing adolescents through the sinister lyrics of heavy metal, sowing destruction through the drug trade, and savaging their own children in Black Mass orgies. The Beast, apparently, was on the prowl, and Americans were compelled to do everything possible to halt its deadly progress.

This wasn't the first time, of course, that fears of this sort had surfaced in America. As recently as the late sixties, a number of events — including the chilling Manson murders and the release of Roman Polanski's *Rosemary's Baby* (1968) — had convinced more than just a few people that a satanic threat was stalking the land. The difference now, however, was the sheer pervasiveness of the threat. If the reports of self-appointed occult-watchers were true, satanism in the 1980s and early 1990s was a vast conspiracy, with a hidden network of lascivious, bloodlusting agents hatching evil on virtually every street corner across the nation.

As in the sixties, there were a number of highly publicized events that lent these satanic-conspiracy fears a resonance of plausibility. In early 1984, for example, the nation caught its first glimpse of a headline-grabbing scandal that was unfolding at a day care center in suburban Los Angeles. According to criminal investigators, there was strong evidence that teachers at the McMartin Preschool, quite possibly in complicity with other adults in the community, had been systematically abusing their students for well over a decade. From the looks of it, moreover, this wasn't just garden-variety abuse. In interviews with child-welfare officials, students at the school spoke of having been exposed to grisly graveyard rituals and gruesome animal torture and of being forced to participate in a startling range of perverse sexual activity, sometimes in deserted candlelit churches. In one particularly graphic testimony, the mother of a former McMartin student claimed that adults wearing masks and capes had forced her two-year-old son to stick his fingers into a goat's anus and to drink the blood of a murdered infant. After McMartin the floodgates opened, and allegations of horrific abuse surfaced at dozens of other day care centers throughout the country. And more often than not there was a macabre cast to these allegations. In case after case, children confided (or reportedly confided) being sexually accosted by their teachers and other adults while in the presence of pentagrams, dismembered body parts, and other accouterments of the occult. Almost overnight, "satanic ritual abuse" (as it was christened by the media) seemed to have become a national epidemic.[8]

As the decade wore on, accusations of ritual abuse were increasingly raised not against just workers in day care centers but also against parents themselves—quite often by grown children who claimed to have recovered their memories of parental abuse while undergoing intensive psychotherapy. "Recovered memory" cases multiplied at a furious rate during the late eighties, and by the turn of the decade they had taken on the predictable, ritualized stages of a well-worn fable. First there was the therapeutic epiphany: the sudden, miraculous recovery of horrific abuse-memories that had been completely repressed—completely lost to consciousness—since early childhood. Next, the disclosure of these memories to the supposedly abusive parent or parents. Then the shocked denials. The anguished soul-searching. The escalation of hostility. And then finally, as in all good American fables, the squalid court battles. Not all of these cases involved specific allegations of satanism, but those that did were generally accorded front-page treatment by the popular media. A truly American carnival of lost souls.[9]

Nor was this the end of it. Alongside the furor over ritual abuse there was widespread concern during the 1980s and early 1990s that America's adolescents were being seduced into satanism by the popular entertainment industry. The chief (though by no means exclusive) culprit here was heavy metal music. In addition to glorifying satanism through their elaborate neo-Gothic stage sets, heavy metal acts such as Ozzy Osbourne and Mötley Crüe were widely suspected of smuggling into their music subliminal messages of gloom and doom and destruction. Public concern over such "hidden messages" was considerably heightened in late 1985, when two Nevada teenagers entered into a suicide pact after a drug-hazed day of listening to records by the English metal band Judas Priest. (One of the youths died instantly of self-inflicted shotgun wounds, and the second, who succeeded only in blowing his face off in the initial suicide attempt, died three years later from an overdose of prescription painkillers.) In 1986 the families of both teenagers filed suit against Judas Priest and their recording company, CBS Records, alleging that satanic messages had been covertly planted (or "backmasked") into the band's music. The case went to trial in Reno in 1990, and although the court ruled in favor of the defendants, heavy metal music continued to be regarded by many Americans as a staging ground for the occult.[10]

In the meantime there were even more serious threats to contend with. Throughout the 1980s satanists were also suspected of abducting runaway teenagers and other vulnerable youths and then slaying them in bloody nocturnal rituals. (Female adolescents seem to have gotten a marginally better deal than males here: Rather than being murdered, many were reportedly kept alive and pressed into service as satanic breeders, thus ensuring a steady supply of sacrificial babies for their kidnappers.) Although the precise body count was impossible to determine, one widely quoted source estimated that no fewer than forty thousand people annually were the victims of ritual homicide in the United States.[11]

And then, finally, there was the sheer insidiousness of it all. For the most part, according to occult-watchers, modern-day satanists knew better than to wear their colors in public. Rather than advertising their beliefs, they had made an art of blending in: For all anyone knew, the contemporary satanist was the colleague schmoozing at the office water cooler, the racquetball partner showering in the next stall, the gardener manicuring the neighbor's lawn. In their outward appearance, satanists had succeeded in becoming diabolically respectable, and tracking them down was an exceedingly tricky business.

Not that this dissuaded people from trying. Among the conspiracy-minded, satanist-hunting was a deadly serious sport during the 1980s, and along the way there were some surprising targets. In 1986, for example, a group of conservative Protestants in the Midwest published a special newsletter asserting that the president of Procter & Gamble was a dedicated adherent of an obscure cult called the Church of Satan, and that his company's secret logo was the satanic number 666. The newsletter urged readers to boycott Procter & Gamble products, and also to take whatever steps might be necessary to smoke other surreptitious satanists into the open.[12]

As it turns out, the accusations against Procter & Gamble and its president were wildly overblown, and so, too, apparently, were many of the other satanist scares of the 1980s. Despite the determined efforts of prosecutors, allegations of ritual abuse at day care centers very rarely resulted in criminal convictions. Recovered memory cases were frequently found to hinge less on reality than on the high-pressure salesmanship of overzealous therapists and the heightened suggestibility of their clients. Far from being a tool of mass damnation, heavy metal music proved to be not much more than another passing youth fad. And ritual homicide seems to have been a national scourge mainly in the overcharged imaginations of antisatanic mythmakers. In a 1989 report, Special Agent Kenneth Lanning, the FBI's resident expert on the occult, claimed that he had yet to identify a single clear-cut case of satanically motivated murder in the United States.[13]

This is not to suggest that there was no satanic activity whatsoever in America during the 1980s. No less (but probably not much more) than in previous decades, children undoubtedly suffered cruel abuse

at the hands of self-styled occultists, and adolescents undoubtedly created mischief (and occasionally brought harm to themselves and others) while experimenting with satanic rituals. Moreover, while their
combined membership was slight and their public influence negligible,
the Church of Satan and several offshoot organizations did in fact exist during the eighties, and it's certainly possible that more than a few
ostensibly upstanding citizens secretly belonged to them. And although hard evidence has been slow to materialize, it wouldn't be surprising if at least some occult-related murders were committed over
the course of the decade. On balance, however, all of this activity was
disjointed and sporadic—a far cry from the closely choreographed
conspiracy that antisatanists seemed desperate to uncover. While satanism was alive, in other words, it wasn't nearly as rampant or well-
regimented as popular rumor suggested.[14]

In America's media-driven culture, however, a good story is rarely
inconvenienced by reality, and this one was too good to pass up. In addition to playing a pivotal role in getting the satanic-conspiracy story
started, the popular culture industry succeeded during the eighties in
milking it for all it was worth. At the nation's bookstores, True
Confessions of satanic cult survivors, from the reality-challenged
Michelle Remembers (1980) to the reality-distressed *Satan's Underground*
(1988), were reliably hot sellers, and Oprah Winfrey, Sally Jessy
Raphaël, and other tabloid talk show hosts had a field day document-
ing satanism's hidden reign of terror. A two-hour Geraldo Rivera special called "Devil Worship," which featured supposedly firsthand
accounts of satanic breeding and ritual cannibalism, was the most
widely watched syndicated talk show of 1988.[15]

A ll this satanism talk, of course, was potentially good business for
exorcism, and no one was better equipped to capitalize on it than
Malachi Martin. On April 30, 1987, Martin appeared on *The Oprah
Winfrey Show* with a Lutheran minister named Pastor Erwin Prange,
who claimed to be an expert on satanism and a veteran of more than

fifteen hundred exorcisms, and a young woman named Helen Chitwood, whose rather more limited expertise consisted of having had sex with demons during her midteens. Despite having good stories to tell, Pastor Prange and Chitwood were clearly secondary attractions. In a hushed, almost reverential tone evidently due a genuine hero-exorcist (or perhaps even a would-be one), Oprah introduced Martin as "an outspoken Catholic priest who has assisted in hundreds of exorcisms" and the "author of a book on possession, *Hostage to the Devil*, which will be rereleased this summer." Oprah went on, "For Father Martin, the forces of good and evil are so real and so powerful, he says, that the fact that he is appearing on this show today could open him up to the wrath of demonic forces."

Martin was clearly expected to perform, and he didn't disappoint. With his Irish charm in full lilt, and the studio audience obviously spellbound, he insisted that diabolical possession was a surprisingly frequent phenomenon and that many of its victims were currently being warehoused in asylums throughout the country. ("But certain it is that I've met the heads of state hospitals . . . who tell me that fifty percent at least of the people they have behind bars, tied down, in padded cells are certainly beyond repair by psychiatry because they're really possessed.") He referred to a mysterious study of possession with which he himself had presumably helped out, and cautioned against drawing hasty conclusions on the subject. ("Well, we tried to make a profile, Oprah, of the possessed person. And we went through thousands, literally, and we found that neither sex nor race nor color nor education nor poverty nor background— It was a zigzag profile. I know men and women who are very naughty, you know, really naughty, in every sense of the word, but they're not possessed.") And, best of all, he discussed some of the juicier details of cases with which he'd personally been involved, and emphasized that exorcists themselves were always at grave risk, during the course of duty, of being invaded by the demonic. ("And that's one of the reasons why I was never an exorcist; I'm always an assistant exorcist. Because I have one basic character flaw: I'm intellectually curious. And I could start asking [the demon] questions out of intellectual curiosity, whereas the basic weapon of an exorcist is commands. . . . If it asks you a question, you never answer. You command all the time. But I am built in such a way, I know that I'd say, 'Oh, really. Well, tell me.' You know?")

Besides affording Malachi Martin an occasional star turn on the talk show circuit, the satanism scares of the eighties went a long way toward reinvigorating America's popular market for exorcisms. As was the case in the years immediately following the release of Blatty's trendsetting movie, thousands of people suddenly became convinced that they themselves (or perhaps an acquaintance or loved one) had fallen under the sway of demonic forces, and many of these people sent out calls for emergency assistance. Once again, however, the institutional Catholic Church was almost entirely unresponsive to these cries for help, and it was left to others to pick up the slack. The Warrens continued to do their part, as did underground priests such as Father McKenna, and the charismatic renewal movement continued to offer deliverance ministry as a sort of bargain-basement alternative to full-fledged exorcism.

At the same time there were some surprising reinforcements on the demon-expulsion front. Partly because of the heightened satanism scares of the day, exorcism had succeeded during the early eighties in gaining favor within certain sectors of evangelical Protestantism, and by mid-decade dozens of evangelical-based exorcism (or deliverance) ministries had sprung up across the country. Even for seasoned observers of the evangelical scene, this was hardly an expected development. For several decades prior to the eighties, evangelicalism in the United States had presented itself as an exceedingly sober and strait-laced affair. Casting out devils seemed to fit its profile about as well as snake-handling or break-dancing. But now evangelicals (or at least a significant minority of them) found themselves, along with a motley assortment of tongue-speaking charismatics and underground priests, right in the thick of the action, diagnosing demonic affliction in people from all walks of life and performing deliverance in their churches, in their homes, and sometimes even in their places of work.

It would be foolish to argue that the popular media, with their intensive coverage of satanism, were entirely responsible for this turn of events. Far from taking their cues directly from Oprah and Geraldo and so forth, evangelicals played a leading role themselves during the 1980s in fomenting public concern over satanism, and, as we shall see later on, their embracement of exorcism was facilitated as much by internal theological dynamics as by external cultural ones. Nevertheless, it would also be foolish, here as elsewhere, to discount the importance of the popular media. In addition to stimulating the market for exorcisms and thereby ensuring a steady stream of business for evangelical deliverance ministers, the tabloid industry's endless glitz-and-gloom treatment of satanism during the eighties served, at the very least, as powerful secondary legitimation for the growing number of evangelicals in America who were convinced that the time had arrived to gird themselves for spiritual warfare. With so many people confessing their satanic sins on television and so many frothy tales of demonic conspiracy appearing in the popular press, could there really be any doubt that satanism was on the rampage? While evangelicals may have come to exorcism of their own accord, in other words, the popular culture industry was unquestionably helpful in smoothing the path.

5.

The priest-exorcist as Hero—Revisited

While fascinating in its own right, evangelical and charismatic deliverance ministry never really succeeded during the 1980s in capturing the imagination of the broader American public. Deliverance inspired no blockbuster movies or best-selling books; there was no William Peter Blatty or Malachi Martin waiting in the wings to convert it into a full-fledged cultural icon. Indeed, the popular entertainment industry tended for the most part to treat deliverance as a distinctly second-string phenomenon—a minor-league diversion perhaps worth scouting now and then, but hardly the stuff of prime-time legend.

For big-league wallop there was still no substitute, apparently, for exorcisms officially sanctioned by the Roman Catholic Church and performed by bona fide hero-priests under the direction of their bishops. Although few and far between, these were the exorcisms the popular media feasted on, that served as the inescapable standard by which all other forms of exorcism were measured. While evangelicals and charismatics were expelling demons by the busload without attracting much more than passing notice, the slightest mention of an officially sanctioned Roman Catholic exorcism was all it took to bring the media scrambling to full attention. By almost universal consensus this was the genuine article, the truly epic struggle between supernatural good and evil. Everything else was pale imitation.

The national media were brought to full attention in March 1990, in fact, when John Cardinal O'Connor, the archbishop of New York, delivered a sermon at St. Patrick's Cathedral on the plague of satanism in contemporary America. The cardinal denounced heavy metal music for promoting satanism in its lyrics and videos, and he claimed that "diabolically instigated violence" was on the increase throughout the nation. He also asserted that demonic possession was an acutely real (if relatively rare) phenomenon and suggested that Catholics could learn more about possession through the "gruesomely realistic" depiction of it in William Peter Blatty's novel and film. (Here was the clincher: the most powerful Roman Catholic prelate in America defending the reality of demonic possession by invoking Hollywood's greatest melodrama on the subject. Is there anything more that needs to be said regarding the symbiotic connection between religion and popular culture in contemporary America?) What's more, as if this weren't enough, the cardinal also told reporters after Mass that two officially approved exorcisms had recently been carried out in the New York Archdiocese. "As far as we know," he said, "they have been successful."

Cardinal O'Connor couldn't have attracted more attention if he had announced the end of the world. For several weeks afterward the news media scrutinized his sermon from every imaginable angle, and cultural celebrities from almost every imaginable corner chimed in with their own specialized observations. Heavy metal rocker Ozzy Osbourne complained that the cardinal had "insulted the intelligence of rock fans all over the world," and Father Richard McBrien, chair of the theology department at the University of Notre Dame, dismissed the very notion of a personal devil as "premodern and precritical." Coming to the cardinal's defense was none other than William Peter Blatty, who observed that "the devil has been soft-pedaled and de-emphasized" by the Catholic Church in the United States and elsewhere in the years since the Second Vatican Council. And then there was the matter of those two mysterious exorcisms. Precisely where, and under what circumstances, had they been carried out, and who were the principals involved?[1]

While reporters were still seeking answers to these questions, a baffling (and entirely unprecedented) development unfolded on the Catholic exorcism front. On April 5, 1991, following weeks of back-room negotiations between church officials and network executives, ABC televised a genuine, real-life exorcism on its prime-time news-magazine show *20/20*. The ritual, which took place in Florida and involved a deeply disturbed teenager named Gina, was performed by a mystery exorcist, who was identified only as "Father A," with the assistance of a New York priest and close consultant to Cardinal O'Connor named Father James LeBar.

As if not quite believing their luck at being privy to so rare and forbidding a procedure, ABC's studio hosts Barbara Walters and Hugh Downs, and field reporter Tom Jarriel, presided over the telecast with a sort of blushing solemnity. "When the subject is Roman Catholicism," Barbara Walters declared at the outset, "nothing is more provocative, more terrifying, more fascinating than the subject of exorcism." Tom Jarriel observed that "interest in exorcism [was] rekindled in 1973 with the release of the movie *The Exorcist,*" and then he introduced viewers to Gina, a heavyset sixteen-year-old with long, straggly brown hair and wearing a loose-fitting white dress. For some years, apparently, Gina had been tormented by demonic visions and voices and by violent seizures, and several members of her family claimed that they had actually seen her levitating. Her mother, a Colombian immigrant, had taken her to a psychic healer, and Gina had also spent two months in a Miami psychiatric hospital, but none of this had had any effect on her condition.

Despite ABC's rapid-fire editing, the exorcism itself seemed an oddly brittle, indecisive affair. Strapped to a chair, Gina writhed and babbled, screamed and grimaced, all the while struggling to break free of her constraints. At one point, during the ritual's preliminary stages, she announced in a screeching, infantile voice, "My name is Minga," whereupon Father A, his face carefully kept hidden from the cameras, shot back, "You want pain; I'll give you pain," while he pressed a crucifix against Gina's forehead. At the ritual's climax Father A, in a loud, sonorous voice, commanded the demons by name to depart, and when Gina then seemed to calm down, he told her to kiss the crucifix and said that her mother could now take her home.

The segment concluded with a dreamy tableau of Father A in silhouette, breviary in hand, meditating on the shores of a small lake at twilight, with Tom Jarriel and the exorcist himself providing the solemn voice-over.

"Father A believes that with each ritual something dies inside him," Jarriel said. "He spends lonely days and sleepless nights tormented from having incurred the direct displeasure of pure hatred. This, he says, is the price the exorcist pays."

"It is the devil himself trying to weaken and destroy me," Father A said, softly.

"Why do this?"

"[Gina] has a right to a normal life like you and I, and she has turned to the church asking for help."

Back at the studio, the main drama now complete, Barbara Walters and Hugh Downs seemed genuinely awestruck. "That was extraordinary," Walters volunteered, and then, a moment later, on a rather more ambiguous note, she added, "This certainly isn't for everybody."

A scoop of this magnitude clearly couldn't be dealt with adequately in just one show, and so later the same evening ABC's hard-hitting news program *Nightline* also joined the action.

"It has never been seen before—a real-life exorcism of someone said to be a victim of demonic possession," *Nightline* correspondent Jeff Greenfield announced, before segueing into an interview with *20/20* segments producer Rob Wallace, who had overseen the filming of Gina's exorcism. Although he and his crew had anticipated more satanic fireworks, Wallace said, the exorcism had still left a deep impression on them. "I came away believing that possession was possible, and that it can happen, and, in fact, we may have witnessed possession and the exorcism of demons."

Father Richard McBrien of Notre Dame wasn't nearly so impressed. In an animated exchange with *Nightline* host Ted Koppel, McBrien slammed the exorcism for "hold[ing] the Catholic faith up to ridicule" and promoting the delusional belief that demons (rather than people themselves) were responsible for the world's evil. In response to this tirade, Father James LeBar, who had assisted with the exorcism and played a key role in arranging its filming, insisted that demonic possession was a tragic fact of life even in the modern world and suggested that anyone wishing to learn more about possession and exorcism would do well to consult Malachi Martin's *Hostage to the Devil.*

When Ted Koppel, in his closing remarks, observed that there seemed to be "an endless degree of fascination with exorcism" in America, LeBar, after more pooh-poohing from McBrien, acknowledged that poverty and other social evils deserved every bit as much attention from the Catholic Church as supernatural evil. Nevertheless, he went on, "Occasionally people may be infected by demonic presences, and the Church must also help them. And television is a powerful and effective medium for informing people that the Church does in fact offer help."[2]

S orting out the irony in all this would constitute a full day's work. For almost two decades the popular culture industry in America had been knocking itself out glamorizing exorcism, especially Roman Catholic exorcism, while the institutional Catholic Church had consistently played hard to get. Despite possessing the hottest and most seductive property on the street, the church had banished its rite of exorcism to the darkest shadows and thereby forced prospective customers to make do with tawdrier, less desirable alternatives. But now, in a remarkable turnabout, all modesty had been cast aside, and this most secret and exotic of Catholic rituals was being advertised in neon. And the popular media, which had so often in the past annoyed the institutional church by sensationalizing exorcism, now found themselves in the peculiar position of promoting the ritual on the church's behalf. This was a partnership that even Malachi Martin would have had difficulty conjuring up.

So what exactly was going on here? After years of secrecy and denial, why had Catholic officials suddenly elected to out–Malachi Malachi and permit the full prime-time airing of their church's rarest and most clandestine ritual? The person who seemed best qualified to address this was Father James LeBar, the priest who had helped orchestrate the filming of Gina's exorcism, and on a sultry July day in 1996 I met with LeBar for the first time at the Hudson River Psychiatric Center in Poughkeepsie, New York, where he has worked as a chaplain for most of the past two decades.

For sheer atmospherics the location would have been tough to beat. The psychiatric center was founded in 1871 as the Hudson River State Hospital for the Insane, and driving onto its rambling grounds was like entering the vast set of some neo-Gothic Hollywood thriller. Faded redbrick structures in various stages of disrepair, many with their windows boarded, were scattered across the property, and looming at the heart of the complex, about a quarter of a mile along a winding roadway, was a large and forbidding brick-brocaded building with arched entries that seemed, in the hazy gloom of the late afternoon, almost to groan with the dead ghosts of paraldehyde and electric shock. A bit farther along there was a patient-run car wash with a painted sign beckoning passersby to ROLL IN AND SHINE, and also a small museum that housed, among other marvels of nineteenth- and early-twentieth-century psychiatry, a ghastly restraining bed with a lockable lid known as a "Utica Crib" and a wooden prison box called the "Rush Tranquilizing Chair," thoughtfully designed with a strategic opening in the seat.

I found Father LeBar at a rustic, stone-walled chapel on the fringes of the hospital property, and he escorted me to a cluttered upstairs office whose walls were lined with citations from the Cult Awareness Network and the Citizens' Freedom Foundation praising him, in the words of one, "for his efforts [in] focus[ing] public attention on the dangers of destructive cults." A rumpled, plain-spoken, intelligent man in his early sixties, LeBar seemed initially ill at ease discussing exorcism with an outsider (he told me that he had already taken "a tremendous amount of heat" for his supporting role in the *20/20* affair), but a bit later, over coffee at a nearby diner, he gradually warmed to the subject.

I asked whether the decision to televise Gina's exorcism was a gamble that hadn't quite paid off: In addition to corroding the mystique of Catholic exorcism, wasn't it ill advised putting the emotional travails of a helpless teenager—harnessed to a chair!—on display before an audience of millions?

"This wasn't something that was undertaken lightly," Father LeBar answered. "We only decided to proceed with an exorcism for Gina after a painstaking six-month investigation of her case, and the decision to televise it was based entirely on pastoral considerations. . . . Like it or not, there are many people in this country who are engaged in struggles with what they believe are demonic forces. In the majority of cases these forces are probably the product of an overactive imagination or some definable psychiatric condition, but in some cases, such as Gina's, they are all too real. And because the church, for quite some time now, hasn't done its job in offering help to these people, many have been forced to turn to shady operators for help. And some of these people have suffered terrible damage in the process. It's really very simple: The church has an obligation to help, and for about thirty years now we have offered precious little in the way of help."

And to what extent had Gina herself been helped by the *20/20* exorcism?

"Quite a bit, I think," LeBar said. "By our estimation Gina wasn't suffering from full-scale possession, but rather very severe demonic oppression. While she hadn't been completely taken over by demonic forces, in other words, she was being seriously attacked by them. The exorcism succeeded in getting rid of her demons, but Gina has severe psychological problems that she still hasn't dealt with. She's not hospitalized now; she's up and about, but she's definitely not well."

Although I wasn't entirely comfortable with his role in the *20/20* affair, Father LeBar struck me as sincere and compassionate and impressively forthright, and during a series of meetings in Poughkeepsie over the next several months, he did his best (within the limits of discretion) to fill me in on what had been happening on the American Catholic exorcism front in recent years. Confirming what I had already heard from Father John Nicola and several other insiders, he told me that the rite of exorcism had been languishing on life support for the past several decades and that a good many Catholic bishops and theologians had seemed perfectly willing to pull the plug. Despite the excitement generated by William Peter Blatty and Malachi Martin, no more than one or two American Catholic dioceses at any given time since the mid-seventies had seen fit to have an officially appointed exorcist on call, and the vast majority of requests for exorcism-related help had simply gone unattended.

Nevertheless, Father LeBar suggested, there were strong indications that the situation was improving. Thanks in large part to the revived satanism scares of the late eighties, and also to the publicity stemming from Gina's *20/20* ordeal, a small but growing number of bishops had become more receptive of late to the possibilities of demonism and demonic affliction, and as a result exorcism seemed to be working its way back onto the ecclesiastical charts.

"The *20/20* exorcism definitely made a big difference," he told me during one of our conversations in Poughkeepsie. "For weeks afterward I was besieged by twenty phone calls a day from people looking for help. But now, for the first time since I've been keeping track, we were in a position to offer at least some of these people genuine help. In the past—in the years after Malachi Martin's book came out, for example—this certainly wasn't the case. People would come to the church and be ignored or turned away, because most priests and bishops were completely unsympathetic. The church was dodging its responsibilities, and so people were forced to go to Ed and Lorraine

Warren or Catholic charismatics or even Protestant Pentecostals for help. . . . You know, in some circles the Warrens are looked upon as either kooks or mere opportunists, but I have a different view. Ed and Lorraine helped fill the gap at a time when there were very few bishops and very few priests willing to consider even the possibility of demonism. They helped people secure exorcisms from renegade priests, they took care of people's needs, and in this respect they performed a very valuable service. It wasn't a perfect arrangement, but it was better than nothing, and so I feel grateful to them. But since the *20/20* show an increasing number of bishops appear to have recognized the need for exorcism, and I think the church is gradually reaching the point where it will be able to take care of its own business."

And what of officially appointed priest-exorcists? I asked. Was their number also on the increase in American Catholicism?

"The answer is yes, but this is something that can't happen overnight," LeBar said. "Until quite recently Father A"—the priest-exorcist of *20/20* fame—"was shouldering much of the burden all by himself. After the *20/20* show he was in constant demand, and he was doing about ten exorcisms a year around the country. The problem is that most bishops who are open to exorcism either don't know whom to appoint as exorcist in their diocese or they simply don't have anyone to appoint. I know a priest in Texas who has done two exorcisms with the authorization of the church, and also a priest in Washington State who's done a couple, but these priests haven't been officially appointed to the office of exorcist by their bishops. So various bishops were calling on Father A, and he's simply had too much to do. You can only survive for so long in the job: The pressure is huge, and it takes its toll. Just last year Father A went on sabbatical, and the chances are he won't be doing any more exorcisms. He has told me that he'll probably retire."[3]

While Father LeBar was careful not to reveal anything more specific about Father A, he did inform me that he knew of five priests in various parts of the country who had recently been appointed to the office of exorcist in their respective dioceses. Although none of these priests had yet to pull the trigger on an actual exorcism, LeBar said, they had a combined backlog of more than three hundred cases in various stages of investigation, some of which quite possibly involved full-fledged possession. He also said that at least several of these cases were almost certain to come up for exorcism in the near future, and that it might be possible for me to be present as an observer when they did.

The popular media's investment in exorcism during the early nineties was by no means limited to Gina's televised tribulations on *20/20*. Hollywood continued to churn out its usual run of throwaway movies on the topic; the Warrens and their favorite house exorcist, Father McKenna, rejoined the action with *Werewolf,* a deliciously campy paperback that chronicled the gruntings and growlings of a middle-aged Englishman who had somehow become inhabited by a spirit of lycanthropy; and on the evangelical publishing front, a minister-author named Frank Peretti scored big with a series of plodding (and highly profitable) novels depicting demonic depredation and deliverance in the American heartland.[4] Fully twenty years after William Peter Blatty, exorcism remained a hot ticket in America, and, what's more, the real-life 1949 exorcism that had initially inspired Blatty continued to arouse a fair measure of curiosity. CBS's *Inside Edition* and A&E's *Unsolved Mysteries* both aired episodes on the 1949 exorcism during the early nineties, a number of newspapers and magazines printed retrospectives on it, and it was also given full-length treatment by journalist Thomas Allen in a 1993 book entitled *Possessed*.

Of all these efforts Thomas Allen's was easily the most absorbing. In undertaking research for *Possessed*, Allen succeeded in making personal contact with the Reverend Walter Halloran, one of two surviving Jesuits who had assisted with the 1949 exorcism. Halloran confirmed that the exorcism had been conducted in various installments over a two-month period on a fourteen-year-old working-class boy from Mount Rainier, Maryland, and that its most dramatic moments had taken place in a psychiatric wing of the Alexian Brothers

Hospital in St. Louis. He also told Allen that the chief exorcist in the case had been a Jesuit named Father William Bowdern, who was pastor of St. Xavier Church at St. Louis University. (Bowdern died in 1983, at the age of 85.) With Halloran's help, moreover, Allen managed to secure a copy of a densely packed, twenty-six-page diary that a second Jesuit assistant had kept for Bowdern throughout the course of the ordeal. (This was the same diary, apparently, that William Peter Blatty had consulted prior to writing his novel more than twenty years earlier.) With the diary in hand, and Halloran's eyewitness testimony as added juice, Allen set out to defictionalize Blatty, as it were, and bring the 1949 exorcism and its main players ringingly back to life.

Of course, there wasn't much doubt which of these players would end up stealing the show. On Allen's pages, real-life exorcist Father William Bowdern shone every bit as brightly as the fictional Damien Karras had on Blatty's twenty years earlier. "Short and stocky, black-haired and square-jawed, with a reputation for cool, decisive action," Bowdern was a tough-guy priest, a hard-bitten, chain-smoking former army chaplain whose previous encounters with evil had been decidedly more earthbound than supernatural. When the call for help came, however, Bowdern wasn't in the least hesitant in responding. With a priestly passion no less stirring that that of Damien Karras or Lancaster Merrin, he dedicated himself to the arduous task of expelling the adolescent boy's demons. In the end the exorcism was successful, and the boy's family, largely as a result of watching Bowdern in action, converted from Lutheranism to Roman Catholicism.[5]

And so here it was again: At century's end, in the most technologically advanced nation in the world, the most improbable of all scenarios—the priest-exorcist as hero.

Far more than the Roman Catholic Church or any other religious institution, then, it is the popular entertainment industry in America that has been responsible over the past thirty years for promoting the mystique of exorcism. Thanks in large measure to bestselling writers such as Malachi Martin and Thomas Allen, television shows such as *20/20,* and the Hollywood movie mill, exorcism has been mythologized and commodified and turned into a kind of recurrent pop sensation. In this capacity, in fact, it isn't much of an exaggeration to say that exorcism today is actually the invention of the popular entertainment industry—the product, above all else, of Hollywood hype and Madison Avenue hucksterism. To most Americans, exorcism without the Blatty-Friedkin movie or *Hostage to the Devil* would be just as unimaginable as rock-and-roll without Elvis, top-forty radio, or MTV.

But this, of course, is only part of the story. While exorcism for the majority of Americans is nothing more than a drive-in diversion, a vicarious midnight thrill, there exist certain cultural pockets in the United States where the ritual is taken with utmost, life-and-death seriousness. And while the people who inhabit these pockets have unquestionably been influenced by the popular entertainment industry, they have also drawn on a variety of other resources for their beliefs in demonism and demonic possession. It is to these people—America's true believers in exorcism, as it were—that we now turn.

charismatic Deliverance ministry

6.

Heartland Deliverance

The healing and deliverance session was off to a rough start. Paul, a tall, thin, balding man in his mid-twenties, had driven almost two hundred miles to Kansas City in a desperate quest for help, but he hadn't anticipated that one of his prayer ministers would be a woman. Slouched in an armchair at the front of a dimly lit, bare-walled room on the fourth floor of a nondescript office building, Paul fidgeted and squirmed and finally admitted that he was quite uncomfortable with the arrangement. He asked Ellen, a forty-year-old lay minister with short brown hair and thick glasses, to move her chair so that she wouldn't be directly facing him. Ellen shifted her chair to the perimeter of the room and sat down again, but this still wasn't good enough. Paul asked her to turn her chair sideways so that the contours of her legs beneath her ankle-length dress would be hidden from his view. Ellen did as he asked, but Paul complained that even now she was too provocative a presence for him. Ellen next moved her chair to the back corner of the room and again positioned it sideways, but this time Paul asked her to leave the room altogether—at least until he had managed to find his bearings. With just a hint of a frown, Ellen stood and walked to the door, saying that she'd be waiting down the corridor in case she was needed later on.

This left Paul alone in the room with just myself (I was there as an observer) and Felix, a gaunt, thirty-year-old prayer minister with slicked-back hair and tattooed arms. Felix opened the session with a brief prayer, and then he asked Paul to speak as candidly as possible about the circumstances that had brought him to Kansas City. Still slouching, and still obviously uncomfortable, Paul gave his story in a halting (yet strangely eloquent) monotone. Felix, sitting opposite him with arms folded, listened attentively, only occasionally interrupting with requests for clarification.

Paul said that he had been raised on the West Coast as the second of three children in a nominally Christian family and that his childhood had been distinctly unhappy. His parents, both successful professionals, had spared no financial expense in raising their children (the best schools, customized vacations), but the family environment was an emotional wasteland. Paul's father was engrossed in his work and very rarely found time for anything but the most rudimentary parental affection, and his mother drank heavily and flew into fits of rage at the slightest provocation. By Paul's early adolescence the situation had become almost unbearable for him, and, feeling the need for escape, he began spending one or two nights a week at the house of his closest friend, a boy he'd known since kindergarten. During one of these nights away from home, however, Paul awoke to find his friend performing oral sex on him. Filled with a confusing mixture of revulsion and shame and pleasure, Paul threw on his clothes and spent the rest of the night wandering aimlessly in some nearby woods.

Although Paul tried hard to put it out of his mind, the incident at his friend's house dogged him relentlessly. Over the next several years he fantasized endlessly about fellatio, and his sexual impulses seemed in danger of spinning completely out of control. He masturbated compulsively, four or five times daily, sometimes while sodomizing himself with tampons or other objects and sometimes while wearing his mother's bra and panties. At the age of sixteen he tried to have sex with the next-door neighbor's pet poodle, and the following year he finally succeeded (after many failed attempts) in performing fellatio upon himself. Shortly after mastering this feat of autoeroticism, Paul also began experimenting heavily with hallucinogenic drugs, and on several occasions he experienced nightmarish trips that were highlighted by macabre images of death and destruction.

Paul left home for college at the age of nineteen, and during his sophomore year he befriended a classmate who belonged to a charismatic prayer group that met twice weekly in the basement of an Episcopal church several blocks off campus. Although he had never considered himself particularly religious, Paul decided to check out the prayer meeting personally one evening. It exceeded his wildest expectations. The outbursts of enthusiasm, the spontaneous praying and speaking in tongues, the demonstrations of miraculous healing and intensive fellowship—all of this was astonishingly new to Paul, and he felt that he had finally found a place where he might be truly at home. Over the next several months Paul immersed himself fully in the life of the group, and in the process his sexual miasma and self-doubts gradually seemed to melt away. He studied Scripture and attended special catechetical sessions, he made new friends and cultivated a new religious sensibility, and finally, in what amounted to his full-scale initiation into the charismatic fold, he experienced baptism in the Holy Spirit and suddenly found that he, too, was capable of speaking in tongues.

To his dismay, however, Paul's charismatic conversion wasn't quite the panacea he had hoped for. Within just weeks of his receiving spirit-baptism, all of Paul's old troubles returned with a vengeance: Once again he found himself obsessed with lurid sexual fantasies, and once again he felt himself drowning in doubt and despair. Paul tried to counter his troubles by throwing himself even more fervently into charismatic worship, but his condition seemed to grow progressively worse. He spent entire days locked in his room in a guilt-ridden, masturbatory funk, and, finding it impossible to keep up with his studies, he dropped out of college and took a job driving a cab. It was at this point that Paul became fearful that he might actually be losing his sanity. In the early-morning hours, while waiting outside hotels and restaurants for fares, he began to feel shifting sexual sensations, quite often of orgasmic intensity, in various parts of his body. The sensations normally started out in his chest and then moved on to his head, his groin, and sometimes even his feet, and while rarely lasting more than five minutes or so, they invariably left him numb with shame.

After enduring all of this in grim silence for several months, Paul finally worked up the nerve to discuss his plight with the leadership team of his charismatic prayer group. The team members were sympathetic, and after questioning Paul closely about his personal history, they suggested that his condition was the result of deep-rooted (and still festering) psychological wounds inflicted on him during childhood. In all likelihood, they said, he had felt rejected as a young boy by his emotionally absentee father and alcoholic mother, and his pain and confusion had been exacerbated during adolescence by the traumatic sexual episode at his friend's house. Later the same week they prayed over Paul for "inner healing," calling on Jesus to redeem his fractured psyche and to infuse him with divine love, and this—at least temporarily—somehow seemed to do the trick. In the months that followed, Paul felt as if he had been given a new lease on life. His strange physical symptoms subsided, and his mood brightened; he found a new job managing a small retail outlet; and he began dating a woman from his prayer group.

Just when he was convinced that the worst was behind him, however, Paul's world came crashing in on him again. While riding the bus, or sitting in a coffee shop, or otherwise going about his daily routine, he was sometimes overcome by a bizarre kind of sexual frenzy. He might see a woman, a total stranger, and feel an impulse to commit sexual violence against her; then turn and see a young child and feel a similar impulse; and then begin praying frantically to Jesus, only to end up with an urge to commit sexual violence against Him, Jesus, as well. In addition to this, Paul began to experience new and alarming physical sensations. While lying awake at night, he sometimes felt excruciating pain caused (or so it seemed) by invisible claws clutching at various parts of his body and invisible bonds tightening around his head. As the weeks passed, these sensations seemed to increase in intensity, and for added torture, Paul also began to suffer almost daily from severe headaches and bouts of dizziness. At the urging of his girlfriend he visited a neurologist, but extensive testing revealed absolutely nothing (neurologically, at least) out of the ordinary with him.

In the midst of all this, Paul was acutely uncomfortable attending the meetings of his charismatic prayer group, and he sometimes avoided them altogether for weeks at a time. He blamed himself for his setback, believing that it was due either to lack of faith or to irredeemable perversity, and he worried that the team leaders who had presided over his earlier healing would write him off as a lost cause if they discovered how badly he had fallen. Nevertheless, sensing that something was amiss, several prayer leaders visited Paul at his apartment one evening, and once again they were enormously sympathetic. They assured Paul that he wasn't alone in his struggles, and they urged him not to abandon hope. Although his earlier healing had somehow failed to "take root," they'd be more than happy to try again.

And try again they did. Over the next six months or so the team leaders prayed over Paul for inner healing several additional times — but with frustratingly familiar results. For a period of weeks following each healing session, Paul's symptoms seemed to go into remission, only to spring cruelly (and predictably) back to life. At the end of it all he was no better off than before, and in some respects quite a bit worse. His girlfriend moved out of state and became engaged to another man, he lost his job and was forced to borrow money from his parents, and he increasingly came to regard suicide as possibly his best option.

Paul continued to attend meetings of his charismatic prayer group throughout these tough times, but sporadically and without nearly as much conviction as when he'd first started. Just when he was on the verge of dropping out altogether, however, he was approached one evening by a middle-aged woman who had recently returned to the group after a decade-long absence. She told Paul that she had heard of his troubles and that if only half of what she had heard was true, it seemed a good bet he was suffering from some form of demonic affliction. Rather than prayer for inner healing, she said, what Paul probably needed was an informal exorcism known in charismatic circles as "deliverance." She said that deliverance was commonly practiced in the prayer group when she first started attending its meetings almost twenty years earlier, but that it had gradually fallen into disfavor. She also lent Paul a book she thought he might find illuminating. The book was Malachi Martin's *Hostage to the Devil.*

Paul devoured *Hostage* in a single sitting, and suddenly everything seemed to fall into place. His bizarre emotional seizures, his frantic sexual fantasies, the sensations of claws clutching at his body—all these were symptoms, he was now convinced, of demonic affliction. At some point, possibly during the night of infamy at his friend's house, Paul thought, he had inadvertently opened himself to demonic influence, and while he wasn't yet fully possessed, it was clear that decisive action needed to be taken as soon as possible.

Paul may have been primed for action, but the leaders of his prayer group weren't so sure. When he asked them, several days after reading *Hostage,* if they would be willing to pray over him for deliverance, they suggested that he consider seeing a psychiatrist instead. They told him that the prayer group had given up on deliverance in the late seventies, mainly because it had proven far too unruly and unedifying a procedure. At the time, they said, people from the group were routinely blaming almost everything imaginable, from marital infidelity to depression, on demonic affliction and then coming to prayer meetings looking for an instant fix. Some of these people may have benefited from inner healing and some from a combination of inner healing and psychotherapy, the prayer leaders said, but deliverance was clearly not the answer. It was a cop-out for them, they said, and it would just as surely be a cop-out for Paul as well.

Still convinced, even after this rebuff, that he was suffering from demonic affliction, Paul arranged a meeting with a local Catholic priest to inquire about the possibility of receiving an official Catholic exorcism. The priest said that the Catholic Church wasn't in the business of providing exorcisms, and he, too, suggested that Paul see a psychiatrist. Paul received similar responses from several other priests whom he contacted over the next several weeks, and finally, just when he was on the brink of giving up, an acquaintance from his prayer group informed him that there was an ecumenical charismatic ministry in Kansas City that regularly performed both inner healing and deliverance. Paul contacted the ministry by phone, gave a brief description of his condition, and made an appointment for the following week.

Upon finishing his story, Paul, looking visibly relieved, told Felix that he now felt comfortable enough for Ellen to rejoin us. Ellen came back into the room and asked to be briefed on what had taken place in her absence. Then she and Felix stood over Paul and, laying their hands on his back and shoulders, prayed over him for inner healing. Softly and solicitously, they asked Jesus to heal Paul's wounded memories, to grant him the grace to forgive those who had abused or neglected him, and to fill the empty spaces in his life with love. For the opening three or four minutes of this prayer, Paul sat absolutely still, head bowed and arms folded, but suddenly, his face contorted and his eyes burning, he lurched menacingly out of his chair and stood facing Ellen and Felix, growling like a wounded animal. Ellen and Felix backed up several steps, exchanged worried whispers, and then, calmly and authoritatively, they prayed in unison:

> In the name of the Lord Jesus Christ, and by the power of God's Word, and the shed blood of Jesus Christ and the Holy Spirit, we bind the evil spirits that are tormenting Paul. In the name of Jesus, we forbid you evil spirits from manifesting yourselves in any way, or from interfering in any way with our prayers. In the name of Jesus.

These words seemed to stop Paul in his tracks, and he slumped back into his chair, once again bowing his head and folding his arms. Without missing a beat, Ellen and Felix positioned themselves directly in front of Paul and began the rite of deliverance. With arms outstretched and palms turned upward, they prayed that "the power of the blood of Christ surround and protect every person in the room" and that "the evil spirits tormenting Paul lose their power to resist." There were more preliminary prayers, then Ellen recited Psalm 34:17 ("Thank You Lord that when the righteous cry, You hear them and deliver them out of all their troubles"), and then both she and Felix real aloud from the Gospel of Luke: "I saw Satan fall like lightning from heaven. Behold, I have given you authority to tread upon serpents and scorpions, and over all the power of the enemy; and nothing shall hurt you." [10:17–19]

Leaning forward, Ellen next began to pray softly in tongues, and after two or three minutes she straightened up and said that with the guidance of the Holy Spirit she had succeeded in discerning the identities of Paul's demons. Since his adolescence, and possibly even earlier, Ellen said, Paul had been tormented by evil spirits of guilt and shame, rejection and unforgiveness, sexual perversion, masturbation, and hatred of women. She told Paul that these spirits had placed him under the bondage of sin, and she asked whether he was now prepared "to renounce this sin and renew his commitment to Jesus Christ as Lord and Savior." Clasping his arms tightly around his chest and gently crying, Paul nodded in agreement, and Ellen led him in a short prayer of repentance.

And then the climax. Raising her voice ever so slightly, and standing ramrod straight, Ellen began the serious business of expelling Paul's demons:

> In the name of Jesus Christ, and by the power of His Blood and the Holy Spirit, I command you, spirit of guilt, to leave Paul now, without entering into or otherwise bringing harm to anyone else in this room, and I send you straight to the Creator to be dealt with as He sees fit.

Ellen repeated this formula six more times, once each for Paul's additional demons of shame and rejection and sexual perversion and so forth, and each time Paul responded by coughing and spasmodically jerking his head. At the end of it all he shrugged his shoulders, smiled meekly, and said, "I really think it's happened. I think that they're gone."

And that was it. No pyrotechnics. No acrobatics or spinning heads. The whole business orderly and efficient. Over and done with in less than fifteen minutes. Aside from Paul's coughing and head-jerking, a calm, controlled, almost decorous procedure.

Paul, now grinning broadly, stood up and exchanged hugs with Ellen and Felix. Ellen encouraged him to return to his prayer group and to work hard at strengthening his spiritual life. Although his demons had apparently departed, she said, it was imperative that he not allow them an opportunity to return. She also recommended that he undergo extensive counseling ("You've gotten rid of your demons, but you still have lots more work to do," she said), and she promised that she'd give him the name of a good Christian psychotherapist in his area.

Finally, a postscript. Six months after his deliverance, I spoke with Paul by phone. He told me that he had taken Ellen's advice and was seeing a Christian psychotherapist on a regular basis. He also said that he had experienced none of his old symptoms since his deliverance, and that for the first time in his life he felt truly at peace with himself.[1]

This was my first encounter of any kind with charismatic deliverance ministry. It took me rather by surprise. Here, wrapped up in a single ritual package, were elements from primitive shamanism, backwoods Pentecostalism, and middle-class psychotherapy. Yet, strange assemblage that it was, the ritual played seamlessly, like a finished stage performance whose kinks had been ironed out through endless rehearsal. And this, in fact, wasn't far from the truth. As I would soon discover, deliverance first stumbled onto the charismatic scene during the late sixties, it picked up considerable momentum during the early to mid-seventies, and ever since it has been revised and experimented with and refined into something of an art form.

I should hasten to add, however, that deliverance has never been universally embraced by charismatics in the United States. Over the past thirty years some charismatic prayer groups have flatly rejected the ritual, while others (such as the one attended by Paul) have given up on it after periods of experimentation. Still, the fact remains: Since the late sixties a surprising number of mostly white, mostly middle-class Americans have been convinced that the modern world is heavily populated with demons. Not merely metaphorical demons or the man-wrought demons of barbed wire and ethnic cleansing, but real supernatural entities, with their own identities and missions, their own strengths and foibles, and sometimes even their own telltale odors. To understand how this has come to pass, it is necessary first of all to re-trace the early history of the charismatic renewal movement in the United States.

pentecostalism joins the mainstream

During the summer of 1960 both *Time* and *Newsweek* ran stories on a religious brushfire of sorts that had broken out at an upper-middle-class parish in Southern California. Earlier that year approximately seventy members of St. Mark's Episcopal Church in the Los Angeles suburb of Van Nuys had suddenly started speaking in tongues and engaging in other kinds of ecstatic worship after experiencing baptism in the Holy Spirit. Needless to say, not everyone at St. Mark's was thrilled by this distinctly un-Episcopalian behavior. Some parishioners threatened to pull out unless the "gang of seventy" was brought into line, and others demanded the resignation of St. Mark's rector—Dennis Bennett, a middle-aged convert to the Episcopal Church—for his role in helping to promote this strange outburst of enthusiasm. Under heavy pressure, and widely vilified as a religious crackpot, Bennett was eventually forced to give up his post at St. Mark's, and shortly afterward the Episcopal bishop of Los Angeles, Francis Bloy, issued a statement forbidding any more tongue-speaking under church auspices in his diocese.[1]

An intriguing intramural squabble, to be sure, but why the national media coverage? By 1960 there was nothing particularly unusual about people receiving baptism in the Holy Spirit or speaking in tongues in the United States, and nothing in the least unusual about their doing so in Los Angeles. Fifty-four years earlier, in 1906, the City of Angels had served as the staging ground for a major outpouring of spirit-baptism and tongue-speaking across America when an itinerant black preacher named William Seymour proclaimed the dawning of a new Pentecost no less powerful or marvelous in its effects than the original Pentecost that took place in Jerusalem somewhere around A.D. 34. Operating out of a ramshackle mission at 312 Azusa Street in Los Angeles, Seymour assured his congregation that they were living in the last days and that as a prelude to the Second Coming of Jesus Christ and in fulfillment of biblical promises, the Holy Spirit was once again empowering Christians to speak in strange tongues and to carry out miraculous healings and conversions. Seymour's words caught fire, and over the next two decades missionaries from Azusa Street helped bring into existence the worldwide religious movement that became known as Pentecostalism.[2]

The big difference between St. Mark's and Azusa Street, of course, and the biggest reason for *Time*'s and *Newsweek*'s coverage of the squabble at St. Mark's, was social class. For the most part William Seymour's Azusa Street congregation was poor and black, and as Pentecostalism spread beyond Azusa Street in the years after 1906, it exercised appeal primarily among economically fragile and politically marginal blacks and whites in America's downtrodden urban ghettos and forgotten rural outposts. With its emotional extravagance and end-of-history expectancy, Pentecostalism was the religion of the cultural hinterland—a backwater faith for those of thwarted worldly prospects and feverish otherworldly hopes.[3]

St. Mark's, however, was another story entirely. In the starchy and meticulously manicured world of Episcopalianism, spirit-baptism and tongue-speaking seemed to make about as much sense as Jerry Lee Lewis or camp meetings. And yet here it was: In a bizarre kind of cultural crossover that no one could have reasonably anticipated, the religion of no-'count whites and disprivileged blacks had somehow succeeded in finding a place for itself in the uptown pews.

And St. Mark's was only the beginning. Shortly after being forced out of his position in Van Nuys, Dennis Bennett became vicar of a small Episcopal church in Seattle, and within just a matter of months almost a hundred members of his new congregation had also received baptism in the Holy Spirit and were speaking in tongues. Meanwhile, back in Los Angeles, a well-heeled Episcopal laywoman named Jean Stone, who had worked closely with Bennett in launching the St. Mark's revival, founded a fellowship called the Blessed Trinity Society for the purpose of spreading the news concerning the surprising work of the Holy Spirit that was taking place in American Episcopalianism. The news spread quickly, and not just within Episcopal circles. By the end of 1966, spirit-baptism and tongue-speaking had made significant inroads within Lutheranism and Presbyterianism and virtually every other mainline Protestant denomination in the United States, and one of the only questions remaining was whether Roman Catholicism might be next.[4]

The answer to this wasn't long in coming. In late 1966 William Storey and Ralph Keifer, both faculty members at Duquesne, a Catholic university in Pittsburgh, became interested in Pentecostalism after reading David Wilkerson's *The Cross and the Switchblade* and John Sherrill's *They Speak with Other Tongues*. Wilkerson's book was a vivid chronicle of the author's Pentecostal ministry among drug addicts and teenage delinquents on the mean streets of New York City, and Sherrill's was a highly sympathetic account of the recent outbreak of Pentecostal enthusiasm within mainline Protestantism. Their curiosity piqued, the two professors decided to attend an interdenominational prayer meeting in the Pittsburgh area, led by a charismatic Presbyterian named Florence Dodge; and in January 1967 both men received baptism in the Holy Spirit and began speaking in tongues. The next month Storey and Keifer took thirty Duquesne students on a weekend retreat, and before it was over, almost the entire group had fallen under the Pentecostal spell. Over the next several months word of the Duquesne Weekend spread rapidly throughout the Catholic college network, precipitating similar outbreaks of enthusiasm at

Notre Dame and a dozen other campuses, and by the end of 1967 there were almost as many Roman Catholics participating in Pentecostal worship in the United States as mainline Protestants.[5]

Not that anyone would have confused this upstart, middle-class Pentecostalism with the real thing, as it were, that came out of Azusa Street. In the storefront missions and creaky country churches that served as its main stomping grounds in the decades after Azusa Street, Pentecostalism was a boisterous and rawboned affair, with gut-growling music, sweat-stained dancing and shouting, and end-of-the-world prophesying. In the hands of its newly enthused, middle-class practitioners, however, the old-time faith underwent a sweeping gentrification. The pawnshop saxophones and screeching country fiddles were replaced with sweetly strumming guitars and soothing "Hallelujah" choruses, the fervent praying and praising were trimmed and softened and snuggled into coffee-scented ritual formats, and the anticipation of an imminent and catastrophic end to world history was converted into a quest for spiritual growth and intimacy. Even the label itself was changed: Rather than "Pentecostals," the new enthusiasts from the mainline churches generally referred to themselves as "charismatics" (and to their shared enterprise as the charismatic renewal movement) after the so-called charismata, or "gifts of the Holy Spirit," as set forth in the New Testament epistles of Romans, 1 Corinthians, and Ephesians.

Although quite a bit was lost in this middle-class translation, the chief defining characteristics of classical Pentecostalism came through mostly unscathed. No less than the direct descendants of Azusa Street, both Protestant and Catholic charismatics placed primary emphasis on baptism in the Holy Spirit, which they regarded as an utterly wondrous and transformative experience of God's power, a kind of drenching of the interior self with divine love, and which they believed was accompanied by such extraordinary spiritual gifts (or "charisms") as prophecy, wisdom, healing, and speaking in tongues. Of these various charisms, speaking in tongues ("glossolalia") was regarded by charismatics as the signature gift of spirit-baptism, and it was the practice of tongue-speaking, above all else, that caused many people in the mainline churches to feel uneasy with the charismatic renewal movement during its formative years.

Even today this sense of uneasiness isn't difficult to comprehend. To the outside observer, charismatic tongue-speaking comes across as little more than gibberish, as a bewildering nursery school kind of babble, and virtually all scholarly investigations of the phenomenon, according to the historian of religion Robert Mapes Anderson, have concluded "that speaking in tongues is incoherent, repetitive syllabification having neither the form nor the structure of human speech."[6] In the view of charismatics, however, tongue-speaking is inexpressibly beautiful and moving, a divinely inspired and rapturous mode of speech that transcends ordinary linguistic conventions. As the New Testament writings of Paul and Luke amply attest, charismatics say, tongue-speaking was commonly practiced during the early years of Christianity, and now, almost two thousand years later, the practice has been restored to the Christian Church through the marvelous workings of the Holy Spirit.

Despite taking almost everyone by surprise at the time, this middle-class Pentecostalism was quite possibly a movement just waiting to happen. By the late sixties, as Harvey Cox has recently pointed out, a spiritual restlessness of sorts was making its presence felt across the United States. As evidenced by the growing popularity of Asian mysticism and various experimental new religions, a significant number of Americans were looking for something deeper and more spiritually satisfying than the one-dimensional consumerism of the prevailing culture. If the early adherents of the charismatic renewal movement held anything in common, it was precisely this same sense of restlessness. In an age of worrisome affluence they felt vaguely discontented with the preprogrammed pieties and business-as-usual approach of the established denominations, and participation in the charismatic movement afforded them an emotionally richer and decidedly more spontaneous experience of faith.[7]

This didn't mean, however, that charismatics were in any way schismatic. Rather than conspiring to break away from the established churches, they were committed to staying and trying to revitalize them from within. And this meant, first of all, convincing the authorities of the churches that the charismatic renewal movement was a legitimate enterprise of faith. The practice of speaking in tongues was clearly an impediment in this regard, and so, too, was that of miraculous healing. But there was (potentially) no greater impediment to charismatics' winning full acceptance within the mainline churches than the practice of deliverance.

The Rise of charismatic Deliverance Ministry

In one sense it was only to be expected that deliverance would succeed in working its way into charismatic circles. The charismatic renewal movement was deeply influenced by classical Pentecostalism, after all, and deliverance (or exorcism) was commonly practiced among Pentecostals in the United States from the earliest days of Azusa Street. Just as they had been empowered by the Holy Spirit to perform miraculous healings, Pentecostals believed, so, too, had they been empowered to cast out demons. During the first several decades after Azusa Street, in fact, Pentecostals tended to view miraculous healing and exorcism as two sides of the same coin. Sickness was generally regarded by them as a kind of "demonic assault," and as Robert Mapes Anderson points out, miraculous healing was "a process of driving out the evil spirits through the greater power of the Holy Spirit." When praying for healing during these early decades, Pentecostals almost always commanded the "cancer demon" or the "arthritis demon" or the "alcohol demon" or whatever to "come out in the name of Jesus." As Vinson Synan, the ranking dean of Pentecostal studies in America, told me in a recent interview, there was "no shortage of enthusiastic deliverance ministers prepared to discover a demon behind every tree."[8]

During the late 1930s and early 1940s, however, this emphasis on demonism was considerably toned down. As more and more

Pentecostals began to enter the economic mainstream of American society, exorcism and faith-healing tended to recede into the background of their ritual life—still practiced, but without nearly as much frequency or urgency as before. Having attained a measure of social respectability, many Pentecostals quite naturally craved religious respectability as well, and chasing after demons no longer seemed to fit the bill. As cultural alienation gave way to cultural accommodation, in other words, exorcism was consigned to the back room, out of sight and, mostly, out of mind.

"During the early years Pentecostals were guilty of terrific excess when it came to demon-expulsion," Synan told me. "But for a variety of reasons, more sociological than theological, exorcism or deliverance fell out of favor around the time of the Second World War. This was especially true of Pentecostals connected to mainly white denominations such as the Assemblies of God and the [International Church of the] Foursquare Gospel. It resurfaced here and there, mainly in connection with healing revivals, and it continued to be practiced to some extent by independent Pentecostal preachers in out-of-the-way rural areas. For the most part, however, exorcism fell into a state of dormancy for almost thirty years. It was the charismatics, or neo-Pentecostals, who brought it back."[9]

Nevertheless, it took some time for exorcism (or deliverance) to catch on within charismatic circles—and even then it never caught on entirely. At its heart the charismatic renewal movement was an upbeat, joy-to-the-world kind of affair, a celebration of the new life that was available to believers through immersion in the Holy Spirit. Charismatics wanted to feel good about themselves and their prospects for future salvation, and this, especially during the fledgling years of their movement, left little room for demons or supernatural evil.

Eventually, however, demons came knocking at the back door, and one of the first charismatics to hear them was a forty-year-old Disciples of Christ minister named Don Basham. In 1964 Basham left a charismatic ministry in Toronto to become pastor of a merged Baptist and Disciples of Christ congregation in the small mill town of Sharon, Pennsylvania. Over the next couple of years, as he recounts in a chirpy memoir entitled *Deliver Us from Evil*, a combination of events complicated his hitherto sanguine view of the world. A middle-aged, and rather intimidating, woman from his new congregation came to him for help, claiming that she was tormented almost daily by inner voices whispering lewd and blasphemous messages. While reading in his den, or sitting over his morning coffee, Basham began to suffer alarming (and medically inexplicable) physical seizures. And more ominous still, a Pentecostal prophetess from the Pennsylvania coal-mining hills informed him that she had received a revelation that he would "be greatly used in a ministry of deliverance, discerning and casting out evil spirits."[10]

Basham was perplexed. His liberal theological training hadn't prepared him for this sort of thing, and as late as 1966 he still wasn't sure that he believed in a personal devil—let alone legions of demons hatching evil in the lives of ordinary women and men. Nevertheless, Basham was nothing if not open-minded, and in best ministerial fashion he resolved to work through his perplexity by taking a fresh look at the Christian Scriptures.

As he did so, his perplexity rapidly gave way to amazement. How, he asked himself, had he gotten through seminary without noticing that the New Testament was crawling with references to demons and demonism? In the Gospels there were several striking instances of Jesus' freeing entire groups of people from evil spirits, including the following account in Matthew 8:16: "That evening they brought to him many who were possessed with demons; and he cast out the spirits with a word, and healed all who were sick."[11] And there were also seven separate instances in which Jesus expelled demons from specific individuals: the woman with a spirit of infirmity as reported in Luke 13:10–17, for example; the man in the synagogue tormented by an unclean spirit (Mark 1:21–28; Luke 4:31–37); the Syrophoenician woman's daughter (Matthew 15:21–28; Mark 7:24–30); and, most memorable of all, the following episode as recounted in Matthew 8:28–32:

> When he came to the other side, to the country of the Gadarenes, two demoniacs coming out of the tombs met him.

They were so fierce that no one could pass that way. Suddenly they shouted, "What have you to do with us, Son of God? Have you come here to torment us before the time?" Now a large herd of swine was feeding at some distance from them. The demons begged him, "If you cast us out, send us into the herd of swine." And he said to them, "Go!" So they came out and entered the swine; and suddenly, the whole herd rushed down the steep bank into the sea and perished in the water.[12]

What's more, Jesus apparently fully expected his followers to take up his ministry of exorcism. "Lord, in your name even the demons submit to us," the seventy disciples reported to him after returning from their first major preaching expedition, whereupon Jesus replied, "See, I have given you authority to tread on snakes and scorpions, and over all the power of the enemy; and nothing will hurt you." (Luke 10:17–19) And at the end of the Gospel of Mark (in a passage whose authorship is contested by Scripture scholars), Jesus gave His disciples some startlingly explicit instructions:

Go into all the world and proclaim the good news to the whole creation. The one who believes and is baptized will be saved; but the one who does not believe will be condemned. And these signs will accompany those who believe: by using my name they will cast out demons; they will speak in new tongues; they will pick up snakes in their hands, and if they drink any deadly thing, it will not hurt them; they will lay their hands on the sick, and they will recover. (Mark 16:15–18)

Basham wasn't sure at first what to make of all this. Thanks to his seminary training, he was passingly familiar with modern biblical criticism, and it seemed quite possible to him that none of this demon-talk was meant to be taken literally. Perhaps Jesus was only speaking in the popular idiom, or cultural vernacular, of His times, and the people reported in the Scriptures as demon-possessed were really suffering from what we would regard today as psychological or biochemical disorders. But was this really the point? Basham asked himself. Whether or not demons were actually involved, the exorcisms performed by Jesus seemed remarkably effective. At a stroke, people were cured instantly of whatever it was that ailed them—demonic affliction, psychological pathology, or whatever else. And if exorcism worked for Jesus, and if His followers had been commissioned to take up the ministry after Him, was it not something worth trying even today? As he informs us in *Deliver Us from Evil,* Basham decided that it was. "What if, for a few days or a few weeks, I were to act *as if* demons existed? Never mind trying to rationalize it. Just follow the Bible pattern exactly. Do what Jesus did—and see."[13]

While still not completely sold on the notion of demonic affliction, then, Basham in late 1966 began performing occasional exorcisms on an experimental basis. The outcome of his first several procedures gave him reason to believe that he was on the right track: His subjects seemed relieved, at least for the time being, of whatever spiritual or psychological torments they had been experiencing. In the fall of 1967 he resigned his pastorship in Sharon and embarked on a new career as an itinerant preacher and part-time exorcism minister.

Shortly into this new career, however, Basham was forced to deal with a nagging theological issue. Up to this point every single person who had come to him for an exorcism was a Christian—a born-again, spirit-baptized Christian no less. How could this be? As several of his charismatic acquaintances were quick to point out, the idea that someone could be simultaneously spirit-filled and demon-possessed was completely at odds with New Testament teaching and classical Pentecostal theology. (By then most leading Pentecostals were in agreement that a true Christian couldn't be taken over by demonic forces.)[14] Finding himself at a loss on the matter, Basham decided to consult a well-known, Cambridge-educated Pentecostal minister named Derek Prince, who was then residing in Fort Lauderdale, Florida. In 1964, while serving as pastor of a Pentecostal church in Seattle, Prince had started a high-profile exorcism ministry of his own, and to the chagrin of many leading Pentecostals, his clientele had also been made up almost entirely of Christians.

The crucial distinction, Prince told Basham, was between demonic possession and affliction. While it was highly unlikely that true spirit-baptized Christians could actually become possessed, which meant falling completely under the sway of Satan, there was no reason to think that they couldn't be tormented or afflicted in some area of their lives by demonic powers. The New Testament provided no straight-forward evidence of Christians' falling victim to demonic affliction, Prince conceded, but the pastoral evidence was overwhelming. In every Christian congregation that he knew of, he said, there were people who were tormented by some compulsive appetite or haunting fear that no amount of prayer or personal resolve seemed capable of conquering. Rather than simply struggling against their "old selves," or carnal natures, Prince said, many of these people were undoubtedly afflicted by evil spirits. And what's more, he added, there was nothing in the least surprising about this. Considering that spirit-baptized Christians posed a significant threat to Satan's kingdom, it stood to reason that they would be singled out for special treatment.[15]

This settled, Basham got down to serious business. In the winter of 1968 he teamed up with a veteran Canadian-based Pentecostal exorcist named H. A. Maxwell Whyte to deliver a Cleveland boy of a spirit of epilepsy. Upon returning to his new home base in Florida, he delivered a middle-aged, alcoholic woman of twenty-two quarrelsome demons, "each one arguing and complaining before it left." Indeed, now that he was secure in his ministry, Basham seemed to find demons everywhere. He delivered his preschool daughter of a "spirit of fear" and a neighboring woman of forty-one separate demons, and while visiting his chiropractor, he delivered a young man named Mark of a demon of insanity, which insisted on licking up Mark's vomit from the floor before vacating the premises. Along the way Basham also developed an extremely close working relationship with Derek Prince, and during the late sixties the two men barnstormed across the country, preaching (and demonstrating) the gospel of deliverance at every opportunity. Toward the end of the decade they even added a new wrinkle to their ministry: group deliverance conducted in public — an arrangement that permitted entire roomfuls of people, in a collective rush of thrashing and wailing, to be freed of their demons all at once.[16]

F rom the very beginning Basham was fervently forthright about his deliverance ministry, but relatively few charismatics seemed interested in taking his lead. Within certain sectors of the renewal movement, in fact, he was regarded as something of a loose cannon, and his talk of demons and demonization was widely dismissed as utter nonsense. Nevertheless, by 1967 a small number of additional charismatics, some of them emboldened by Basham's (and Prince's) example, were also trying their hand at deliverance. One of these was the Episcopalian Dennis Bennett, now based in Seattle following his misadventures in Van Nuys, California. Another was Erwin Prange, a Lutheran pastor based in St. Paul, Minnesota. And on the Presbyterian side there was Bob Whittaker, whom I will discuss shortly; Jim Brown, a minister who worked out of the Philadelphia area; and Leonard Evans, who was pastor of a church in New York City before moving to Toronto and then Ohio. With the possible exception of Erwin Prange, these men weren't nearly as prolific as Basham or Derek Prince in performing deliverance—and they also weren't nearly as open about it.[17]

And for good reason. Consider, for example, the case of Bob Whittaker, who was a pioneering deliverance minister in the Presbyterian wing of the charismatic renewal movement. Whittaker was born and raised in Philadelphia, and after graduating from Yale Divinity School in 1955, he was ordained by the Presbyterian Church (U.S.A.). Following a brief stint in the Appalachian mission field, he became pastor of a middle-class church in Chandler, Arizona, in 1957, and five years later he experienced baptism in the Holy Spirit. In 1966 Whittaker was introduced to deliverance firsthand by a woman of Dutch Reformed background named Corrie ten Boom.

"I was probably one of the very few deliverance ministers at the time who wasn't directly influenced by Don Basham or Derek

Prince," Whittaker told me during a recent conversation. "I knew of Basham and Prince, of course. They were very, very controversial. Pentecostals were suspicious of them, and so were most charismatics. But the person who really had the greatest influence on me was Corrie ten Boom. She had been in a Nazi concentration camp, and she became convinced that the Nazis were demon-possessed. There was no other way to account for their atrocities. After the war she became a famous deliverance minister in Europe. She came to Arizona in 1966 and preached at my church, and after the service I watched her perform a successful deliverance on an alcoholic man from my congregation. He had been oppressed by demons, and I personally watched him being healed. Needless to say, I was convinced."

After watching Corrie ten Boom in action, Whittaker began to perform occasional deliverances himself—but with painful consequences.

"I discovered that I had a spiritual gift in this area, and I made deliverance part of my ongoing ministry," he told me. "It was a team approach. Discerning spirits has never been one of my gifts, and so I worked with one or two other people who were responsible for discerning the presence of demons, and it was my job to drive them out. I thought that we were very discreet, but some people in my church found out about the deliverances, and I was suddenly in the middle of a major controversy. Things came to a boil in 1967, and the local presbytery demanded that I renounce my exorcism ministry. I refused to do so. By this point healing and exorcism were an important part of my overall ministry; they were part of who I was. So the presbytery put me out of my church in Chandler; they put me out of my manse. And my wife and I had five small children at the time. I was blackballed. I appealed to the General Assembly, and this became the first Presbyterian test case involving deliverance. The General Assembly vindicated me the next year, ruling that the presbytery had no right to put me out, but by this time I was serving as associate pastor at a church in Glendale, California. I kept up my exorcism ministry over the years, but I always made a point of being low-key about it."

8.

The Heyday of charismatic Deliverance

At the end of the 1960s deliverance was still very much a guerrilla operation within the charismatic renewal movement — carried out on the run-and-bluster by Don Basham and Derek Prince, and mostly undercover by Bob Whittaker and a handful of others. Many prominent charismatics wanted nothing to do with the ritual, and some worried that it might jeopardize their movement's still-fragile credibility. The real action, however, was yet to come. During the early to late seventies deliverance enjoyed a surprising run of popularity within charismatic circles, and in the process it was openly embraced by some of the renewal movement's leading personalities.

By almost all accounts the most important of these personalities was a Dominican priest named Francis MacNutt. If Basham and Prince were the hit-and-run specialists of deliverance, MacNutt was the consummate ambassador — cool, articulate, unfailingly gracious. Born in St. Louis and educated at Harvard and Catholic University, MacNutt entered the Dominican Order in 1950 and was ordained six years later, at the age of thirty-one. After earning a doctorate in theology and taking over as president of the Catholic Homiletic Society, he returned to St. Louis in 1964 and opened a resource and training center for Catholic preaching. From his earliest adolescence MacNutt had been interested in exploring new dimensions of religious faith, and in the summer of 1967, at the suggestion of a friend, he decided to attend a charismatic retreat called Camp Farthest Out in Knoxville, Tennessee. The experience, he told me several years ago in Jacksonville, where he now lives, proved far more than he had bargained for.

"Camp Farthest Out changed my life," he said. "Most of those in attendance were charismatic Protestants, and I saw them as really turned-on Christians. The main focus of the retreat was healing. This was a subject I had always been interested in — when I first started at Harvard, my plan had been to go on to medical school. Agnes Sanford and Tommy Tyson and some other big names in Pentecostal-charismatic healing ministry gave talks on the need for the Christian churches to rediscover the power of praying for the sick, and I was pretty much won over. I also experienced baptism of the Holy Spirit at the retreat. It was an extraordinary happening. I was one of the first Roman Catholic priests in the United States to become charismatic."

The next summer MacNutt attended a workshop on faith healing that was run by Agnes Sanford in Whitinsville, Massachusetts, and any lingering doubts he might still have harbored were put to rest. The Gospels, he was now convinced, were perfectly clear. During his earthly ministry Jesus had been concerned with liberating women and men not just from sin but also from sickness and both physical and emotional suffering. Healing was an essential part of the Good News that Jesus had come to proclaim; it was a sign of the New Kingdom, and the gift of healing had been transmitted directly by Jesus to his church. Over the centuries, however, the major Christian churches had lost sight of this gift. Rather than seeing sickness and suffering as evils that might potentially be overcome by healing prayer, the churches had resigned themselves to suffering and even assigned it positive redemptive value. Earlier in the century, classical Pentecostals had attempted to reclaim the gift of healing, and Protestant charismatics had been trying to do likewise since the early sixties. There was no reason, MacNutt thought, that Catholic charismatics shouldn't do their part as well. And there was also no reason that he himself, as a charismatic priest, shouldn't take the lead.

Shortly after the Whitinsville workshop, MacNutt prayed for a charismatic woman who was suffering from severe depression, and almost at once her condition improved dramatically. Bolstered by this success, he began to pray for other sick or disturbed people on a fairly regular basis, and he quickly gained a reputation within charismatic circles as an up-and-coming faith healer. Along the way, however, there were some troubling incidents. Sometimes the people he was praying over would shake convulsively, or break into fits of profanity, or even threaten to strangle him. MacNutt wasn't sure at first how to deal with any of this, but in the summer of 1969, at a charismatic retreat in Racine, Wisconsin, he met a woman named Barbara Shlemon who introduced him to the concept of deliverance.

Shlemon was a registered nurse at a hospital on the outskirts of Chicago, and she had been praying deliverance for the benefit of some of her patients since the mid-sixties. (Although Roman Catholic herself, she had first learned about deliverance in 1965 while attending a charismatic prayer group at Trinity Episcopal Church in Wheaton, Illinois.) She told MacNutt that it wasn't accidental that Jesus, as reported in Luke 9:1–2, had commanded His disciples to both heal the sick *and* drive out evil spirits. Jesus recognized that there was sometimes a demonic dimension to sickness and that full healing couldn't be accomplished without attending to it. The bizarre symptoms that MacNutt had encountered in his own healing ministry, she said, were undoubtedly manifestations of the demonic, and it was only through deliverance that they could be properly addressed.[1]

MacNutt was intrigued, and at Shlemon's suggestion he listened to a series of tapes by Derek Prince on deliverance and demonology and found out as much as he could about Prince and Basham's deliverance ministry. "Barbara Shlemon was a big influence on me, and so were Don Basham and Derek Prince," he told me. "But the biggest influence was experience. When you're praying for healing often enough, you inevitably come into contact with evil spirits. These spirits come out of people—bizarre, ugly manifestations. This stuff gets your attention, so eventually you say that healing and deliverance go together. Barbara helped me to make sense of this, and in early 1970 I incorporated deliverance into my healing ministry."

MacNutt's embracement of deliverance was no small deal. During the early to mid-seventies he was at the height of his powers in the charismatic renewal movement. Tall and handsome and (as a Dominican priest) seductively inaccessible, he was the movement's first true sex symbol, a star attraction at healing services and a commanding presence at charismatic leadership conferences. In his public performances, moreover, he was the personification of ecumenical goodwill, always happy to pay tribute to Agnes Sanford, Kathryn Kuhlman, and other well-known Protestant faith healers, and to acknowledge indebtedness to trailblazing deliverance ministers such as Don Basham and Derek Prince. His own gifts for healing were generally held in high regard, and he was widely admired by both Protestant and Catholic charismatics for his sangfroid and intellectual balance. (When I spoke with the pioneering Lutheran exorcist Erwin Prange in the spring of 1998, Prange said that he had always regarded MacNutt as "a personal hero.") With MacNutt on the scene, deliverance no longer seemed (especially to Roman Catholic charismatics) quite so fantastic a proposition.

It was among Catholic charismatics, in fact, that deliverance made its most significant inroads during the 1970s. Not long after MacNutt's conversion to the cause, the predominantly Catholic (and hugely influential) Word of God prayer community in Ann Arbor, Michigan, brought in Don Basham and Derek Prince for several days of intensive consultation. "This was a time of real ferment for us," Randall Cirner, a Catholic layman with deep personal ties to the Word of God community, told me in a recent interview. "Along with the People of Praise community in South Bend, [Indiana], we were a major center of the Catholic renewal at the time, and we were certainly becoming more and more interested in deliverance. An Anglican in England named Michael Harper had written a book on the subject. Francis MacNutt had gotten involved, and he had a genuine gift for the ministry. And then, of course, there were Don Basham and Derek

Prince, who were the biggest names on the scene. We sensed that there were things happening in our community that perhaps warranted deliverance, and so we invited Basham and Prince to come and speak with us. We learned a great deal from them, but their approach wasn't the best match for us. They were big into physical manifestations of demons leaving—retching, puking into buckets, this sort of thing. I personally thought this was very weird. But we began practicing deliverance ourselves shortly afterward. It could sometimes be a daunting and sickening experience, but we were doing it, and so was the People of Praise community in South Bend. . . . As Catholics we were in a bit of an awkward position. We were performing deliverance, which is a kind of informal exorcism, not the formal ritual of exorcism, which requires the explicit permission of the bishop and which can only be performed by a priest appointed by the bishop. We were mostly laypeople, and we didn't have the approval of our bishops. This was admittedly a gray area, and not everyone felt comfortable with it."[2]

Probably the first Catholic charismatic to perform deliverance with the explicit approval of his bishop was a Franciscan priest named Michael Scanlan. A graduate of Williams College and Harvard Law, Scanlan was ordained to the priesthood in 1964, at the age of thirty-three, and baptized in the Spirit several years later. Partly through MacNutt's influence he first became interested in deliverance in about 1970, while he was serving as rector of St. Francis Seminary in Loretto, Pennsylvania, and in 1972 he published a booklet on the sacrament of penance proposing the confessional as an ideal setting for waging battle against evil spirits. *The Power of Penance* attracted a great deal of attention within Catholic charismatic circles, and Scanlan was soon being sought out by a wide variety of people in quest of help for demon-related problems. "In one of my earliest cases," he told me several years ago at the Franciscan University of Steubenville, where he has served as president since 1974, "I commanded a spirit to leave a woman, and the spirit said, 'You can't throw me out; you don't have the authority of your bishop.' So I went to the local bishop of Altoona-

Johnstown for authorization to proceed, and he said, 'Go ahead. Better you than me, Michael.' "

Scanlan, however, was the exception. Very few Catholic charismatics during the early seventies thought it necessary to seek episcopal approval for deliverance, and some, such as a rough-and-tumble, El Paso–based Jesuit named Richard Thomas, seemed only too happy operating outside of official church channels. Born and raised near Plant City, Florida, Thomas was ordained in 1958 and baptized in the Spirit in 1969. In late 1970 he attended a workshop on deliverance at a charismatic conference in Ann Arbor, and shortly after returning to El Paso, he was dealt his first real-life case.

"A woman asked me to bless her house, and while I was sprinkling holy water around, just out of plain playfulness, I threw some on her," he told me. "When I did this, she threw herself on the floor, screaming, howling, banging. I said, 'You didn't like the holy water, did you?' She just sat there looking distraught, and then she asked me to pray over her for deliverance. But I didn't know anything about anything. All I'd ever done was take one workshop on deliverance."

To his immense relief, however, Thomas wasn't forced to go it alone. "This woman wasn't a Catholic," he said. "She went to a Foursquare Pentecostal church, and I knew her minister. He was one of the few Pentecostal ministers around who believed that a Christian could have a demon, and he agreed to help out. We prayed over her eight to ten hours, two days straight. He did most of the heavy work, and I watched everything he did. He taught me a lot. Together we cleared the demons right out of her."

This case led to others, and Thomas soon discovered that he had "a special gift for casting out demons." Unlike most Catholic charismatics, moreover, he wasn't in the least hesitant about tackling cases not just of demonic affliction but also of outright possession. On the strength of his own experience, in fact, he soon became convinced that possession was far more common than most people realized. "Oh yeah, I saw lots of possessions in those early years, and I continue to see them all the time. I saw one just yesterday," he said. "The difference between affliction and possession is one of degree. With affliction you do a basic deliverance, and with possession you do an exorcism. It's like the difference between washing and scrubbing. I've done a bunch of exorcisms, but I've rarely used the Catholic Church's official ritual of exorcism. Because then I'd have to get permission from the bishop, and I usually don't have time to get permission. I see a need, and I respond to it."

Thomas also told me that he has generally avoided discussing his demon-expulsion ministry with his fellow Jesuits. "Most of them can't find their way out of the library," he said. "I'm not going to get into arguing and theorizing with these Jesuits. Over the years they usually haven't even been able to find me. I have the real experience. My provincial once asked me if I did exorcisms, and I said yes. He said nothing more about it. No point kicking an ant hive; just walk around it. No sense talking to people about it—especially to people who are educated. They already know better. But when ordinary people say, 'I've got something in me; please help me,' I try to help."

Although his fellow Jesuits might have had difficulty tracking him down, Thomas was well known among charismatics during the seventies for his deliverance ministry—and especially for a kick-out-the-jams, shake-the-rafters approach that made even Don Basham and Derek Prince seem timid in comparison. I asked him if he had toned down his act over the years.

"Oh, sure, when I first started out in this, we used to have fireworks all the time. It was crazy—like riding a busting bronco. The demons would be manifesting; I'd be arguing with them; there was screaming, fighting, and vomiting all over the place. I learned through trial and error. I never used to bind the spirits. Now I bind them all the time—I command them to shut up and stop their interfering. I'm not interested in fireworks any longer. And I never get into a fight I can't win. I've got no intention of getting whipped. I'm only interested in winning. If it looks like I might not win, I cut things off.

"A short time ago I did an exorcism on a sixteen-year-old boy. His family had wired him to a pole inside a small, windowless house. They lived in a separate house about thirty yards away. He was uncontrollable. He'd eat his own excrement and throw it at visitors. He didn't get many visitors. He made horrible, animal-like noises. The boy was possessed. Not insane—possessed. When I went to see him, the first thing I did was bind his demons to stop them from manifesting. I wouldn't have done this when I first started out. I probably would have had shit thrown all over me. And there's a chance I might have thrown it back."

It wasn't just Roman Catholic charismatics who were throwing themselves into deliverance during the early seventies. On the Episcopal side the action was almost as intense. By 1975 virtually all charismatic Episcopal prayer groups in the United States had done some experimenting with deliverance, and many had incorporated the ritual into their regular healing ministries. One of the most prominent, and quite possibly the busiest, of these was run by the husband-and-wife team of Virginia and David Collins out of St. Philip's Cathedral in Atlanta. Virginia Collins, the real driving force behind the St. Philip's ministry, was raised as an only child in a middle-class family in Carlinville, Illinois. After graduating high school, she moved to New York City with dreams of making a career for herself in the theater, and in April 1945 she joined the original Broadway company of *Carousel* as an understudy. Later the same year she married David Collins, an aspiring clergyman from Hot Springs, Arkansas, and in August 1946 the couple moved to Sewanee, Tennessee, where David completed his theological studies and received ordination. Two decades (and four children) later they settled in Atlanta, where David was appointed dean of the Cathedral of St. Philip.

Virginia received baptism in the Holy Spirit in 1972, a year or so before her husband, but the experience wasn't nearly as transformative as she had hoped. Now in her seventies, and still bright and vivacious, she recently told me what happened next.

"I became charismatic, but I had difficulty receiving the release of tongues," she said. "I felt there was something inside me, holding me back, dragging me down, but I didn't know what it was. At the time I was attending a prayer group that was led by a Catholic man and his wife, who was Methodist. We would meet in their home. They had some experience with deliverance, and they'd been influenced, as I re-call, by Derek Prince and Maxwell Whyte. One evening they dis-cerned that I was in need of deliverance. They prayed over me, and several spirits—spirits of anger and resentment and rejection—began manifesting themselves. This was a major deliverance, very dramatic, and when it was over, I felt truly freed. After this I felt called to the ministry myself. David and myself put together a team, and at our Thursday-evening prayer and praise meetings at the cathedral, we be-gan to perform deliverances. Many of them, especially at first, came with horrific manifestations. We became very well known, and we got referrals from all over the country. By the late seventies there were fif-teen charismatic prayer groups at the cathedral, and five of these spe-cialized in deliverance."

No less significant were the efforts, also during the seventies, of an Episcopal priest named Charles Irish. A former Marine, and veteran of the Korean War, Irish was baptized in the Spirit in 1970, just a year after becoming rector of St. Luke's Episcopal Church in Akron, Ohio. In 1971 a local charismatic group called the Northern Ohio Christian Conference brought Don Basham up from Florida for a seminar on deliverance, and Irish made a special point of attending.

"Like quite a few charismatics at the time, I was hungry for the full ministry of the Spirit, and although deliverance sounded a bit weird, I wanted to hear what Basham had to say," Irish, a soft-spoken, self-effacing man in his late sixties, told me recently in Akron. "Basham gave a talk, and then he performed a public deliverance. It was amaz-ing. The entire room came unglued. People were shrieking and shak-ing and vomiting while getting freed of their demons, and afterwards a real peace came over the place. I'd never seen anything like it."

Sensing that he was on the trail of something important, Irish set up a deliverance ministry of his own at St. Luke's, and even he and his colleagues were surprised at how quickly word got around.

"We worked as a team—myself and three women—and we tried to be very discreet," he said. "No public deliverances or anything of that sort. No advertising. Everything was done privately in my office. But we were busy. We were the only ones doing deliverance in northern

Ohio at the time, and people were contacting us from all over. The ministry really took off after 1975, and it was featured in a full-page story in the *Akron Beacon Journal.* Most of the people who came to us for help were charismatic Episcopalians, and we had some really dramatic cases. Early on, we delivered a woman of seventy different demons—demons of lust and violence and duplicity—they just kept manifesting. Not that we didn't make mistakes. Looking back now, I'd say we were a bit reckless and immature. We were seeing demons everywhere."

In 1978 Irish was appointed national coordinator of an organization called the Episcopal Charismatic Fellowship (ECF), and this gave him an expanded opportunity for spreading the gospel of deliverance. "The ECF represented all charismatic Episcopalians in the country," he said. "We ran conferences and workshops, and in my role as coordinator I made sure that we featured deliverance. This gave deliverance a huge national profile. Not all Episcopal charismatics were sold on deliverance by the late seventies, but there's no question that everybody was aware of it."[3]

Deliverance had many other worthy advocates during the seventies—and not all of them were Roman Catholic or Episcopalian. Don Basham and Derek Prince continued to do their part, albeit with less frequency as the decade wore on. Brick Bradford, a Presbyterian based in Oklahoma City, proved himself a solid defender of the cause. And in St. Paul, Minnesota, a Lutheran pastor named Morris Vaagenes presided over a flourishing deliverance ministry at one of the country's largest charismatic churches.

Vaagenes in particular deserves special mention. Now in his late sixties, stolid, deliberate, Norwegian, the very picture of ministerial rectitude, Vaagenes came to deliverance along a rather different path. Raised in Madagascar as the son of Lutheran missionaries, he was exposed to talk of demons and exorcism from his earliest childhood. He grew up listening to his parents swap exorcism stories with other missionaries around the kitchen table, grew up in a world where demons were part of the taken-for-granted reality, a world where his two older sisters died of malaria before reaching their teens. When he became charismatic, in the early seventies, Vaagenes didn't need Don Basham or Derek Prince (or even Francis MacNutt) to convince him that demons were real.

When Vaagenes became charismatic, he was already firmly ensconced as head pastor of North Heights Lutheran Church in St. Paul, and within months virtually his entire congregation followed him into the charismatic fold. Behind all the Spirit-drenched enthusiasm, however, trouble was brewing.

"It was in 1972 that we began to run into serious problems with demons," Vaagenes told me during a recent interview at his church office. "This was the same year that North Heights came into the charismatic renewal. It got started when a woman who was married to a former Roman Catholic priest—by this time they were both members of our congregation—came to me for help. She was severely demonized. I exorcised her several times over a period of weeks until she was released from bondage. Then the floodgates opened. I was in constant demand for exorcisms, and during the mid-seventies everything seemed to really escalate. For a while it was pretty frantic around here."

So frantic, in fact, that Vaagenes eventually felt compelled to ask Erwin Prange, a Lutheran minister with a growing reputation on the demon-expulsion front, to come up from Baltimore, where he was then living, and help straighten things out. Prange was only too happy to oblige, and in 1976 he was appointed the official house exorcist of North Heights, making him the only person in America (and quite possibly the entire world) to hold such a position.[4]

A nd then, of course, there were the books. If any charismatic somehow missed finding out about deliverance through the Basham-Prince-MacNutt conference circuit or through personal experience, the books were bound to do the trick. The 1970s resulted in a flurry of books on the subject, almost all of them written by charismatics and meant for a specifically charismatic audience.

Not that the books by themselves stood much of a chance of persuading anyone not already open to being persuaded of the benefits of deliverance. For the most part they were tedious, slipshod affairs, deadeningly repetitious, a patchwork of shopworn anecdote, wooden testimonial, and play-it-as-it-goes theology. With very few exceptions, to have read one is to have read them all.

Among the exceptions are Don Basham's *Deliver Us from Evil* (1972), to which I've already referred, and the slightly earlier *Can a Christian Have a Demon?* (1971), in which Basham tried to lay out a practical theology of deliverance for the benefit of the charismatic renewal movement as a whole. The fundamentals of Basham's theology are easily summarized: Demons are real supernatural agencies with a capacity for working evil in the lives of ordinary men and women. This is as true today as it was two thousand years ago. Christians, no less than anyone else, are susceptible to demonic affliction, though not (in all likelihood) to outright demonic possession. Thankfully, however, Spirit-baptized Christians are empowered to deliver demonized people from their torments and restore them to a state of spiritual freedom. All this we know (directly or indirectly) from the Christian Scriptures, and it is amply corroborated by pastoral experience.

Basham's practical theology has withstood the test of time within the charismatic renewal movement—save one notable disagreement. On the whole, Roman Catholic, Episcopal, and Lutheran charismatics have tended to be far more open than Basham to the possibility of Christians' falling prey to full-scale possession. Indeed, the Jesuit Richard Thomas, the Lutheran Erwin Prange, and a handful of others have gone so far as to suggest that possession is nearly as frequent an occurrence among Christians as is simple affliction.[5]

Almost as important as Basham's efforts was a slim volume entitled *Pigs in the Parlor,* which was written by a charismatic Baptist couple named Frank and Ida Mae Hammond. First published in 1973, and now boasting more than a million copies in print, *Pigs in the Parlor* was designed as a practical guide to almost everything anyone could possibly want to know about deliverance—with results ranging from the ludicrously open-ended to the impossibly specific. Hence we're told that the seven "most common symptoms of indwelling demons" are "1. Emotional Problems . . . 2. Mental Problems . . . 3. Speech Problems . . . 4. Sex Problems . . . 5. Addictions . . . 6. Physical Infirmities . . . [and] 7. Religious Error." Anyone exhibiting such symptoms (singly or in combination) would, presumably, be a candidate for deliverance. (Is there anyone who wouldn't be a candidate for deliverance?) We're also told that indwelling demons normally cluster in family groupings around a ruling demon (or "strong man"). Anyone infected by the ruling demon of Rebellion, for example, will also likely be infected by the subordinate demons of Self-will, Stubbornness, Disobedience, and Anti-submissiveness. The ruling demon of Gluttony will normally be accompanied by the subordinate demons of Nervousness, Compulsive eating, Resentment, Frustration, Idleness, Self-pity, and Self-reward; the ruling demon of Indecision by demons of Procrastination, Compromise, Confusion, Forgetfulness, and Indifference; and the demon of Cursing by lesser demons of Blasphemy, Coarse jesting, Gossip, Criticism, Backbiting, Mockery, Belittling, and Railing. And on and on. A mind-numbing catalog of demonic groupings. Fifty-three groupings in all, and this, the Hammonds advise, is just the tip of the iceberg.

Never mind how anyone could know all this—and know it with such serene self-assurance. To readers of *Pigs in the Parlor* this was impressive, curiously consoling stuff. With their intricate taxonomy, their demons' directory, the Hammonds had laid the groundwork for an intoxicating new world, a thoroughly desecularized and reenchanted world in which every facet of human experience was charged with supernatural energy, enlisted in cosmic conspiracy. A dangerous world also, to be sure, with demons lurking in every crevice of daily life, brushing up against every bad habit, every thought and action, but (and here's the consoling part) the danger was capable of being contained, managed, and, finally, conquered. All that was needed was to properly map out enemy territory, and then, as frequently as necessary, to bring the enemy into line through the correct administration of deliverance.

Of course, this wasn't so much a new world as a revived version of a much earlier one. The Hammonds (and many charismatics with them) were committed to a project of historical reversal, trying to bring demons and spirits back into the equation after science and technology had spent centuries knocking them out. Bad habits, defects of character, temptation—demons were behind all of this, but they were also behind emotional disability, physical infirmity, and mental illness. Demons of schizophrenia. Demons of depression. Demons of diabetes. Demons of everything. Science may have succeeded over the centuries in medicalizing the demonic, but now the Hammonds and their allies, trying to reverse the trend, were doing their utmost to re-demonize the medical.[6]

Rather less strident than *Pigs in the Parlor,* and vastly more nuanced, was a 1974 book by Francis MacNutt entitled *Healing.* Here, as elsewhere in his writings, MacNutt is a gracious presence on the page, solicitous, inviting, employing none of the scare tactics favored by some of his colleagues. While demons undoubtedly exist, he says, it is senseless to blame them for all sickness and suffering or to treat deliverance as the answer to all of life's problems. In the normal course of things, he says, Christian healing ministers can expect to encounter several different kinds of sickness, each one calling for a particular kind of response. There is sickness of the spirit, which is occasioned by our own personal sin and whose proper remedy is repentance. There is physical sickness, caused by disease or accident, which should be responded to through prayer for physical healing *and* professional medical help. (MacNutt insists that charismatic healing ministers should refrain from setting up "an artificial opposition between prayer and medicine.") And there is also sickness of the emotions, stemming from the emotional wounds of our past, which should be addressed through prayer for inner healing (or the healing of memories) and, perhaps, psychological counseling.

Finally, MacNutt says, any of these sicknesses—but especially the third kind, emotional sickness—may occasionally be caused by demons or aggravated by demons, and it's here that deliverance enters the picture. But great caution must be exercised: Deliverance should never be the first option of healing ministers, he says. It should be undertaken only if prayer for inner healing has proven ineffective and if the officiating ministers feel certain that they have discerned the presence of evil spirits. Deliverance is a loaded gun, MacNutt warns, and if entrusted to the wrong people or carried out recklessly, it can cause considerable damage. "Because [deliverance] is a prayer of command, involving confrontation, persons with aggressive tendencies may feel called to this work, when in reality they are working out their own aggressions. Since their motivation is mixed, the results of their ministry are likely to be mixed. The sensitivities of the person being prayed for may be deeply hurt by what one observer once described as 'spiritual rape.'"

And further, "Simplistic people who tend to see everything in terms of black or white often seem drawn to a deliverance ministry where they help some people while they harm many others. This, in turn, gives deliverance a bad image, frightening away the very persons who might be best able to exercise a discerning ministry of deliverance."[7]

Discerning Demons

MacNutt was right. In the hands of some of its practitioners, deliverance wasn't always the most edifying of procedures. By the early seventies, in fact, there were already two strikingly different approaches to the ritual within the renewal movement: The gunslinging approach, as it were, fast and furious, where demons were assumed to be present in almost every circumstance and the goal was to draw them into the open and then send them packing; and the more temperate and therapeutic approach favored by MacNutt (and which we saw in action in Kansas City at the outset of this part), where demons were dealt with only out of perceived necessity, and always within a broader context of healing prayer.

Quite apart from the conflicting personal styles of its practitioners, however—and here's the more significant point—deliverance continued to rise in popularity throughout the seventies. While some charismatics persisted in regarding it as a genetic accident of their movement, a freakish offspring best kept chained up in the cellar, the ritual gave absolutely no indication of fading away. For a while, in fact, there seemed no limit to its expanding appeal. There were public deliverances in which demons were expelled in droves from packed

auditoriums, private deliverances with muffled shriekings and thump-
ings behind locked basement doors, and laid-back deliverances, over
and done with in scarcely a whisper. Tens of thousands of people (the
number is only a rough approximation) who previously wouldn't have
given a thought to demons now seemed obsessed with extricating
themselves from demonic influence.

And so the question: how to account for all this activity, all this
demon-related activity, involving so many people (mostly white,
middle-class people).

There are several ways of getting at this—without forcing the issue, one way or another, as to whether demons might actually exist. In
the first place it's worth emphasizing that charismatic deliverance ministries were in the business, by and large, of expelling demons from
charismatics. Not from ordinary, run-of-the-mill Christians. Not from
the religiously unwashed or the spiritually unawakened. But from
charismatics: true Spirit-baptized, tongue-speaking charismatics. It's
not that they weren't open to taking business from elsewhere, or that
there wasn't business from elsewhere to be taken. Charismatic deliverance ministries had all they could handle just dealing with the
demon-related problems of charismatics. And among charismatics, apparently, there was an epidemic of demon-related problems during the
1970s.

So many charismatics suffering symptoms of demonic affliction:
hardly the best advertisement, it would seem, for the renewal movement. Wasn't there something suspect, something invalidating, about
a religious movement that left so many of its members acutely susceptible to the demonic realm? Why should anyone (anyone not actually
courting the demonic, that is) want to join such a movement?

This was an issue I raised with more than a dozen prominent deliverance ministers, all of whom responded in one of two ways. It simply wasn't the case, some said, that charismatics were more vulnerable
than anyone else to the depredations of the demonic. Charismatics, it
was true, complained more about demonic interference in their lives
than just about anyone else, but this was only testimony to their
heightened spiritual sensitivities. Demons were a ubiquitous fact of

life in the modern world, so much so that they were (colloquially) stinking up the joint; but most people were so hemmed in by exclusively material considerations, so blinkered by banality, as to be incapable of noticing. Most people were contaminated in some area of their lives by demonic presences, without even being aware of it. But charismatics were aware. This was what set them apart: They were humanity's advance guard into the spirit world; their surveillance equipment finely tuned, they were capable of seeing things, experiencing things, that those still on the home front could scarcely imagine.

About half of my respondents saw it in a somewhat different way. It was quite true, they said, that charismatics were especially vulnerable to demonic attack during the 1970s and early 1980s. But why should this be surprising? Why should this be construed as a defect of the charismatic renewal movement? If anything, it proved that the movement was on the right track. It stood to reason that Satan would pay special attention to those whom he regarded as the most serious threat to his kingdom. And charismatics, by virtue of their baptism in the Spirit and their passionate commitment to Christ, were unquestionably a serious threat. Charismatics were forced to endure far more than their share of demonic harassment not because they were patsies, not because their movement was somehow defective, but because they had been specifically targeted for abuse by Satan. They were martyrs for their faith, shouldering burdens that ordinary Christians (once again) could scarcely imagine.

Either of these accounts may be true. Perhaps they're both true. But there's another possibility. Perhaps charismatics experienced far more than their share of demonic harassment during the seventies and early eighties because they were expected to, they were encouraged to, and (in some cases) they wanted to.

It's no secret that small groups can exert enormous influence over their individual members, shaping perceptions, inducing conformity, and so forth. All the more so when the groups in question are fiercely partisan, in the grip of some transcendent passion. Charismatic prayer groups during the 1970s, particularly those that practiced deliverance, were nothing if not partisan and impassioned. Their members were encouraged to see themselves as latter-day pilgrims, breathing the exhilarating air of a new spiritual age, marking the territory of a new dispensation. As pilgrims, of course, they were also expected to contend with obstacles, with deadly opposition, and was there anything (or anyone) better suited to serving as opposition than demons? In the intensely supernatural world inhabited by charismatics, demons played an indispensable role. They completed the roster, so to speak, of the cosmic drama. They were scripted into the charismatic worldview. Simply being charismatic meant (to some extent at least) being concerned with demons.

Consider also the distinctive style of so many charismatic prayer groups: the ecstatic worship, the gushing emotionalism, the breathless solidarity. All of this gave rise, as often as not, to an atmosphere of heightened suggestibility, of hothouse conformity. Individual charismatics, even relative newcomers, easily surmised what was expected of them in the way of belief and conduct, and there was no shortage of cues to help them along. Imagine a fairly new recruit to the renewal movement, impressionable, eager to please, seeing two or three, or fifteen or sixteen spiritual brethren writhing and moaning in demon-induced torment. And then seeing the performance repeated time and again. It would take an iron act of will, arguably, for such a person not to go along for the ride.

Frequently the cues were far subtler—but no less effective. Not long ago I sat in on a charismatic healing service in a small Midwestern city. Among those seeking help was a well-educated woman in her early thirties who reported that she had been plagued by depression and anxiety since the recent breakup of her engagement. The prayer minister, an earnest and well-meaning man, asked her if she had felt burdened by some strange force.

"I'm not sure what you mean," she said.

"You know, is there a sense in which you haven't been yourself? Experiencing things which really don't fit in with how you define yourself, with the person you think you are?"

"Well, I guess so. I mean, I've been very depressed and scared. I've just felt like shutting myself off from everything. And this isn't really me. I've always thought of myself as being pretty active and outgoing."

"So there might be something foreign to you, something intrusive, that's been getting in the way of who you really are?"

"Well . . ."

"Don't worry, we don't want to come on heavy, but it's our experience that sometimes there's a foreign reality behind the depression, the hurt, that we're feeling. Sometimes this reality, this force, detects a weakness in us and then clings on. And it's not our fault. But we won't be healed unless we get rid of it."

"Hmm." Nodding, chin in hands.

"Do you understand? I'm talking about evil spirits."

"Yes." Still nodding. "I think I understand. I've certainly heard of this."

Indeed. The woman got the picture, and half an hour later she was moaning and trembling while getting freed of her demons.

Leading the witness like this is bad enough, but still nothing compared to the blatant emotional manipulation that seems to have taken place in some prayer groups. I had heard about this from time to time—the tremendous emotional pressure that could sometimes be brought to bear to convince people that they were demonized—but it wasn't until quite recently that I had an opportunity to observe something of the sort firsthand.

In the summer of 1997 I was invited to a symposium on deliverance that was sponsored by an association of charismatic nurses in a small Southern city. Before the discussion even had a chance to get started, while I was still in the process of introducing myself, in fact, a large middle-aged woman, who was seated to my immediate right, broke into a distracting singsong of tongue-speaking. I tried to carry on as if nothing were the matter, but after a minute or so the tongue-speaker threw up her hands and boomed out "Hold it! Hold it!"

"Where did this guy come from? What's this guy doing here?" she continued, clearly agitated. "I'm getting a strong discernment here. I'm seeing evil spirits here."

"You think I'm demonized?" I said.

"What I think is that you've been doing very dangerous research. This has brought you into contact with spirits of darkness. And what protection have you had against these evil spirits?"

"I'm not sure what you mean."

"Look, you're not charismatic. We know you're not charismatic. Have you done anything to protect yourself? Hasn't anyone told you about the importance of putting on the armor of God? I'm discerning that you haven't been protected, and you've picked up evil spirits from your research. And I'm concerned for all of us here. Now we're all under threat."

"It's true, Michael," a second woman chimed in. "Has no one ever prayed over you for the baptism of the Holy Spirit? Or for deliverance? For your own protection, have you been covered with the blood of Christ? I'm receiving a word of wisdom. The Holy Spirit's telling me that you've been brought here so we can pray over you."

There were murmurings of approval from several other women around the table.

"You see, Michael," the first woman said, "these kindhearted women are picking up that you're in trouble. They want to help you. All of us have years of experience dealing with the demonic. Are you going to tell us we're wrong? Are you going to question my discernment?"

Open-mindedly skeptical, but skeptical nevertheless, I had little difficulty questioning her discernment. But what if it had been someone else in that room? Someone desperate for approval. Someone seriously committed to the charismatic worldview. Or perhaps someone seriously troubled—without knowing exactly why. It wouldn't be difficult to predict which way this would have gone.

This wasn't the only time, moreover, that I ran into a situation of this sort. Just a couple of weeks later I met with two charismatic Episcopalians, a priest in his late forties and a layman about ten years older, at a restaurant in rural Oregon. The men spent almost an hour telling me about their experiences performing deliverance or exorcism (they used the terms interchangeably), but then the conversation took a more personal turn.

"Tell us something, Michael," the priest said. "Have you yourself ever been exorcised?"

"No. I haven't. Why do you ask?"

"Well, for one thing, how do you expect to understand exorcism, really understand it, without undergoing it yourself? Otherwise, you're just looking at the surface reality. You're not seeing it or experiencing it from the inside. You should really, seriously think about receiving an exorcism yourself."

"Just for the research value of it?"

"No. Also because you need to be exorcised," the layman said. "We both think so."

"When you were in the washroom, Michael, we talked about this. We both have a strong gift of discerning spirits, and we discerned that you're afflicted by demons. Quite a few demons. It's just something that came through loud and clear to us. In our ministry we rely heavily on our gift of discernment. It's our most valuable diagnostic tool. You need an exorcism."

"You feel certain of this? I certainly don't feel that I'm afflicted by demons."

The layman chuckled knowingly. "Most people don't realize at first that they've got problems with demons. But they're there. That's where our discernment comes in."

"It's nothing to be ashamed of," the priest said. "I've even been exorcised myself—several times. It's a terrific feeling getting liberated from demonic influence. Anyone dealing with demons runs the risk of being contaminated. Why should you be different? You've been doing work in this area, and I'm positive that you've come into personal contact with demons. Do you think that you're immune?"

"So how would I go about getting an exorcism?"

"We could do it," the layman offered.

"When would you propose doing it?"

"We could perhaps manage it later today," the priest said.

"Today? Just like that?"

"I'm saying we could possibly do it today. But there's no need to rush. You might want to think about it, pray over it. And we wouldn't want to do it unless you repented of your sins. You have to clean out your spiritual house, so to speak. Otherwise the demons will just come back. You can't allow them a point of reentry."

"Still, I'm a bit surprised that you'd be open to this on such short notice."

"I'm not sure we'd finish it today, but it might be possible to get a start on it. We have all the equipment we'd need out in the car."

"Equipment? What equipment?"

Several minutes later, out in the parking lot, they opened the trunk of a blue Chevrolet and showed me the equipment: belts, handcuffs, and other restraining devices.

"Things can sometimes get a little frantic," the layman said, noticing my frown of puzzlement. "We have this stuff on hand just in case. For everyone's safety."

I told them that I'd take a rain check.

The wild card here, of course, is the gift (or practice) of discerning spirits. Over the years many charismatics involved with deliverance have claimed to possess such a gift, and most of them would readily concede that it defies rational explanation. The gift, apparently, works in different ways. Some charismatics claim that they are able to visualize evil spirits surrounding or inhabiting an individual, and sometimes even to visualize the individual's initial point of contact with these spirits. Others claim that their gift is primarily olfactory, and that they are actually capable of smelling any demons that might come into their vicinity. Some claim to be able to detect the presence of demons within an individual by testing nearby air currents with their outstretched fingers, while still others prefer simply to describe their gift as a mystical, extrasensory kind of perception.

Many of the charismatics I spoke with are enormously proud of their gift of discerning spirits, and supremely confident in its effectiveness as a diagnostic tool. To the outsider, however, the entire business seems bewildering—and more than just a little arbitrary. During my research I was given the diagnostic once-over numerous times, with wildly conflicting results. Sometimes I received an utterly clean bill of health, sometimes I was told that my spiritual condition was dubious, and sometimes I was pronounced to be desperately in need of deliverance. Occasionally all three of these verdicts were rendered (by different individuals) within the space of just a week or two. And once, in upstate New York, I attended a meeting where two women discerned the presence of evil spirits in me while two others discerned spirits of peace and gentleness.

None of this is to suggest that there's anything inherently bogus or manipulative about the practice of discerning spirits. I saw it applied many times—sometimes to compassionate and genuinely therapeutic effect. In the hands of the wrong person, however, the potential for abuse is all too obvious, and during the 1970s and 1980s there is little doubt that it was sometimes used (as it is still sometimes used today) as a spiritual cudgel for coercing people into deliverance. Deliverance ministry has always attracted more than its share of authoritarian cranks, and it would be difficult to imagine anything better suited for power-tripping than telling gullible, needy, and, sometimes, emotionally stricken people that they are afflicted by demons. (And telling them so, it might be added, on apparently unimpeachable authority.)

In a related vein, deliverance seems to have been used by some charismatic groups during the seventies and eighties as a mechanism of social control. Practically from its beginning the renewal movement as a whole was an intensely conservative affair, implacably opposed not just to the theological liberalism of the major Christian churches in the United States but also to the cultural upheavals of the broader society. Feminism, sexual permissiveness, the collapse of traditional authority structures—many leading charismatics regarded these and related developments as unmitigated evils, and they were determined to do whatever they thought necessary to prevent them from taking root in their own prayer communities. Which sometimes meant resorting to deliverance.

Not long ago a woman I'll call Carol sent me a letter recounting her personal experiences with deliverance in a charismatic prayer group in California during the late seventies. Carol had joined the group with her husband, an Episcopal minister, looking to put her life on a fresh track. For years she had felt mounting frustration at having given up her career aspirations for the sake of becoming a full-time wife and mother, and she hoped that getting involved with the renewal movement might be a way of lifting herself out of the doldrums. Such, however, was not the case, at least not initially. During her first several months in the prayer group, Carol felt just as frustrated and embittered as before, and her intransigence didn't go unnoticed.

> [Eventually] the prayer group leaders discerned that there were some of us in the group who needed deliverance ministry. So, one night they set aside the whole prayer meeting, divided us into teams and prayed. . . . Several of the things that they told me I had, I couldn't believe. It was not acceptable for an Episcopal minister's wife to have anger, bitterness, hate, resentment, rejection, rebellion, unforgiveness, and others [*sic*]. And so I had to take on faith what they said. I had been reading so I did know that there was validity in what they were doing. Sure enough, as they prayed, these spirits did manifest themselves in various ways and through their prayers of command, just as Jesus did in the New Testament, each one came out.

This accomplished, Carol, now a true believer, resolved to carry the battle directly into her home.

> My household was oppressed—a hellish atmosphere full of confusion, disorder, disobedience, a house divided against itself . . . Because of what I saw and because of where our household was, I started what I call "spiritual warfare" in my home . . . I began to bind every spirit which I saw manifested in my children. I commanded these spirits to be loosened so that God could have His way with them. I began to battle for that land that had been taken over in my husband and I began to do the same thing for my children. I did some strange things . . . I waited until after they were asleep at night to slip into their bedroom and anoint them for healing and command those spirits to be loosed and to leave. By then I had found out that in your own household, those *under* your au-

thority *could* be delivered from demons. My husband at this point was not at that place where he could do the anointing, but he allowed me to do so. I went all over the house, I anointed the windows and the door posts. I anointed the recordings that came into the house—anything that I thought was demonic in source, that was not blessing our children and leading them to Jesus. I prayed over their clothes as I took them out of the washing machine . . . Now, my husband and I pray for each other as we discern things still controlling us that are not of Jesus Christ.[1]

A bit overripe in the telling perhaps, but hardly an exceptional case. During the 1970s and 1980s it wasn't uncommon for charismatic women to be put through the deliverance wringer for betraying unhappiness over their subordinate status as full-time wives and mothers. Such unhappiness, arguably, was feminism trying to claw its way into their consciousness, and the best strategy for dealing with feminism, in the view of some charismatics, was to demonize it and banish it to the outer boroughs. Of course, there was more involved with deliverances of this sort than just ideological policing. Not unlike certain secular psychotherapies of the day, they were sometimes a coping mechanism for women caught in dissatisfying domestic situations. And as Carol's case vividly attests (all that binding and loosing, all that anointing), they were sometimes also a highly effective means of intensifying commitment to the charismatic cause.

There is another angle worth pursuing, on this issue of deliverance as a mechanism of social control. During the 1970s many charismatic communities in the United States became deeply involved with an initiative known variously as "shepherding," "discipling," or "covenanting." Leading the way on this, as with so much else, were Don Basham and Derek Prince. As early as the late sixties, Basham and Prince were convinced that the renewal movement as a whole was in need of some serious stocktaking. Just a decade or so into its existence, in their view, the movement was showing signs of slippage. Its energies were scattered, its voice divided, and its future far from certain. Many older charismatics seemed to be losing some of their original fire, and

newcomers weren't always receiving adequate grounding in the requirements of faith. Quite simply, according to Basham and Prince,
the honeymoon was over; it was now time for laying down the law, setting the house in order.

As a step in this direction, Basham and Prince and several other
prominent charismatics, most notably a Southern Baptist minister
named Charles Simpson and an independent evangelist named Bob
Mumford, founded an organization in Fort Lauderdale that eventually
became known as Christian Growth Ministries. Harmless enough,
one might suppose, but to its detractors the organization might just as
well have been called Charismatic Cult Ministries. In the interests of
tightening discipline within the renewal movement and promoting a
more intensive level of discipleship, Basham, Prince, and company set
themselves up as a kind of infallible leadership caste. They claimed
that they had been especially empowered by the Holy Spirit to define
strict lines of authority for charismatic prayer groups across the country. And they also claimed that individual charismatics were required
to submit themselves, totally and unflinchingly, to the authority of spe-
cially designated elders or "shepherds" from their local communities.

During the early to mid-seventies Christian Growth Ministries
succeeded in fashioning an extensive network of rigidly authoritarian
prayer groups throughout the Protestant wing of the renewal. Not
everyone, however, bought into the plan. Many prominent charismatics (and more than just a few classical Pentecostals) complained that
the entire business reeked of spiritual megalomania and that the
Christian Growth people were placing the renewal movement as a
whole at grave risk.

"This was a really dreadful episode in the life of the renewal; it
threatened to tear us apart," the Lutheran Morris Vaagenes told me in
St. Paul. "Charismatics had always been committed to working within
their own denominations, but Don Basham and the shepherding people seemed to want to create a separate charismatic sect. And some of
the so-called shepherds or elders were exercising a completely un-
scriptural authority over people, forcing them to divulge the most intimate details of their personal business, trying to control every aspect

of their lives. The joke going about was that in some shepherding communities you had to get the permission of an elder just to go to the bathroom. This was the biggest internal controversy that we ever faced; bigger even than deliverance."[2]

At just about the same time, moreover, the Roman Catholic wing of the renewal movement was facing an almost identical controversy. During the early seventies, in a similar effort to promote greater discipline and dedication among the troops, Catholic charismatic leaders in Ann Arbor, South Bend, and elsewhere began setting up what they referred to as "covenant communities." These were relatively small, self-enclosed affairs—charismatic cells, as it were—occasionally organized in residential units called "households," and governed, more often than not, according to a quasi-monastic ethic of strict obedience and spiritual conformity.

As the decade advanced, dozens of covenant communities sprang up throughout the Catholic wing of the renewal—but not without rumblings of protest. Critics charged that many of the communities were being run as petty fiefdoms, with arrogant, brook-no-dissent prayer leaders lording it over rank-and-file members. Disaffected members (or ex-members) of some communities complained of being subjected to rituals of humiliation, of having their perceived shortcomings openly discussed at household meetings, and of being force-fed a reactionary, antiworldly theology that sometimes verged on the apocalyptic and the downright paranoid.[3]

Some of these accusations, on both the Protestant and the Catholic side, were undoubtedly exaggerated, and it would be ill advised in any event to tar all shepherding/covenanting communities with the same brush. Nevertheless, there is little question that a good many of them were committed to a kind of spiritual engineering, trying to transform ordinary charismatics into entirely new and submissive children of God. And there is also little question that they sometimes deployed demon-expulsion toward this end. If someone stepped out of line or appeared insufficiently cooperative, insufficiently submissive, there was better than a decent chance that he or she (especially *she*) would be diagnosed as demonized and subjected to remedial deliverance.

During my research I heard numerous accounts of people receiving deliverances of precisely this sort. Here is just one, considerably abridged, told me by a woman who belonged to a Catholic covenant community in the Midwest during the 1970s:

> At first it was pretty exciting being part of the group. I was in my early twenties, and I was thrilled. I thought, This is what the earliest Christian communities must have been like; this was what we were capturing—the joy, the togetherness, the strength. We were all single, seven women and six men, and we lived together in a big old house. No sexual hanky-panky, at least none I was aware of. We were committed to celibacy, and to supporting one another in prayer. . . .
>
> After about a month I started to feel uncomfortable. I was starting graduate studies in theology, and I knew that I was pretty smart. I used to contribute a lot in class discussion, but then I'd go home and I was expected to be this little passive, subservient thing, not say anything, not question anything. I don't know how it happened, but a couple of the men suddenly were claiming more authority than the Pope. The rest of us were supposed to submit to them, which I did for a while, but then I started asking questions. I said that this kind of hierarchical arrangement didn't seem true to the real meaning of the charismatic renewal. I said that we were all brothers and sisters, equal under the Spirit. One of the men, who was one of our leaders, spoke to me in private and admonished me. He said I was assertive and disruptive. Then the next night, after dinner, he talked about me and my so-called problems in front of the whole household. He told everyone to pray for me.
>
> This did it for me. I thought he was the one with the problem—not me. I guess I kind of lost my temper and said I wasn't there to be anyone's doormat. There was complete silence for a while. Then the same guy and one of the women—thanks a lot, sister!—said that they were discerning spirits of rebellion and rage in me and that I needed deliverance. By this point I felt badly

about losing my temper, and I felt that maybe I was going to be responsible for destroying our group, and so I went along with it.
And do you know the really weird part? When I was being delivered, I really did feel that evil spirits were leaving me. Afterward
I cried my eyes out, and we all hugged. A few weeks later, though,
I started to feel the same frustration over being a second-class cit-
izen, over failing their expectations. And by now I wasn't buying
into any talk of demons and deliverance. I made my own decision.
I was right, they weren't; and so I left.

Of course, not all charismatics who underwent deliverance during
the 1970s were manipulated or browbeaten into doing so. Some ea-
gerly sought it out, for reasons, not least of all, of spiritual glamour
and prestige. In some charismatic circles at the time, being diagnosed
as demon-afflicted and receiving deliverance carried considerable ca-
chet. It was a badge of honor, a surefire indication that one was fully
in the game. Indeed, *not* having to undergo deliverance might well
have been taken as a negative commentary on one's spiritual condition, as if Satan and his minions had more important fish to fry.

Quite apart from these internal dynamics, there is also a broader
cultural explanation for the attractiveness of deliverance within
certain sectors of the renewal movement during this period. It was
during the late sixties and the seventies that much of mainstream
America came under the sway of what may be described as a new
therapeutic ethic, a freewheeling, whine-and-divine ethic of personal
growth and self-transformation. Picking their way out of the rubble of
the sixties, large numbers of middle-class Americans seemed only too
happy putting political activism aside and casting their attention in-
ward instead. Forget about changing the world, the sentiment ran; the
truly important (and far more workable) task was changing the self.
The self was the new project, the thing to be worked on: the infinitely
malleable self, the experimental self, the self of limitless potential. To

help with the project there was a colorful assortment of "human potential" groups, such as Scientology, *est,* and Synanon, and a stroll-
down-the-aisle, fill-up-the-basket variety of personal-growth books,
personal-growth therapies, personal-growth infomercials.

All of this, needless to say, was nicely tied in with the assumptions
of middle-class consumerism. The idea was that no one should actually have to work terribly hard at attaining personal growth. The rig-
ors of asceticism, the self-sacrifice of traditional spiritual discipline,
the dark night of the soul—all of this was unnecessary; it was all easily bypassed. What most of these personal growth groups and books
and therapies offered their customers instead were laborsaving techniques, seven-day nostrums, which allowed for the enhancement of
personality and the maximization of potential without any inconven-
ient alteration in middle-class lifestyle. All in all, psychosalvation by
gimmickry, a paint-by-numbers approach to transforming the self.[4]

Although most charismatics would have been loath to admit it, deliverance also fit in quite nicely with this new therapeutic ethic. No
less than any of the rather more secular techniques in vogue at the
time, the ritual was held up as a rapid-fire, relatively convenient way
of improving the self and transcending personal limitations. It could
be engaged in as often as anyone wanted, usually without undue pain
or duress, and for virtually any reason under the sun. Think of *Pigs in
the Parlor* and all those demonic groupings, all those ruling demons and
subordinate demons, representing almost every human frailty, foible,
and shortcoming imaginable. If an individual charismatic complained
of being afflicted by demons of cigarette-smoking, or demons of marital infidelity, or demons of anything in between, the solution was close
at hand. Deliverance promised new possibilities for the self, the possibility of an endlessly redeemed self, a self renewed and improved at a
single stroke. Despite being cloaked in the time-orphaned language of
demons and supernatural evil, deliverance was surprisingly at home in
the brightly lit, fulfillment-on-demand culture of post-sixties America.[5]

Deliverance was a product or, better, a reflection of its times in another respect as well. By almost all accounts the ritual attained its height of popularity within the charismatic renewal movement during the mid- to late seventies. These were the years when it was in greatest demand, when there seemed almost to be an epidemic of demonism within certain circles of the renewal movement. And this, as I have already indicated, was by no means accidental. That deliverance came on strongest during this period was due, at least in part, to the tremendous cultural buzz generated by the release of *The Exorcist* in 1973 and the publication of *Hostage to the Devil* three years later. Blatty's movie, Malachi Martin's book, and the more general media hype regarding demonism at the time substantially increased the demand for charismatic deliverance. More than ever now, demonism was in the air, and this only made deliverance that much more attractive, that much more sought-after.

Most of the veteran deliverance ministers I interviewed told me that they regarded Blatty's film in particular as something of a mixed blessing. On the one hand they were pleased that the film had publicized the issue of demonization, ushered it, so to speak, into the bright lights of the cultural mainstream. Thanks to Blatty and company, demonization had become part of the national vocabulary, a diagnostic category that might compete with the relentlessly secular categories of the medical and psychiatric professions. Individual charismatics (and Americans more generally) who might not otherwise have even considered the possibility that their problems were demonic in nature now had positive cultural incentive for doing so.

On the other hand, however, they were also convinced that the movie had had a negative impact. Its graphic depictions of diabolism and possession, in their view, were like an electric charge, activating demonic energies that quite possibly had been lying dormant in the American psyche for generations. Was it merely happenstance, they asked, that reports of occult activity and satanic ritualism seemed to increase exponentially in the years immediately following the movie's release?

Concerns of this sort were expressed by charismatics as far back as the mid-seventies—and not just by those in the United States. In 1973, for example, a charismatic Church of England prelate named Morris Selby was asked by the Archbishop of York to head up an advisory committee with the goal of producing pastoral guidelines for exorcism and deliverance ministry in the York diocese. The committee was given three years to complete its work, but in 1974 Selby felt compelled to submit a hurry-up report to the archbishop, two years ahead of schedule. And the reason for the rush? "The news that the film called 'The Exorcist' was about to cross the Atlantic, tornado-like, leaving a trail of damage behind it, together with an apparent increase of demand here for such a ministry," Selby wrote in his cover letter, "has led us to offer your Grace this report, which you may care to pass on to the parish priests of the diocese, together with your own pastoral guidance."[6]

10.

Exorcism as Therapy

During the 1980s charismatic deliverance ministry in the
United States seemed intent on settling down, finding its
bearings, getting a grip on itself. After the excesses and exu-
berance of the seventies, this was its period of introspective middle
age, its time for cleaning out the drawers.

Much the same can be said for the charismatic renewal movement
as a whole. After facing bitter opposition during its earliest years, the
renewal movement had succeeded by the early seventies in winning
acceptance within most of the major Christian denominations in the
United States. Throughout much of the seventies, in fact, the movement experienced vigorous growth, and by the end of the decade, according to a 1979 Gallup survey, a striking 19 percent of the total U.S.
adult population identified themselves as either charismatic or
Pentecostal.[1] As growth slowed substantially (and eventually came to
a standstill) during the early eighties, however, the movement went
into a period of strategic retreat, taking inventory, trying to determine
exactly where it stood, where it should be headed.

Deliverance continued to be practiced within the renewal movement during this period—with Roman Catholics and Episcopalians,
more than ever, taking the lead. For a variety of reasons the ritual had

proven especially congenial to Catholic and Episcopal charismatics. Both belonged to religious traditions that endorsed the value of exorcism or deliverance and made concrete provision for its occasional performance. The Roman Catholic rite of exorcism, so effectively dramatized in Blatty's movie, was first formally laid down in the *Rituale Romanum* of 1614, and the 1917 Code of Canon Law, which was in effect until 1983, mandated that every bishop officially appoint an exorcist for his diocese. (As we've seen, however, this wasn't always followed through in places such as the United States.) Historically, the position of the Church of England, the parent body of Episcopalianism in the United States, has been quite similar to that of Roman Catholicism. The Canons of 1603/4 (most of which were repealed in 1969) made explicit provision for exorcism, and a commission appointed by the Anglican bishop of Exeter in 1972 recommended that "it is much to be desired that every diocesan bishop should appoint a priest as diocesan exorcist, and that in each province centres of training should be established."[2]

At a more modest level, exorcism (or the idea behind it) has also been woven into the very fabric of Roman Catholic and Episcopal sacramental life. In various ritual settings both traditions have employed incense, the sign of the cross, holy oils and salts, and other accouterments of worship as symbolic vehicles for cleansing people of evil, converting darkness into light. The Roman Catholic baptismal rite still contains prayers for the exorcism of the candidate, and similar prayers have been restored to Anglicanism through the Alternative Service Book of 1980. And prior to the reform of their liturgy after the Second Vatican Council, Roman Catholics recited the following prayer, which was composed by Pope Leo XIII in 1886, at the end of every Mass.

> *St. Michael the Archangel, defend us in battle;*
> *be our protection against the wiles and wickedness of the devil.*
> *We humbly beseech thee, O God, to restrain him,*
> *and do thou, the Prince of the heavenly hosts,*
> *cast into hell Satan and all the evil spirits,*
> *who roam through the world seeking the ruin of souls.*[3]

Curiously enough, moreover, quite a few Roman Catholic and Episcopal priests with long-standing involvement in deliverance told me that they had actually benefited from the hierarchical structure of their respective churches, with lines of authority extending downward from the local bishop. This meant that they weren't at the mercy of prominent members of their home congregations who might have disapproved of deliverance and taken steps to stamp it out. Most Catholic and Episcopal bishops, for their part, seem to have adopted the ecclesiastical equivalent of a "don't ask, don't tell" policy. Providing that deliverance ministers comported themselves with discretion and didn't take on suspected cases of full-fledged possession without first seeking official approval, they were mostly permitted to go about their business unimpeded. (Of course, many bishops, on both the Roman Catholic and the Episcopal sides, looked upon the entire business as utter foolishness and tolerated it mainly because it would have been too much trouble to do otherwise.)

Roman Catholic and Episcopal charismatics were by no means alone in practicing deliverance during the 1980s. The ritual was kept alive also within the more properly Protestant sectors of the movement, and it remained a major concern of freelance preachers such as Don Basham and Derek Prince. (At the same time, it was also gaining popularity among people who weren't, strictly speaking, part of the renewal movement, but I shall leave this part of the story for later.) For the reasons I've suggested, however, it was among Catholic and Episcopal charismatics that the ritual became most fully institutionalized—not openly advertised, to be sure, still conducted mostly in the shadows, but generally accepted and widely available.[4]

In the hands of many of its Catholic and Episcopal practitioners, moreover, deliverance underwent a kind of domestication during the 1980s. This happened in two ways. First of all (and here the influence of Francis MacNutt figured prominently), the ritual was completely integrated by an increasing number of prominent charismatics into comprehensive healing ministries, which involved prayer for spiritual healing, inner emotional healing, and sometimes also physical healing. Gone were the days (at least among most Episcopalians and Roman

Catholics) when deliverance was a separate and specialized ministry, carried out by single-minded zealots whose first and only thought was the casting out of demons. It was now part of a more general therapeutic process, a process in which demons might not even play a featured role. "It had always made me nervous when someone told me that they had a deliverance ministry," Barbara Shlemon told me. "This usually meant that they were mainly interested in expelling demons, at any cost, not in ministering to the total person. Deliverance must always take place within a broader context of healing. Francis MacNutt had always understood this, and so had some others, but finally it started to sink in more widely, especially among Catholics and Episcopalians. This was a real growth in maturity for us."

In a related development, deliverance was also considerably toned down by many Catholic and Episcopal charismatics during the 1980s. Prior to this, as we've seen, the ritual was frequently a noisy and unkempt affair, with shrieking, cursing, slobbering—and sometimes worse. For some charismatics, in fact, this was a large part of its appeal; the dramatic manifestations were like a certificate of authenticity, the surest, most visceral proof that demons—real spitting, jeering, profanity-addled demons—were actually being engaged in combat. The uglier and more gut-wrenching the manifestations, the better. Toward the end of the seventies, however, a number of prominent charismatics declared their unhappiness with this state of affairs. The growling, the howling, and all the rest of it, they claimed, were turning deliverance into a permanent sideshow and thus preventing its true value from being more widely appreciated. And what's more, they said, all of this grotesquerie was completely avoidable. Regardless of whether it was demons making a nuisance of themselves or the subjects of deliverance simply playing to the occasion, there was no excuse for such histrionics. Demons needed to be kept in their place, the subjects of deliverance needed to be restrained from acting out, and it was the responsibility of deliverance ministers to ensure that proceedings were conducted in a dignified manner. And how could this best be done? Quite simply, by binding the demons. By commanding them, in the name of Jesus Christ, to hold their peace. This would take care of the demons, and it would also serve notice to subjects of deliverance that any acting out was unnecessary and unacceptable.

This notion of binding the demons—of placing them under strategic house arrest, as it were—was rapidly picked up in the Catholic and Episcopal wings of the renewal movement, and among Roman Catholics in particular it soon became an almost obligatory procedure. No one was more responsible for making it so than Father Richard McAlear and Betty Brennan, a priest-housewife team and without question two of the most engaging personalities on the charismatic deliverance scene throughout the 1980s.

Richard McAlear was born in Boston in 1943 and raised in an Irish-Italian, working-class family as the second of five boys. He joined the Oblates of Mary Immaculate in 1964 and then spent seven years in Rome preparing for ordination. Upon returning to the United States, he became deeply involved with the renewal movement, and in 1976 he started his own healing and deliverance center at a defunct seminary in Newburgh, New York. One of his earliest clients was Betty Brennan, a large, blond, plainspoken woman, who was a recent convert to the charismatic renewal—and quite an exceptional convert at that.

"Betty had been experiencing serious personal problems before becoming charismatic, and she came to the center for deliverance," McAlear, a tall, good-looking man with a salt-and-pepper beard and pouches under his eyes, told me in the summer of 1997 at a parish rectory he was visiting in Queens, New York. "But when I got to know her better, I discovered that she had a remarkable ability for discerning spirits. Not just spirits, but someone's entire psychological condition. I'm talking about a major gift, a wonderful gift, a powerful gift of infused knowledge. Benedict Groeschel, who was closely familiar with our work in Newburgh, was tremendously impressed. It was simply extraordinary. I first became aware of it when a woman in her sixties came to the center for healing. She had an inner ear problem that was wreaking havoc with her balance. Betty was sitting at the back; she'd never met the woman or her husband. She came up to me and said, 'Here's the problem. The husband has been sexually unfaithful. Now he wants to retire and travel. But the wife's sickness forces him to stay home and, for the first time, give her his attention.' And she was right. This was the way it really was. Remarkable.

"We started working together as a team in 1977, and our reputation built up by word of mouth. A lot of priests came to us for deliverance. There are so many priests suffering serious demonic affliction; priests are sitting ducks. As time went by, Betty became quite famous within the renewal movement. She was in tremendous demand. Her gift of discernment blows everyone else's out of the water. Francis MacNutt works with women who have impressive gifts of discernment, but these women aren't even remotely in Betty's league. Don't get me wrong: Betty inspires respect far more readily than affection. She's so blunt and outspoken that she's turned some people off. She's bruised a lot of egos. But the gift is for real."

Betty Brennan, the woman behind the gift, spent her earliest childhood in Brooklyn. When her father, who was a New York City cop, died of a massive coronary at the age of forty-one, she moved to Ireland with her mother and brother and was educated in a convent boarding school run by the Loretto Sisters. She moved back to New York City when she was twenty, got married and started a family, and eventually settled in a small upstate town where her husband found work as a firefighter. During the early seventies she went through a painful personal crisis but she regained her moorings soon after becoming charismatic.

I spoke briefly with Betty Brennan at a retreat house just north of New York City shortly after my meeting with Father McAlear and at much greater length by phone several months later. I had been warned by several people that she could be intimidatingly brusque, but I found her smart and charming, with a habit (perhaps an echo of her Brooklyn girlhood) of punctuating her sentences with "You know what I'm saying? Do you know what I'm saying, Michael?"

I asked about her gift, of which McAlear and a number of other charismatics had spoken so highly.

"It's true that I have this gift," she said, "but it's so far beyond me that it's very difficult for me even to talk about. But look, I want to be clear. The gift doesn't make me special, it's no measure of holiness, it's something I've got to give back to God. A lot of people with gifts of discernment are prima donnas. The gift is not my identity. My husband is a retired firefighter; I've got three kids in graduate school. This is who I am. If I ever told my neighbors around here what I do—discerning spirits and praying for deliverance—they'd die laughing. One of my daughters once said to me when she was having friends over, 'Whatever you do, Mom, don't tell them what you do. Don't tell them you're an exorcist.' "

She also told me that her work in deliverance hasn't always been duly appreciated.

"I am probably the most experienced deliverance minister in American Catholicism. Over twenty-two years now I have seen thousands upon thousands of cases. A lot of these cases have just involved minor spirits, and some of them could have been dealt with through the sacrament of confession, but I've also had many major cases. And lots of people have resented me for this. There is so much jealousy. Also, I'm a laywoman, and I'll tell you, Michael, I've had to put up with so much resistance and opposition over the years because I'm a laywoman and involved with this ministry. A lot of priests, including charismatic priests, have resented me for this. This has sometimes hurt. And I'm totally loyal to Rome; I'm not interested in being a woman-priest. While we were ministering together, Father McAlear placed me under his protection, and this was what helped me carry on."

And what about the practice of binding spirits, as a way of eliminating untoward manifestations during deliverance? How had this come to pass? I asked.

"When Father McAlear and myself really got into the ministry in a big way, we couldn't believe all the nonsense that was going on," Brennan said. "The screaming, the swearing, the spitting and vomiting. You name it. We thought that this was ridiculous and unedifying and completely unnecessary. All of these manifestations are pure Hollywood stuff. It's like people saw *The Exorcist* and figured this was how they were supposed to carry on if they were truly demonized. A lot of it is also primal psychological stuff—people acting out their pains and frustrations and problems and getting a lot of attention for it, and maybe even getting complimented for it. But none of this means that evil spirits are present. Come on, all of these theatrics don't give evidence of demons. They might be evidence of psychological break-down, or emotional neediness, or something else. But this is part of the problem: So many charismatics don't take psychology seriously. A lot of these cases can be treated without deliverance—with medication and counseling—but they aren't. So many charismatics want to think in terms of demons, and then no one has to take responsibility.

"So this was the situation that Father McAlear and myself faced. We saw all of these theatrics and we were convinced they were just getting in the way. And in those cases where demons really were involved, why stand by and permit these theatrics to take place? This is giving far too much control to Satan. When we're doing deliverance, we're acting by the authority of Jesus Christ. And in the name of Jesus we can prohibit the demons from manifesting. The Scriptures speak of the importance of binding, and so this is what we decided to do.[5] We tried it, and it worked. The demons were forced to cooperate, and it sent out a message to the people we were praying over that there was no need for any nonsense. We would walk in and take the whole drama out of it. During the eighties the word spread, and lots of deliverance ministers started using our approach."

Several months earlier I had also raised the issue of binding spirits with Father McAlear.

"This was our major contribution to deliverance ministry," he told me. "There's so much autosuggestion and therapeutic pressure at play when you pray over people for deliverance. If you tell them the demon will come out in a bucket of vomit, they'll vomit. If you tell them it will come out in a scream, they'll scream. If you tell them not to be surprised if they thrash on the floor, they'll thrash on the floor. So much of this stuff is psychological neediness. You're being driven by the train. People come to you, they're acting out, you're praying over them, they're needy and acting out more. They have a vested interest in being demonized; they're getting all this attention. Betty and myself didn't want all this acting out. We proved that deliverance didn't need to be a sideshow."

I spoke with Father McAlear for almost three hours, and for the greater portion of the conversation I was struck by a nagging thought. Was it possible that this talented and articulate man, who had been so major an influence in American Catholic deliverance ministry, didn't actually believe in demons? Or, at least, didn't believe in them in a strictly literal sense? Was "demonization," in his usage, simply a metaphor for psychological and emotional sickness, or for old-fashioned sin? In his deliverance ministry had he simply been meeting true-believing charismatics on their own ground, binding (and then expelling) imaginary demons as a way of getting at the real problems of mind and heart? And if McAlear was a metaphorist, might not others I had interviewed also be?

I put this to him as our conversation was winding down, and he said that the best way of answering was to tell me about two cases he had personally been involved with some years back.

"In the early eighties, when we were really going strong in Newburgh, a number of priests in the area complained to the bishop," he said. "These priests were suspicious; they didn't know exactly what was going on. Maybe they thought we were performing some kind of Catholic voodoo. Maybe they were jealous of Betty Brennan. Anyway, the bishop told us not to do any more deliverance pending investigation. Benedict Groeschel was put in charge of investigating us, and so for a while we were forced to close up shop. During this time a teenage girl from North Carolina was brought to us. Betty and myself were convinced that this girl really did have a serious problem with a demon, but we were under strict orders from the bishop not to perform deliverance. The girl took my hand and said, 'Please, help me.' I was really torn. Out of love I wanted to do it, but I couldn't be disobedient to the bishop. For Catholics in this ministry, obedience to the church, being at one with the church, is the main criterion of success. If you're disobedient, you're setting yourself up for failure. So when this tortured girl was holding my hand, the demon in her said to me, 'I dare you to do it.' And I had no doubt this was an actual demon speaking through her. I've been involved with plenty of cases where I wasn't so sure. Here I was sure."

McAlear's second case, which also took place in the early eighties, was clearly more difficult for him to talk about.

"You're going to find some of this hard to believe, and if I were in your shoes, I'd also find it hard to believe," he said. "But I was there, and I can only report what I saw. And I was sober and sane. I have only mentioned this particular case to a few people, but feel free to write it up. It really happened.

"There was a woman in her early forties who went to a charismatic prayer group in [a Great Lakes city] for healing. She was a single woman, grossly overweight, and she wanted the group to pray over her weight problem. But during the prayers she threw herself on the floor, and then she levitated. The group tried to perform deliverance on her over a period of weeks, and they eventually put in a call to Betty and me. We went out, and she levitated right before our eyes. She was the first case of full-fledged possession we'd ever seen. She had an entire hierarchy of evil spirits in her. We got permission from the local bishop to do an actual exorcism. While I was performing the exorcism, she was sticking her tongue out right down to her belly button, with an absolutely hideous, lascivious leer on her face. This was the evil spirits mocking me, challenging me. It was so revolting that I couldn't stand it any longer, and so I went behind her. But when I did this she rotated her head 180 degrees, without turning her body, and looked me right in the eyes. It was incredible. There was blood on the wall, the furniture was shaking. The exorcism itself took just one afternoon, but the woman required years of follow-up therapy. It's really a very happy outcome. Today she is a fully functioning, happy, and productive member of her community."

(McAlear also told me about a second, rather less dramatic exorcism with which he and Betty Brennan had been involved, and when I spoke with Brennan several months later, she corroborated the essential details of both cases.)

Before leaving, I told McAlear that I was convinced that the popular entertainment industry, especially Blatty's movie and Malachi

Martin's *Hostage to the Devil,* had played a major role in stimulating the market for exorcism and deliverance in the United States.

"Yes. Yes. You're absolutely right," he said. "And I think this has especially been true for Catholics, because it is mostly Catholic exorcisms which have been depicted in the media. This is a big reason why exorcism and deliverance have come easier for Roman Catholics.

"Everyone knows about the movie, *The Exorcist,* but *Hostage to the Devil* was widely read by Catholic charismatics," he added. "I'm actually very impressed by it. It rings true with my experience. I believe it's authentic. Malachi Martin knows how people get possessed."[6]

D eliverance, as McAlear suggests, may have come easier for Roman Catholic charismatics than for just about anyone else, but this doesn't mean the ride was always smooth. In 1980 Francis MacNutt sent shock waves throughout the Catholic wing of the renewal when he left the priesthood and, without receiving dispensation from his vow of celibacy, married a woman named Judith Sewell, whom he'd met in Jerusalem five years earlier. The fortunes of Catholic deliverance in the United States had always been closely tied to MacNutt, and now many Catholic charismatics wondered whether their longtime star performer, their franchise player, had himself fallen prey to demonic temptation.

It wasn't long after this, moreover, that deliverance finally came under fire from certain sectors of the Catholic hierarchy. In early 1983 Bishop Rembert Weakland of Milwaukee issued an order temporarily forbidding the ritual from being practiced in his diocese. Weakland was concerned that charismatic Catholics in the Milwaukee area were becoming obsessed with casting out demons, and at least one of my interviewees seemed convinced that the bishop was right. "A lot of people were very upset with this ban on deliverance, but there's no question that things were getting completely out of control," Father Lou Lussier, a Milwaukee-based priest-physician and veteran charismatic, told me in a recent interview. "People were picking up demons left and right. Deliverance was being done over the phone. There was no solid discernment, and very little competent follow-up. This is not a ministry that is meant to be a witch-hunt."[7]

Later the same year Catholic deliverance was dealt an even more serious blow when it was sharply criticized by Cardinal Léon-Joseph Suenens of Belgium in a report entitled *Renewal and the Powers of Darkness*. Cardinal Suenens could hardly be classified as a hostile witness: Charismatic himself, he had long been an enthusiastic supporter of the renewal movement and its chief emissary within the Catholic hierarchy, all of which lent his critique added wallop. While their hearts were probably in the right place, the cardinal wrote, many Catholic charismatics involved with deliverance appeared to have surrendered to a kind of demonomania. They were seeing demons everywhere, fantasizing demons, blaming almost everything on demons. And what's more, the cardinal claimed, it was highly questionable whether deliverance, as it was practiced by Catholic charismatics, was even a legitimate ministry.

This issue of legitimacy was especially troublesome. Practically from the beginning, most Catholic charismatics involved with deliverance had recognized that they were operating in murky territory. The laws of their church stipulated that exorcism could be performed only by a duly appointed priest with the express permission of his bishop. And yet Catholic charismatics, priests and laypeople alike, were routinely performing a kind of exorcism, and doing so without any permission whatsoever. The last thing Catholic charismatics wanted was to be tagged as disloyal or rebellious, and so during the 1970s they had worked out a practical defense, a psycho-theological apologia, for their practice of deliverance. The linchpin of this defense was the distinction between "solemn" exorcism and possession on the one hand and "simple" exorcism and demonic affliction on the other. Solemn exorcism, or the formal ritual of exorcism as laid out in the *Rituale Romanum,* according to charismatics, was intended by the church primarily for cases of full-fledged possession, in which an individual's personality was completely taken over by Satan. It was this kind of exorcism that was restricted to an officially appointed priest—acting in the name of the church and with the explicit permission of his bishop.

But an individual could also be afflicted or tormented by demons without succumbing to full-fledged possession, charismatics insisted. And for cases of this sort it was perfectly legitimate for any Catholic, priest or not, to perform a simple exorcism without being obliged to seek episcopal approval. There was a long tradition of simple exorcism (or deliverance) within the Catholic Church, charismatics claimed, but it had fallen into neglect before being revived by Francis MacNutt and others during the 1970s. Providing they didn't try to tackle cases of outright possession or make use of the church's solemn ritual of exorcism, Catholic deliverance ministers were simply acting as good Catholics.[8]

Cardinal Suenens was unimpressed by this line of reasoning. In the first place, he said, the distinction between solemn and simple exorcism, possession and affliction, wasn't nearly as clear-cut in Catholic teaching as charismatics wanted to believe. And in the second place, the distinction (whatever its merits) was hardly justification for the kind of demons-in-the-cupboard, demons-under-the-blankets deliverance ministry with which so many Catholic charismatics were engaged. As much as charismatics might want to deny it, the cardinal said, things had unquestionably gotten out of hand, and it was probably best if no deliverance whatsoever were henceforth carried out without the prior approval of the local bishop.[9]

Cardinal Suenens's call to sobriety received mixed reviews among Catholic charismatics in the United States. Some charismatics, agreeing with the cardinal that a large segment of the renewal movement had become virtually drunk with demons, decided that this was as good a time as any to back off from deliverance ministry altogether. Others, while conceding the need for greater moderation, strongly disagreed that deliverance should be carried out only with episcopal approval. "I think that the cardinal had the best interests of the renewal movement in mind," Father Michael Scanlan, the pioneering Catholic deliverance minister, told me in Steubenville, Ohio. "He was rightly concerned with certain excesses. He wanted everything to be tested and prudent. For more serious cases of demonism I fully agree that the approval of the local bishop should be sought. But for the majority of cases I don't think this would be sound pastoral practice. It would be redundant, almost like asking permission to pray with someone."

For many practitioners of deliverance, Protestant as well as Catholic, the sting of Cardinal Suenens's critique was considerably allayed by the publication, also in 1983, of M. Scott Peck's *People of the Lie.* Peck's book was a great and unexpected gift. Here was the most famous psychiatrist in America preaching what charismatics had always known: Demons were real agents of evil in the modern world, fully capable of infiltrating ordinary women and men, and the only effective means of dealing with them was exorcism or deliverance. Many charismatics, in fact, saw *People of the Lie* as the breakthrough for which they had long awaited. After generations of denial, of derisory dismissal, perhaps now the medical and psychiatric establishments would be persuaded to take demonism seriously.

Probably no one was more appreciative of *People of the Lie,* or more hopeful of its leading to even better things, than charismatics who were themselves health care professionals. The renewal movement had always attracted its fair share of doctors, nurses, and therapists, at least some of whom were committed to performing deliverance while in the line of duty. More often than not, however, this meant leading a kind of double life: conducting one's official business by the book and then praying deliverance over patients or clients behind closed doors, furtively, always fearful of being found out. *People of the Lie* offered hope that the days of secrecy were finally coming to an end and that deliverance might soon find its place of respectability.

"For some of us Peck's book was one of those 'Aha, this is finally it' moments," a charismatic psychotherapist from the Midwest told me. "We hoped that the book would wake up the nation, shake up the establishment. It isn't easy doing deliverance when you're trying to hide it from your peers, hide it from the professional watchdog and licensing bodies, knowing full well that if they ever found out, you'd be a laughingstock and probably forced out of business. We were hoping that *People of the Lie* would change all of this. So far it hasn't, but we're still hoping."

Justifiably concerned for their reputations, most of the charismatic health care professionals I interviewed insisted on anonymity. Dr. William P. Wilson, on the other hand, a veteran deliverance minister from North Carolina who's now living in retirement, told me that he no longer has anything to hide. Born in Fayetteville in 1922, and raised in a middle-class Methodist family, Wilson earned degrees in medicine and psychiatry at Duke University during the forties and then went on to a distinguished career in teaching and research. Besides publishing dozens of scholarly articles and becoming a respected authority on epilepsy, he served a long and fruitful stint as head of Duke's division of biological psychiatry.

During his lengthy medical apprenticeship, Wilson had fallen away from his childhood faith, but in 1966 he returned to the Methodist fold, and the following year he became charismatic. Four years later he performed his first exorcism or deliverance.

"For the first few years after my baptism in the Spirit, I wasn't interested in demon-possession," he told me. "I thought the whole idea was extremist and crazy. But in 1971 I came across a woman who was incredibly violent. She threw herself to the floor, and then she picked up a nurse and hurtled her right across the room. I was an epileptologist, and she had been referred to me. She had what looked like epilepsy, but I wasn't so sure. I had just read Francis MacNutt's book on healing and deliverance, and it had had a profound influence on me. I thought she might be possessed. So I cleared the room and exorcised her. This was my very first case, and it was completely successful. After the exorcism she was cured instantly."

From here Dr. Wilson went on to perform dozens of additional exorcisms, mostly outside the United States. "I have only been involved with seven or eight exorcisms here," he said, "but I've done thirty to forty in Madagascar. And I've also done quite a few at a mental hospital in Juárez, Mexico, with Father Rick Thomas, a Jesuit in El Paso who's a very dear friend." I asked Wilson whether any of his professional colleagues had known about his involvement with exorcism or deliverance. "I'm pretty sure they had no inkling what I was up to," he said. "I kept it secret, even after M. Scott Peck's book came out. I was doing exorcisms while I was on the faculty at Duke. No one there knew about it. The psychiatrists in my department would have thought I was crazy. For people in the medical professions, I've got to say, it could be pretty lonely and isolated doing exorcisms during the 1980s."[10]

To some extent such loneliness and isolation was offset by an organization called the Association of Christian Therapists (ACT). Founded in 1975 by Francis MacNutt and several colleagues as a fellowship group for charismatic health care professionals, ACT experienced rapid growth during its first decade of existence, and by the mid-eighties it boasted a membership of almost two thousand. While not all of its members practiced deliverance, the organization regularly sponsored national and regional conferences where the subject was at least assured a sympathetic hearing.

The mid-eighties, as it turns out, were probably the high-water mark of the Association of Christian Therapists. The organization still exists today (with headquarters in Laurel, Maryland), but internal bickering and upheaval within its leadership ranks have taken their toll. Its membership is less than half what it was fifteen years ago, and even some of its own spokespeople seem worried that its time may have passed. Despite its recent troubles, however, ACT remains the organization of record for charismatic health care professionals in the United States, and in the fall of 1998 I met with some of its leading members in the hope of finding out how widely deliverance was still being practiced by charismatics in medical offices and consultation rooms across the nation.[11]

The subject is a sensitive one (again the insistence on anonymity) — and all the more so as a result of several recent cases in which health-care professionals have been sued for malpractice after attempting to expel demons from their patients or clients. In the most publicized of these cases a forty-five-year-old woman from Appleton, Wisconsin, named Nadean Cool received a $2.4 million out-of-court settlement from a psychiatrist who had diagnosed her as not only diabolically possessed but as having 126 separate personalities, one of which was the bride of Satan, another a duck. After being rebuffed by local Catholic officials, the psychiatrist, Dr. Kenneth C. Olson, attempted to carry out an exorcism himself, with the help (one can only imagine) of a fire extinguisher he purchased at a discount department store. The diagnosis, and attempted cure, proved more than Ms. Cool could handle, however, and over a period of several months she repeatedly tried to commit suicide, once slashing her abdomen so severely that she spent five days in a coma. "I couldn't stand the thought that I had Satan inside my body. I couldn't stand the thought that I believed I had murdered children and eaten them," Cool told reporters in November 1997, shortly after agreeing to the out-of-court settlement.[12]

Although Dr. Olson wasn't charismatic himself, the significance of his case wasn't lost on my interviewees. "First of all, I want to say that Olson's conduct was disgraceful, and I seriously doubt you'd find ACT people carrying on so recklessly," a charismatic psychiatrist based in the Great Lakes region told me. "I do some deliverance as part of my work, and so do some of my colleagues, but we're very cautious and discreet. In counseling you have to be perfectly clear. You tell people that deliverance is not part of your professional treatment package. You get their consent, and you draw strict lines. You might move the proceedings out of your professional office to another setting. You might bring in completely different people to help. The important thing is to establish boundaries. Otherwise you'll be raked over the coals by lawyers."

Another of my interviewees, a psychiatric nurse at a large hospital in the Midwest, told me that she has been performing deliverance at work since the mid-seventies. "After becoming charismatic, I got involved with spiritual healing, but I eventually saw that healing by itself was sometimes inadequate," she said. "I became convinced that there was sometimes another dimension involved—a demonic dimension. A patient can have a serious psychiatric problem and at the same time have a problem with demonic affliction. Frequently one leads to the other. It's not an either/or deal. After getting my M.A., I started to pray deliverance over some of my patients. I've usually worked by myself, not as part of a team. I perform simple deliverance, a quiet prayer with the patient. Sometimes the patient isn't even aware I'm doing it. My ministry is very quiet and discreet. I have no interest in getting involved with the sensational. Most of my cases I wouldn't describe as terribly serious."

Not that more serious cases haven't occasionally come calling. "About two years ago I was contacted by a Jesuit priest who's on the pastoral team of a nearby Catholic hospital," the nurse told me. "A twenty-six-year-old man had just been admitted to his hospital. He was Lutheran, from a very respectable, middle-class family, and he had a raft of physiological symptoms. He was pre-Parkinsonian. The Jesuit sensed the presence of something demonic, and so I went over and spoke with the man. He said that he'd been seduced into the occult by a girlfriend, and he'd picked up a horrible spirit of lust. He said he could have raped a sheet. Just for kicks one day he rented a video of *The Exorcist*, and watching the movie for the first time was what convinced him he was demonized. So he tried to seek out a Jesuit to perform an exorcism, but he couldn't find anyone who took his story seriously until he was admitted to the hospital. I wound up performing deliverance over him for several weeks, but always with my Jesuit friend present. This was a major case, and I needed support. When the deliverance was completed, all of the young man's symptoms disappeared. He's now in wonderful condition. The interesting thing is, without the movie it wouldn't even have occurred to him that he was demonized."

Just about everyone else I spoke with similarly favored a quiet and discreet approach to deliverance.

"I usually combine prayers for both healing and deliverance, and I'm very low-key about it," a soft-spoken, middle-aged physician with a private practice in a small Pennsylvania city told me. "My specialization is proctology; some of my patients are concerned about colon cancer, some are homosexuals suffering from rectal problems. But sometimes I get the sense there's something more happening beyond this. I ask if they have traditional faith to fall back on. I ask about their prayer life. I'll say to them, 'I believe in healing prayer. Could we pray together?' Only once in twenty years has a patient declined. I think that my patients appreciate my concern for their total being. They don't want a doctor who's just a technician. In the course of healing prayer I'll also pray aloud this deliverance prayer: 'If there is anything here not of the Lord Jesus Christ, I bind that in His name and cast it into the fires of His heart.' "

Altogether I met with twelve charismatic health care professionals, and only one, an intense and voluble physician based on the Atlantic seaboard, admitted to experiencing any fallout from his on-the-job demon-expulsion.

"This happened just a few years ago," he said. "A woman came to see me with a thyroid problem. She was very agitated, far more so than what you would expect, and I asked her consent to pray for healing and deliverance. I get lots of patients referred to me through the charismatic grapevine, but this particular woman had come on her own. She said that she wasn't particularly religious, but she told me to go ahead. After the deliverance she was vastly improved. She said she'd never felt better, and she thanked me profusely. A few months later I got a letter from the folks at the state health department, saying they wanted to meet with me. Apparently this woman, or someone she knew, had contacted them, and they said they had concerns about my 'irregular procedures.' I wasn't being accused of professional misconduct, but the whole business was nerve-racking. I met with them several times and told them about my commitment to holistic healing. They listened, they were respectful, and I haven't heard anything more about it since. What the whole episode reinforced for me is that we have to be constantly on our guard."

And did this mean, I asked, that he was now a bit gun-shy about performing deliverance in his professional capacity?

"Not in the least," he answered. "I still do it. Right in this room. Right where we're sitting. I have patients referred to me all the time who are seeking deliverance. Some of them have major problems with demonic affliction."

I asked what had initially prompted him to get involved with deliverance ministry.

"Some years back I got a call from one of my longtime patients ask-

ing me to come to her home," he said. "We were in the same charismatic prayer group, and I knew that she was distraught because her
husband had gotten deeply involved in the occult—tarot cards, chan-
neling, the whole nine yards. I sensed there was real evil here, so I
phoned people from my prayer group and asked for backup prayer
support. I went to the house, and I found Tom, the husband—a huge
guy, well over six feet and two hundred pounds—huddled up in a fetal position in a corner of a bed. I started praying over him silently:
'Lord Jesus, please help him.' He lurched violently, and then I began
stroking his back, all the while praying silently. Then he lurched again,
and suddenly he was like the Incredible Hulk springing to life. He
jumped off the bed, growling and snorting. His eyes were like two golf
balls of flame. Then he sprung down the stairs but missed the door
and crashed through the wall. He ran to a construction site where
they were building a new mall. He started hurling heavy beams and
cement blocks, tossing them sixty to seventy yards effortlessly. Then
he threw himself on the ground, and the police and an ambulance
came while he was lying in a fetal position. I prayed silently over him
again, and he jumped up like a maniac and went lurching down the
road. Finally he went back to his house and seemed to calm down. I
was convinced that here was real supernatural evil.

"I knew about deliverance from reading Basham and MacNutt,
and so I got some people from my prayer group together, and we
prayed deliverance over Tom that very night. The next day Tom
couldn't remember that any of this had happened, but he was well on
the way toward being healed. This episode taught me the power of the
name of Jesus. We did follow-up counseling with Tom, and we eventually found that his father's brother, Tom's uncle, had died six years
before Tom was even born. Tom used to feel great rage whenever his
uncle's name was mentioned. We suspect that there was an element of
intergenerational evil at work here, some demon or curse that had
been transmitted to Tom through the family tree."

Intergenerational evil? Demons inherited from ancestors? Never mind trying to square this with medical science; the concept seems equally at odds with traditional Christian teaching regarding free will and individual responsibility. And yet this strange notion, that demons and curses may be passed down the family line, has been widely embraced by charismatic health-care professionals in recent years. Indeed, treating cases of transgenerational evil (congenital demonism, as it were) is now the hottest specialty within the charismatic deliverance field.

I first heard about the concept early on in my research, when I met with a former Episcopal pastor who was working as a car salesman in Maryland. He told me that for much of his life he'd had enormous difficulty sustaining personal commitments. He dropped out of college several courses short of graduation and then went through a string of short-lived romances. He got married and had a child, but his wife soon left him and moved with their two-year-old daughter to California. He received ordination and became pastor of a small rural parish, but after repeated run-ins with his church board he resigned his position and took a series of dead-end jobs in the service sector. Finally, in the late eighties, he became charismatic, and a member of his prayer group gave him a copy of *Healing the Family Tree,* a slender volume written by a Church of England clergyman named Kenneth McAll.

"I'd gone through some really tough times, broken vows, broken promises, a sense of never being in charge of my life," he said. "At times it was terrible. During the first few months of my marriage it was as if there were three of us in bed—my wife, myself, and some evil presence. McAll's book opened my eyes; it helped me resolve these conflicts. I learned that an entire family line can be cursed by demons. Somehow this evil gets into the family, and then it's passed on generationally. Generation after generation is contaminated by it, unless steps are taken to break the curse, to purify the familial lineage. You have to undergo a special kind of deliverance for this. In my case I found out that males in my family dating back three or four generations seem to have had a similar problem with commitment. Our family line had become demonically infected, and it took deliverance to put an end to it."

Here again I wasn't sure if I was meant to take all of this literally, and my body language must have betrayed a measure of incredulity.

"I know this isn't the kind of thing you're used to hearing," the ex-pastor said, "but consider the possibilities. We now know that so much about our physical health is genetically conditioned. The same might also be true for our spiritual health. Why exclude the possibility? It seems the best way of testing this is through practical experience. Treat deliverance as a kind of experiment. Does it work or not? In my case, it seems definitely to have worked. I think we should have an open mind about this sort of thing. Remember also the biblical passage in Exodus 20:5, where it says that the Lord is a jealous God, punishing the sins of the fathers to the third and fourth generations. For someone such as yourself, the best thing would be to witness the process in action. See if any opportunity presents itself for you to sit in on an actual healing and deliverance session dealing with this kind of problem."[13]

Such an opportunity finally presented itself in the late fall of 1998, when I visited a small Midwestern city to meet with a charismatic psychotherapist whom I'll refer to as Dr. K. A bright and unpretentious woman in her late fifties, Dr. K was just wrapping up an evening counseling session when I arrived at her office, and over tea a bit later she filled me in on some of her personal background. She said that both of her parents died when she was just a young girl, and she was raised with her younger brother in a foster home in Chicago. After graduating high school, she fell into a life of heavy drinking and partying but was "jolted back to reality" when she gave birth to twin boys in her early twenties. Working part-time and raising her twins with the help of her brother, she managed to put herself through college, and she eventually went on to earn a Ph.D. in counseling psychology from a top-rated university on the East Coast. She became charismatic in the late seventies, and upon discovering that she possessed a "powerful gift of discerning spirits," she gradually incorporated deliverance into her regular counseling practice.

"What I found was that my body works as an instrument of discernment," she told me. "When counseling a genuine victim of SRA [Satanic Ritual Abuse], I will feel aches and pains, sometimes quite intense, in my ears, my eyes, my back, sometimes even my teeth. And for people with intergenerational spirits, which is my main specialty, I will usually feel intense pain in my left arm. At the very least my body tells me whether we're actually dealing with evil spirits in any specific case."

Dr. K is well known in charismatic circles for her deliverance ministry, and she routinely gets referrals from as far away as Florida and California. She told me that she had three appointments scheduled for the next day, and she invited me to sit in on the proceedings as an observer.

At nine o'clock the following morning, Dr. K's deliverance team is assembled in her consultation room—all charismatics, but otherwise a rather eclectic group. In addition to Dr. K there's a middle-aged Methodist couple, a young Catholic woman who's planning on becoming a psychotherapist herself, and a fortyish Episcopal woman who works as a nurse at a nearby hospital. The first client of the day is a thirty-five-year-old woman named Margaret, with a horrific story to tell. She says that when she was twelve, she discovered her father's body hanging by a rope in the basement of the family home, and she has been haunted by the memory ever since. Over the past several years she has undergone deliverance for demons of alcohol and marital infidelity, but the inner peace she longs for has proven elusive. She is still struggling to put the grisly basement discovery of her childhood behind her, and she occasionally feels tempted by suicide herself.

Dr. K asks Margaret some gently prodding questions (Had she been happy as a child prior to finding her father's body? Had she ever seriously visualized taking her own life?) and then tells her to wait outside in the reception area while the team looks over her genogram. This is a specialized family history, a kind of genealogical tracking chart, which virtually all therapists working in the area of intergenerational evil ask their clients to prepare for their first appointment, with a view to identifying relatives who have suffered emotional or mental problems, problems with drugs or alcohol—anything whatsoever that may have provided an opening for the demonic. After studying Margaret's genogram in silence for several minutes, the team anoints the walls of the consultation room with holy oil and prays for the binding of all evil spirits. Dr. K then enters what she describes as her "phase of discernment." For five minutes she sits with her head bowed, trembling, sighing audibly, twice breaking into a spasm of weeping, until finally she says that she's getting a strong signal. Do you remember, she says, referring to the genogram we have just looked at, do you remember that when he was in his late seventies Margaret's paternal grandfather was admitted to a sanitarium against his will? Was it not possible that the old man, lonely and embittered, had somehow invited spirits of despair and suicide into the family line? And that Margaret's father, and then Margaret herself, had been forced to pay the price?

The team members nod in affirmation. This, more or less, is what they, too, had been discerning. Margaret is brought back in and informed of the diagnosis, which she seems to take in stride, and then the team encircles her with outstretched arms, praying in tongues.

Dr. K, stifling sobs, places her hands on Margaret's shoulders. "In the name of Jesus, I remove you, spirit of despair and depression, and send you to the cross," she commands. "In the name of Jesus, I remove you, curse of suicide, and send you to the cross."

Margaret says that she felt something leaving her. The Episcopal nurse reports that a departing spirit bit her on the ankle. The Methodist woman says she felt something grabbing her left breast.

Dr. K strokes Margaret's cheeks and forehead and tells her that the next step in the process is to seek inner healing for the emotional wounds she suffered as a child. She asks Margaret to close her eyes and get deeply in touch with the experience of discovering her dead father. Margaret slumps back in her chair and begins weeping. She says that she loved her father but was strangely relieved, almost happy, upon finding his body. He was an angry and abusive man, and she once overheard his own mother, her grandmother, saying, "Thank God the bastard is gone." For years, Margaret says, she has been living with intense guilt, secretly rejoicing over the suicide of the only man she has ever truly loved.

Dr. K prays softly for the "healing of this woundedness," and then she asks Margaret to leave the room again so that she can confer with her team.

"I'm picking up more spirits in her, spirits that still need to be delivered," she says. The team agrees, and the Episcopal nurse says that she specifically discerned spirits of incest and hatred. Dr. K calls Margaret back in, performs a brief ritual of "sealing" or protection over her ("to safeguard against satanic retribution"), and schedules another session for the following week.

There are two more sessions later the same day—both involving women, and both every bit as poignant as the first. Afterward I ask Dr. K whether women make up the bulk of her "intergenerational" clientele.

"Yes, most of our clients are women," she answers. "Women are more intuitive than men, more right-brain-oriented, more open to spiritual processes. This is also why charismatic women tend to have stronger gifts of discernment than men do. They are far more sensitive to the spiritual realm."

While Dr. K takes a phone call in another room, I scan the titles on her bookshelf. The usual run of standard texts—*Psychological Testing,* 4th edition; *Managing Deficit Disorders in Children; Client-Centered Therapy*—but also some more colorful stuff—Ellen Bass and Laura Davis's *The Courage to Heal,* Carol Gilligan's *In a Different Voice,* M. Scott Peck's *People of the Lie . . .*

The call was from one of Dr. K's contacts on the West Coast, asking her to take on a new client.

Does it ever happen that someone will come to you for intergenerational deliverance and you and your team will say, "No, this isn't your problem"? I ask.

"Very rarely," Dr. K says. "I can think of just one example where this happened. You have to realize that people aren't showing up on my doorstep by accident. Most of my clients are charismatics who sense that they are afflicted by some sort of supernatural evil. But they're confused and afraid. They can't put their finger on the problem, and they're not sure how to get better. That's my job."

Rather late in my research I finally managed to meet with Francis MacNutt and the Lutheran Erwin Prange, without question two of the biggest names in charismatic deliverance ministry over the past three decades.

The meeting with Prange was facilitated by a Lutheran minister named Bob Burmeister, an immensely charming, middle-aged man with graying hair and a goatee. Raised in Milwaukee in a blue-collar, churchgoing family, Burmeister became charismatic in 1972, and four years later he was called to serve as assistant pastor at North Heights Lutheran in St. Paul. As it happened, this was the same year that Erwin Prange joined the North Heights pastoral staff as resident exorcist, and Burmeister soon came under his tutelage.

"Prange needed someone to hold people down, and I was tapped for the job. It's sort of like working in a slaughterhouse; no one else wanted to do it," Burmeister told me. "For a ten-year period, from about 1976 to 1986, we were amazingly busy. There were some other well-known Lutheran deliverance ministries in the country—one in Bethlehem, Pennsylvania, another in Charlotte, North Carolina—but North Heights was definitely at the head of the class. We did deliverance every Tuesday and Thursday morning. Prange was in tremendous demand. He really taught me the ropes. Working with him, I learned that you don't always need to use your gifts of spiritual discernment to tell whether someone's truly demonized. There are a number of dead giveaways."

Most of these dead giveaways, which Burmeister proceeded to lay out for me, I had already heard about from other exorcism ministers.

"Sometimes there's a sensation of extreme cold," he said, "almost a sense of invisible ice masses surrounding the demonized person. At other times there's a horrible demonic odor, like sulphur or horse manure. Pastor Prange could just smell them out. And then there's the glazed-over, catatonic eyes. As the saying goes, 'The eyes are windows to the soul.' But most of all, there's a revulsion to sacred things, a revulsion to the church sanctuary and the crucifix, a revulsion to the merest mention of the name and blood of Jesus. I can't tell you how often we'd be bringing someone into the sanctuary for prayer and counseling, only to have them start screaming and wailing and trying to escape. And so then we'd know."

When Prange retired from active ministry in 1988, Burmeister took over the exorcism post at North Heights, and he seems to have followed closely in his mentor's footsteps. He doesn't bind evil spirits during deliverance ("Prange taught me not to do this, because we need to have some indication that progress is being made. We need the spirits manifesting so we can gauge the process of the ministry. Otherwise, it's like performing surgery blindfolded"), and he isn't averse to putting his own physical welfare on the line. "Sometimes it's real wrestling matches. People have tried to hurt me. You don't wear a tie. You could be strangled. I always work with at least two assistants who help to restrain anyone who gets really out of control."

Unlike many of his colleagues in the charismatic movement, however, Burmeister doesn't go hunting for demons, with the intention of always finding them. During my time in St. Paul, I saw him ministering to a middle-aged woman who was convinced that demons were driving her to fantasize about suicide. Gently and skillfully (he doesn't have any formal psychotherapeutic training), Burmeister questioned her and prayed over her, then told her that he was quite certain she wasn't demonized. (He recommended that she seek psychiatric help.)

Ten years into his retirement from full-time ministry, Erwin Prange lives alone in a nondescript trailer on the outskirts of Winona, Minnesota. There is a whiff of scandal about him these days, murmurings within some charismatic circles of broken promises, reckless living, an exorcist gone astray. Several of his former colleagues at North Heights, in fact, hinted that my visiting him might be a waste of time.

When I finally found him, after navigating a maze of unpaved trailer-park lanes, Prange was alert and full of spunk, still dapper, at eighty-one, with white hair and tortoiseshell glasses and wearing beige slacks with black suspenders over a white shirt.

He opened our conversation by telling me that "the exorcism business is plagued by kooks and wannabes." He went on, "You have these guys who have a low opinion of themselves—an opinion which is shared by just about everyone who knows them—and who have never accomplished anything significant in their lives. Now they become exorcists or deliverance ministers, and suddenly they're in touch with the highest powers imaginable. They can't handle it; they become power-trippers. I'm telling you, anything they say you can't take at face value. They're mostly a bunch of hacks."

As for himself, Prange assured me, the job of exorcist was something he had never really wanted, never lobbied for. He was raised near Whitewater, Arkansas, where his father ran a sawmill and general store, and after serving as an interpreter with General Patton's Tenth Armored Division during World War II, he studied theology at Concordia Seminary in St. Louis and was ordained a Lutheran minister (Missouri Synod) in 1954. He pastored churches in St. Louis, Brooklyn, rural Montana, and Baltimore before moving to North Heights, getting married, and raising four children. He became charismatic in 1963, while working in Brooklyn, and shortly afterward he performed his first deliverance, at Morrisania Hospital in the Bronx.

"Becoming charismatic had made me acutely aware of the demonic realm," he said, "and some Puerto Rican friends told me that they needed my help. A family member, a woman in her thirties, had been hospitalized for psychiatric observation, and my friends thought she might be demonized. So I went to see her, and her demon started screaming at me in Spanish, yelling out everything about my past life, every indiscretion. At the time my Spanish wasn't so great, but a nurse told me what the demon was saying, and she said that the Puerto Ricans in the waiting room were having a ball listening to it all. I said, 'I can't be an exorcist. My image can't take it.' Remember, this was before Don Basham and Derek Prince, before Francis MacNutt. But after this experience I didn't perform many more exorcisms until I read MacNutt's book in the early seventies. Francis was a huge influence on me. He once said, 'The Gospel without healing and deliverance is just good advice—not Good News.' And so I got back in the saddle, and in 1976 I received the call to come up to North Heights."

During his first five or six years at North Heights, Prange developed a close working relationship with the man who has been an almost ubiquitous presence on the American exorcism scene over the past thirty years: Malachi Martin. "I read *Hostage to the Devil* and thought it was a terrific book," he said, "and so I got in touch with Malachi by phone and told him about my ministry."

Martin apparently was impressed—enough so, at any rate, that he added Prange to his roster of on-call exorcists.

"We never actually met in person until we did the Oprah show in 1987," Prange said, "but over the years Malachi sent me a lot of people to be exorcised. Some of these people were Roman Catholics who couldn't get Catholic exorcisms. One time he sent me a man who was actually a demon. I phoned Malachi and said, 'Malachi, I think you've sent me a demon.' I sent him back to Malachi, and a few days later Malachi phoned and said, 'Erv, I've taken a closer look at him myself, and you're right: I sent you a demon.' "

A strange story—but nothing compared to what came next. Not long before his retirement from North Heights, Prange said, he was asked by two charismatic psychotherapists to exorcise a young woman who was ("beyond any doubt") the biological daughter of Satan. The exorcism proved a grueling operation, extending over several weeks, and after one especially taxing session Prange himself fell victim to diabolical possession.

"When we finished for the evening, the woman hugged me, and that's when it happened," he said. "It was like a hand grenade going off in every one of my cells. Now I knew what it felt like; I was totally possessed. I couldn't eat or sleep. People were avoiding me. I was reduced to wandering around an abandoned schoolyard in New Brighton with my pet wolf. The wolf was the only one not avoiding me. I didn't feel driven to commit violence. I wasn't out of control sexually. But I knew I was highly possessed. Finally I came out of it when I succeeded in exorcising myself."

It was time for Prange's daily swim at the local community center. "[My experience with possession] gives you an idea of what we're up against," he said, walking me to my car. "It's a tough business. Every once in a while some young guy fresh out of seminary will approach me and say, 'Pastor Prange, I want to be an exorcist.' You know what I tell him? I say, 'You must be crazy.' And then I recommend that he see a psychiatrist."[14]

For Francis MacNutt it's been a long journey back. After leaving the priesthood and getting married in 1980, he suddenly found himself persona non grata in Catholic charismatic circles. ("A lot of people thought I'd been tempted by the devil," he told me. "It was a horrible scandal. The charismatic magazine *New Covenant* did a full-page story saying I was now beyond the pale.") For several years he kept a low profile, running a small healing and deliverance ministry out of Clearwater, Florida, with his wife Judith. As time went on, he began receiving speaking invitations from various Protestant charismatic groups, and in 1987 he and Judith moved their operations, which they were now calling Christian Healing Ministries (CHM), to a former Episcopal parish complex in Jacksonville. During the late eighties and early nineties word got around: MacNutt was back in action, and his gifts for healing and deliverance were as impressive as ever. Before long, CHM was swamped with calls for help, and even quite a few Catholic charismatics seemed more than willing to give MacNutt a second chance.

Christian Healing Ministries occupies a large corner lot in a low-slung, working-class neighborhood on the northern fringes of Jacksonville. Just six or seven blocks to the east is N. Main Street, a lugubrious, crack-infested thoroughfare haunted nightly by zonked-out addicts selling sex for ten dollars a pop. As I discovered when I dropped by for a meeting with Francis MacNutt, however, the CHM staff has far more serious things to worry about than the surrounding neighborhood. Upon arriving, I was ushered into a waiting room in the ministry's main building—a two-story hall with three yellow-stuccoed wings and a courtyard opening out onto an L-shaped chapel. Within minutes three women came into the room on the pretext of introducing themselves and engaging me in small talk. But this was no ordinary small talk. One woman stared intently into my eyes, another slowly circled me two or three times, and the third stood off to the side with upturned nostrils. A pleasant enough exchange in its way, but also a bit unsettling.

Later, over lunch, I mentioned this odd welcome to MacNutt and asked whether I was being scrutinized for indwelling demons.

"Of course you were," he said, laughing. "We have eleven salaried people on our staff, and most of them are charismatic Episcopal women with strong gifts for discerning evil spirits. They can smell them, feel them, sometimes sense them spatially. Sometimes they'll even say to me, 'Francis, there's something on you,' and they'll pray over me."

"And how did I come out in the inspection?"

"You came out fine. You're clean. Otherwise we wouldn't be sitting here having lunch. The thing is, we have to be vigilant about protecting our ministry. Demonic attack can come from anywhere. You came down to see us from New York City. We didn't know much about you, so we didn't want to take any chances."

It isn't hard to see why MacNutt was once the heartthrob of the Catholic renewal movement. While he's now in his early seventies and walks with a slight stoop as a result of a chronic spinal condition, he is tall and lean and movie-star handsome, with a full head of graying hair and a soft and deliberate manner of speaking.

He said that he had mixed feelings about the popular entertainment industry's exploitation of exorcism. "People such as William Peter Blatty and Malachi Martin deserve credit for raising public awareness, but they also created some false impressions. Take *Hostage to the Devil*, for example, where all the priest-exorcists get beaten up in the course of duty. I didn't like this, and I said so directly to Malachi Martin when I met him at a deliverance conference on Staten Island in the early eighties. It says something terrible about the power of

God, that God would permit His priests to be so horribly bloodied and battered. It's sensationalism of this sort that fires up the media and gets them chasing after exorcisms."

I asked MacNutt whether he himself had ever been sought out by the media.

"After Father LeBar's *20/20* show, Sally Jessy Raphaël's people phoned up and asked if they could do a show on us," he said. "They asked if I had done exorcisms. I said, 'No, but I've done hundreds of deliverances.' But this wasn't good enough for them. They wanted a real, full-fledged exorcism performed by a bona fide Catholic priest. Nothing else would do."

For all its medieval overtones, I suggested to MacNutt, deliverance seemed remarkably well attuned to the therapeutic, recovery, twelve-step culture of contemporary America. From my perspective, I said, it seemed a relatively blame-free, fast-track approach to dealing with personal problems.

"In some respects you're probably right," he said. "At Christian Healing Ministries we see ourselves as part of the wider recovery movement. We feel a real affinity with Alcoholics Anonymous and other twelve-step groups. Our position is that Christians, historically, have put too much emphasis on sin and willpower. Very often individuals will have a problem with sex or drinking or something else, and the problem really isn't their fault, and no amount of willpower can cure it. They're afflicted by evil spirits. They need deliverance."[15]

I didn't have an opportunity during my stay in Jacksonville to sit in on an actual deliverance at Christian Healing Ministries. The night before my departure, however, I was taken by two of MacNutt's associates to a suburban Episcopal church where a small, unprepossessing man named Don, an insurance salesman by day, was presiding over a weekly healing and exorcism meeting. We settled into a front pew and watched as Don ministered on the altar steps to a young woman who was retching into a rubber trash container. After the woman's demons were expelled, Don joined us for a moment in our pew and said that he had "six demonic afflictions and two full-scale possessions" still on deck that evening. When he returned to the altar for his next case, one of my companions saw me stifling a yawn and said jokingly, "You'd better watch out. Don believes that demons usually manifest through the victim's mouth. If he sees you yawning, there's a good chance he might run over and start exorcising you."

It was a long evening, and, compared to other exorcism sessions I'd attended, not especially eventful. Just past midnight, however, a severely retarded fourteen-year-old boy, who seemed at first glance not much older than eight or nine, was brought to the front of the church by his father. My companions filled me in on some of the boy's background. His mother had been addicted to heroin when she was pregnant with him, they said, and the father, who was also a drug addict, had physically abused him for several years after he was born. Since then both parents had straightened themselves out, but they worried that their son was demonized. Besides being retarded, he frequently flew into fits of rage, cursing, spitting, and striking out at anyone in range. Don had been praying deliverance over him weekly for several months now.

The boy was brought to the front of the church by his father, and Don sat waiting for him on the altar steps with outstretched arms. Ten yards or so from the front, the boy broke into a clumsy trot and threw himself into Don's lap, snuggling up against his chest. Don stroked the boy's face and ran his fingers through his hair. He talked to the boy about school and baseball. The boy, now giggling, pinched Don's nose and cheeks while his father stood off to the side with arms crossed, beaming. Then, speaking directly into the boy's ear, Don prayed deliverance over him for several minutes. When he was finished, the boy wrapped his arms around Don's neck and kissed him on the cheek. Don told the boy that he loved him and that he hoped to see him again soon. The father said that it was time to go, but for five more minutes the boy stayed on Don's lap, looking into his eyes and smiling.

Were there demons here? I have no idea. But watching this scene unfold, I was convinced that something undeniably positive was tak-

ing place. Through his love and attention, Don had succeeded in forg-
ing a compelling connection with this young boy. Their encounter was
rich and genuine. Don's deliverance, I was almost certain, had done no
harm. If anything, it had been therapeutically beneficial.

And this, I might add, wasn't the only charismatic deliverance I
witnessed that struck me as such. For all the ego-trippers in the business, showing off their dubious powers of discernment, stacking the
spiritual deck, there are also people such as Don and Bob Burmeister
who approach healing and deliverance with real humility and humanity. The Dons and Bob Burmeisters of the deliverance world might not
actually be expelling demons (my evidence on this score is far from
conclusive), but this doesn't mean they're not making some tangible
difference in their clients' lives. In the hands of some of its practitioners, in other words, deliverance might very well possess positive psychotherapeutic value.

Thanks to the researches of cultural anthropology, we now know
that traditional religio-magical methods of healing may sometimes be
as effective in alleviating mental and emotional distress as modern,
secular ones. Indeed, the specific method of healing, the choice of
therapy, isn't nearly as important as one might think. As the psychologist Jerome Frank has pointed out, virtually all therapeutic procedures—regardless of whether they're rooted in primitive shamanism
or Freudian psychodynamics—may confer certain benefits upon their
clients: the hope and expectancy for improvement, the support and attention of the therapist, the discovery of new perspectives on problem-
solving.[16]

So why not deliverance? Over the past thirty years or so, tens of
thousands of charismatics have availed themselves of the ritual, quite
often in the hopes of gaining relief from such diverse problems as depression, anger, or sexual anxiety. And if their personal testimonies are
to be believed, at least some of these people have come out considerably the better for it. In one way or another, arguably, deliverance has
helped them combat despair or demoralization and given them incentive for improving their lives. In some cases this may have been due to
the particular talents of the deliverance minister, including, not least of

all, his or her capacity for inspiring trust and confidence. In other cases it may simply have been a consequence of undergoing the procedure—what is sometimes referred to as the placebo effect: finding oneself the center of attention, having one's emotions engaged, one's demons (quite literally, in this context) identified.

Of course, I wouldn't want to press the point too far. In the absence of rigorous outcome studies, it is impossible to say how many people have experienced long-term, clinically significant improvement as a result of deliverance. Or, conversely, how many have actually been harmed in some way by the procedure. Even the individual deliverances that I personally witnessed raised more questions than they answered. The psychiatric history and family background of the subjects involved, the short- and long-term impact of their deliverances— on all these matters, my data are frustratingly incomplete.

Consider, for example, the seriously disturbed young man named Paul, who was featured in the case study that opened this part. There are a number of issues related to Paul's case that likely would have been flagged in a more properly clinical setting but that his deliverance ministers in Kansas City neglected to pursue. One of these issues concerns Paul's compulsive masturbating as an adolescent, sometimes, it will be recalled, while wearing his mother's bra and panties. What, precisely, were the contents of his masturbatory fantasies? Was he preoccupied with homosexual thoughts? Or, perhaps, with incestuous ones? It would be useful here to know more about Paul's early family history, his relationships with his parents and siblings, as a way of probing possible problems in his psychosexual identification. Another issue concerns the sexual frenzies and violent impulses that Paul experienced as his condition continued to deteriorate. Was there anything in particular that triggered these episodes? There is also a glaring implausibility in Paul's story. In the depths of his despair, apparently, he was convinced by his girlfriend to see a neurologist. But wouldn't any neurologist, finding nothing neurologically wrong with him, have referred Paul for immediate psychiatric help? At no point in his story does Paul indicate ever having seen a psychiatrist.

It isn't difficult to imagine what might have happened if Paul had been steered into professional psychiatric treatment rather than deliverance. In all likelihood he would have been diagnosed as suffering from severe personality disorder, with brief psychotic episodes and massive conflicts around sexuality. His complaints of claws clutching at his body would have been seen as somatic delusions or tactile hallucinations, possibly triggered by memories of incestuous abuse. His conviction that he was demonized might have been attributed, at least partially, to the tremendous suggestive power of Malachi Martin's *Hostage to the Devil.* In the end he probably would have been treated with antipsychotics. For psychiatrists who work regularly with severe personality disorder, a patient such as Paul would not have been especially unusual.

Without long-term follow-up, moreover, most psychiatrists would probably be inclined to regard Paul's apparent recovery in Kansas City as extremely fragile. After undergoing deliverance, Paul may have been engaged in a sweeping denial of his problems, perhaps replacing his delusional cast of demons with an entirely new cast of benevolent, guardian spirits. Even the most dramatic psychiatric symptomatology may occasionally go into spontaneous remission. Despite feeling better after his deliverance, in other words, Paul's underlying pathology might still have been present.[17]

B ut all this is rather beside the point. Regardless of how its therapeutic value might be judged, deliverance or exorcism remains a highly sought-after commodity in contemporary America. And not just among charismatics. In recent years a number of other groups have also embraced the ritual. Some of these groups believe that the best way of taking care of business is to let the wolves howl.

Part Four

The Rough-and-Ready School

11.

The Hegewisch shuffle

Pastor Mike Thierer, a small, balding, amiable man in his early forties, wastes little time getting down to business. Just a minute or two into the deliverance session, he works his way to the front of the brightly lit auditorium and sits down in a metal folding chair beside Brian, a strapping young man with brown wavy hair. Wrapping his arms tightly around Brian's shoulders, he speaks directly into his ear, commanding the demons to reveal themselves. For five minutes or so Brian sits quietly, fidgeting, shifting his feet, his face pressed against Pastor Mike's chest, but then, growling and foaming, he lurches to his feet with Pastor Mike now on his back, clinging to his neck. One of Pastor Mike's assistants, a stocky man in his twenties wearing jeans and a plaid shirt, charges to the front of the room and tries to intervene, but Brian, flailing, kicking, screaming, tosses him aside and starts gyrating furiously, twirling Pastor Mike around and around in an airplane spin, sending his glasses flying.

Just an hour earlier I had eaten dinner with Pastor Mike at a local restaurant, and now, concerned for his safety, I take off my jacket, walk slowly up the center aisle, and throw a headlock on Brian, which stops his gyrating and gives Pastor Mike a chance to climb from his back. Plaid Shirt rejoins the action, and with the help of two more as-

sistants—one bearded and beefy, the other tall and thin and wearing a
shirt and tie—succeeds in wrestling Brian to the floor. Not yet ready
to give up, Brian works a leg free and kicks Plaid Shirt hard in the
mouth, cutting his lip and sending him crashing headfirst against the
front wall. With Brian now lying on his back, I grab one of his arms
by the wrist and hold it down. The bearded assistant grabs the other
arm, while Shirt-and-Tie and Plaid Shirt (making an impressive come-
back) hold down his legs. Pastor Mike retrieves his glasses and throws
himself across Brian's chest, pleading with the demons to depart.
Brian struggles to break free, and in the humid hall his wrist is slippery with sweat. Pastor Mike tells me to be careful not to choke off
the circulation, and when I relax my grip a bit, Brian jams the index
finger of my right hand hard into the floor.

This is just a small piece of the action. Throughout the auditorium,
demoniacs are paired off with exorcism ministers, wailing, thrashing,
regurgitating. Demons are being expelled in gushes of vomit and
strands of mucus, and assistants pick their way through the heaving
mess, handing out paper towels, holding brown paper bags up to peo-
ples' chins. Not more than five yards from me, a teenage girl, eyes
dancing crazily, hurtles herself to a clearing on the floor, where four
women hold her down, one of them praying fervently. Across the hall
an attractive, middle-aged blond woman named Linda wails constantly, a high-pitched air raid siren of a voice. Young children roam
the hall, taking it all in nonchalantly.

Back in our corner, Pastor Mike, sweating heavily, begins insult-
ing Brian's demons. He says that they're sorry excuses for demons,
useless, weak. He laughs at them, scoffs at them.

The demons are outraged. "You fucker, Pastor Mike!" they howl.
"You asshole. You fucking sodomite. Fuck off. You're a faggot, Pastor
Mike."

Exasperated, Pastor Mike says, "Just go. Just leave. Get lost."

Brian tries to spit in my face, then makes direct eye contact with
me and growls, "I'm gonna get that guy. I'm gonna get that fucking
guy." A small blond-haired boy, the son of one of the assistants, kneels
down for a moment by Brian and gently, lovingly caresses his fore-

head. The two assistants pinning Brian's legs start singing softly, to the tune of "Take Me Out to the Ballgame": ". . . and it's one, two, three strikes, and the demon's out."

There's a strange choreography to the entire business. Brian struggles frantically, but he seems to make a tacit deal with me. I notice that when I loosen the pressure on his wrist, he refrains for a while from trying to hit me. When he tries to hit me again, I exert stronger pressure for several minutes, then loosen my grip, and the whole process repeats itself. The assistant holding Brian's other arm periodically lets go of it so Brian can wipe the foam and spittle from his chin, and then he seizes the arm again and the struggle resumes.

After an hour of this, Brian calms down and, with a slight smile, signals us to release our grips. He then embraces Pastor Mike, is helped to his feet by Plaid Shirt, and embraces him also.

I ask Pastor Mike if he's okay. "Oh, sure, I've been involved with worse ones," he says.

He also confides a measure of frustration.

"As our ministry grows, I hope the Lord will give us more power to cast out these demons," he says. "You know, Jesus used to just command demons to depart, and they'd have to leave. It's strange; it should be that way for us, too. These are very tough, stubborn demons we're dealing with here tonight. We pray the Lord will give us more power."

Pastor Mike invites me to join him for a glass of lemonade (there's a table at the back set out with cookies, pretzels, and other refreshments), but his attention is drawn to the near corner where a slim, stylish, white-haired woman named Susan is engaged in wild battle with three female assistants. Pastor Mike grabs her legs, dumps her to the floor, and instructs the assistants to keep her under restraint, then rushes to the assistance of Brian, who, in a marvelous role reversal, is casting demons out of a young black woman. While Pastor Mike is kneeling next to Brian, Susan—thrashing and gobbing and perhaps feeling a bit cheated—repeatedly cries out to him, "Help me, Michael. Do something, Michael."

Finally, at 11:00 P.M., Pastor Mike's colleague, Pastor John, a handsome, brown-haired, fortyish man with a dimpled chin, takes a microphone and calls the proceedings to a halt. He instructs everyone to recite the formula for "binding" or "boxing" all demons that have still not been expelled:

> We take authority over every remaining demon from the Strongman on down to the lowest demon in rank, power, and form and bind you all in Jesus' Name. By binding, we mean you are not to torment, hurt, or harass [anyone]. We loose sufficient numbers of Warrior Angels to put each of you in boxes, cages, or caves five hundred thousand times too small and seal each box, cage, or cave with the Blood of our King, the Lord Jesus Christ.

Pastor Mike does a last-minute cleanup, picking up dozens of soiled paper towels scattered throughout the hall, and then about twenty of us, including Brian and Pastor John, adjourn to a local late-night diner. Over coffee and dessert, Brian, now perfectly calm and lucid, says that he's single and works as an accountant on Long Island, where he also runs a small deliverance ministry of his own. Seated next to him is a slim, tanned, fifty-year-old woman from Akron, with short-cropped white hair and wearing a beige jumpsuit, who tells me that she became involved with deliverance when her husband, a United Methodist minister, divorced her four years earlier.

Pastor Mike advises everyone to prepare for the next day's action by getting a good night's sleep. Walking to the parking lot, he tells me that most of the people in attendance for the weekend workshop are doubling up in dorm rooms at the local college. With just a flash of a frown, he says that his own roommate for the weekend is Brian.

The next morning opens at a comparatively sedentary pace. Pastor John gives a talk slamming "false ecumenicalism," recounting how he recently attended a Promise Keepers meeting where a prominent Protestant minister said, "Now, I want you all to embrace your Catholic brother." Pastor John: "Catholic brother? This is ridiculous. The Catholic brother isn't my brother."

A bit later, chatting by the refreshment table, he says that he once performed an exorcism on a woman who had been a cloistered nun in the Buffalo area. The woman confided to him that priests and older nuns regularly had sex with the young novices. The priests told the novices that they were spilling sacred seed into them. When the young nuns got pregnant, their babies were thrown into a huge vat of acid that was hidden on the convent grounds. One day the woman and another young nun broke free from their superiors for a spell and discovered a maze of tunnels beneath the convent. Fifty yards or so into one of the tunnels, they came across the vat of acid.

During an afternoon break I chat outside the hall with Linda, the wailing woman of the previous evening. Wearing green tights and a short-sleeved sweater over a white blouse, and heavily made up with pink lipstick and pink nail polish, she exudes a kind of churchified mid-American sexiness, softly self-confident, laid-back, nothing doing. She says that she's married without children, that she's a nurse in a small Pennsylvania town a seven-hour drive away. She's been undergoing deliverance for six years now, she says, and she feels immeasurably better than when first starting out. No more vaporizing depression, no more dreams of suicide. Nevertheless, she says, she's still under bondage to evil spirits. Some of these spirits stem from sexual abuse she suffered as a young girl, and many are the result of having been raised a Roman Catholic. She says that her spirits used to manifest through violent thrashing and clawing, but now they mostly limit themselves to incessant screaming. She also says that her husband came with her to a deliverance workshop several years ago, but he thought it was a form of witchcraft and that the deliverance ministers were actually putting demons into her.

I ask if she thinks that some of her demons had been released the night before.

"Yes, some of them. I often have spirits of fear in me. That was part of it last night. But I also had a major spirit of chiropracty [*sic*]. I'd been to a chiropractor in Pennsylvania, and I'd gotten infested. I felt the spirit coiling itself around my abdomen. Finally I was freed of it.

The woman praying over me for deliverance has the power of discernment. She said the evil spirit was released from me in the form of a serpent."

"Do you feel a real sense of relief now?"

"Oh, yes. But there's still so much more work to be done. I still have demons that need expelling—especially Roman Catholic demons."

"Did you sleep well last night?"

"I sure did. From about midnight to seven-thirty. Why? Don't you think I look good?"

"No, it's not that. It's just that you seemed to be going through a real ordeal last night. You look great."

"Thank you. But you'd look great today, too, if you had been covered from head to foot in mud and slime and all of this had just been washed off of you with a hose. Well, that's what happened to me last night."

"Do you think you'll get more deliverance this evening?"

"Probably—yes. What about you, Michael? Will you be getting deliverance for yourself this evening? Getting spiritual freedom from some of the bondage that you're under?"

"I think I'll probably just be observing."

Back inside, there are several more talks, a communion service, a lengthy interval of hymn-singing, and then, finally, the main event. At 9:00 P.M. a rail-thin, deep-voiced, fortyish preacher I haven't seen before, wearing a blue shirt and tie, gray flannel pants, and white running shoes, takes center stage with a clip-on microphone and announces that the time has arrived to begin the mass deliverance session. He leads the fifty adults in attendance through a prayer of confession and repentance, then instructs them all to take their seats.

The preacher goes for the groin first.

"Demons of lust. Go in Jesus' name. Go. Go in Jesus' name," he chants. "Demons of fornication and adultery. Go in Jesus' name. Demons of homosexuality and all sexual perversion. Go in Jesus' name. Go. Go in Jesus' name." Shriekings. Moanings. Slobberings. A riot of demons. A young guy in the back row wearing khakis slaps himself repeatedly in the face with both hands.

The preacher switches themes.

"Demons of anti-Semitism. Go in Jesus' name. Go. Go in Jesus' name. Demons of racism. Go in Jesus' name. All demons of intolerance. Go in Jesus' name. Go. Go in Jesus' name." More shrieking and wailing, but not nearly as much as moments before. Up to this point the demons of sexual perversion are winning the day.

The preacher cranks up the heat.

"Demons of Roman Catholicism. Go in Jesus' name. Go. Go in Jesus' name. Mary of Fatima. Mary of Lourdes. Mary, Queen of Witchcraft. Go in Jesus' name. The Pope of Babylon. Antichrist. Infallibility. Go. Go in Jesus' name. Demons of infant baptism. Demons of scapulars. Go. Go in Jesus' name."

The hall erupts in a cacophony of wailing and shouting. Roman Catholic demons on the rampage, screaming, cursing, protesting. Not far from me a gray-haired man in a wrinkled brown suit belches himself to freedom. Linda, three rows from the front, hands clasped to her face, is already well into her piercing siren wail, intermittently screaming, "Shut up! Shu-u-u-ut up! I told you to shut up!"

The preacher, with the self-satisfied smirk of someone who knows he's on the winning side, varies the cadence.

"Oh, yes, Roman Catholic demons, you've got to go. You've got no choice. You've got to go. Yes. In the name of Jesus, you have to go. Mary, Queen of Harlots. You have to go. Popes of the Antichrist. You have to go. Priest perverts. You have to go. You've got no choice, Catholic demons. You have to go. Yes. In the name of Jesus, you have to go."

Ten minutes' worth of Catholic demons are called out and expelled. And then dozens of other demons, from almost every imaginable category. Demons of fear. Demons of depression. Demons of nightmares. Demons of emotional disability. Demons of heart disorder. Demons of divorce. Rantings. Shriekings. Growlings. Deafening noise.

Standing by the side window, I watch as two police cars pull onto the lot and circle the hall, roof lights flashing. Pastor Mike and Pastor John rush outside with assurances that everything is under control.

Finally, after an hour of casting out demons, the running-shoed preacher unclips his microphone and steps from the stage, which seems to signal a new phase to the proceedings. Despite the pandemonium, almost everyone to this point has remained seated, but now, the mass deliverance brought to a close, a dozen people fling themselves to the floor and begin manifesting demonic presences with just as much ferocity as Brian and Susan had the night before. And once again there's a peculiar protocol to the affair. No one who manifested strongly the previous evening does so now. As if by unwritten rule, people seem to know to give others a chance. Many of the people who were doing the heavy ministering last night are now on the floor being ministered to by people such as Brian and Susan. The roles of demoniac and exorcist are completely interchangeable, rendering the whole business strangely democratic. No one is left out, and no one is made to feel centered out for flying out of control. Everyone is demonized (to a greater or lesser extent), and in this respect everyone is equal. Only Pastor Mike retains his cool.

For a solid hour it's a repeat performance of the night before. Clumps of bodies sprawled out across the floor. Foam-spattered, writhing demoniacs being held down and prayed over. People not directly involved at any given moment stand by the refreshment table chatting, surveying the situation.

I position myself by the rear doors, where five young children are playing on the floor, drawing pictures with crayons, seemingly oblivious to it all. Pastor John's eight-year-old son, sweet-faced and skinny, joins the other kids and says, "We have to draw a happy face. Let's everybody draw a happy face."

Less than ten yards away Pastor John is now putting on a rousing show of his own, squirming in a chair, snarling, barking, cursing ("Fuck! Fuck! Fuck this fucking place!"), with Pastor Mike holding him from behind, praying.

Watching Pastor John, it occurs to me that the demons at this gathering communicate along rather quaint gender lines. When acting out in the men, they blister the paint with foul language, but with the women they mostly restrict themselves to screaming, shrieking, and crying out such innocuities as "I hate this workshop!" or "Shut up!" In addition to cooperating with the staging of the performance, in other words, the demons seem respectful of local norms of public comportment.

At 11:00 P.M., once again, Pastor John announces that the session is finished and instructs everyone to "bind" or "box" any remaining demons. Moments later I ask him what was going on with his own deliverance. He says that his biological father (whom he hasn't seen since he was a young boy) was Jewish, and that he was being delivered of spirits of Jewish pride.

Linda comes up to me and says that she's exhausted but has rarely felt better; many of her Catholic demons were expelled. She strongly recommends that I undergo deliverance myself at the earliest opportunity. "Most people have demons inside them, Michael," she says, "and I'm pretty sure you're no different."

With the weekend's business now wrapped up, quite a few people seem eager to volunteer their personal stories. Susan, wearing an ankle-length blue dress and cool, smart, and articulate after her spitting and sprawling spree of the night before, tells me that both of her parents were college professors and that she herself taught English literature at a university in California for several years in the mid-eighties. She now lives with her husband and three children in Virginia, where she runs a small computer business. She says that she's been receiving deliverance for almost twenty years for demons of anger, rejection, and repression stemming from sexual and emotional abuse she suffered at the hands of her father as a young girl. It isn't easy, however, finding an effective deliverance ministry. She says that she's completely sold on the highly dramatic and confrontational approach of Pastor Mike, but wishes that he operated closer to her home.

"I make the long drive from Virginia for [Pastor] Michael's deliverance as often as possible because it's the only deliverance that really works," she says. "There's other evangelical deliverance ministries I could go to, but I've checked some of them out, and they're complete jokes. They don't want the demons to manifest; they're more concerned with maintaining decorum than entering into direct battle with demonic forces. I think that they're actually afraid of the demons. Michael's not afraid. Of course, most of these other folks would claim that he's crazy."

Susan tells me that she never goes into a trance, or any other altered state, while being delivered. She is acutely aware of her struggle as it is taking place, and she usually remembers every detail. She says that she distinctly recalls my watching her while she was being delivered the night before. She also says that she "feels freer" tonight but still has "a lot of work to do."

I'm also approached by an attractive, forty-three-year-old blond woman, wearing jeans and almond-shaped glasses, who's spent much of the weekend roaming the auditorium, her nine-year-old son in tow, helping other people with their deliverances. She tells me that she moved to the United States from Moscow twenty years ago, and she now lives and works in Manhattan. Her husband was murdered in New York City in 1992, shortly after she converted to evangelical Christianity, and she's been receiving weekly deliverance from Brian ever since.

"After I became a Christian, I read a book—I don't remember the author—that talked about intergenerational family curses," she says. "And then it hit me. My husband and my mother both died at the same age of unnatural causes. This is evidence of an intergenerational curse. I came to realize that I'm afflicted by curses and evil spirits that entered my family through Russian folk religion and Russian Orthodoxy. And I also know that I'm afflicted by spirits of whoredom."

Before leaving, I check in with Pastor Mike, who's looking a bit frazzled after the weekend ordeal. I ask him if there's a chance he might take a day or two off to recuperate. He says he'd love some time off, but he has exorcisms scheduled for the next day in a town two hundred miles away.[1]

P astor Mike is the hardest-working exorcist in America. And also one of the least pretentious. What you see is what you get. No cheap tricks or hidden hustles, no running up the deck. Toiling in obscurity, he has no interest in talk-show celebrity or in publicity of almost any other kind. He doesn't charge for his services (though donations are always welcome), and he doesn't submit prospective clients to a test of orthodoxy. Everyone is welcome; no one is turned away.

As such matters go, Pastor Mike came to the job honestly. Raised with two brothers and a sister in a working-class Catholic family in Chicago, he left school after grade ten, and in 1973, after knocking about for several years, he joined the Marines. He was court-martialed in 1977 for dealing heroin on his base in Quantico, Virginia, and, returning to Chicago, he fell into a bleary-eyed life of endless drugs and petty crime.

"I was high twenty-four hours a day," he told me during one of our first meetings, at a restaurant in a distant suburb of Chicago. "My life revolved around drugs, selling them and using them. I did so much PCP it was unbelievable. I was shooting heroin. I was a total drug fanatic. I probably shouldn't even be alive today."

Pastor Mike had several scrapes with the law during these tough times, including an arrest for illegal possession of a firearm. In 1979 he tried to straighten himself out by taking a job in a machine shop, but his old habits proved tough to break.

"I was supposed to be learning how to be a machinist, but I was a wreck," he told me. "I was snorting coke in the bathroom. I had long hair. I was real sleazy-looking. The new job wasn't working out."

Several weeks into the job, however, a co-worker convinced him to attend services at a place called Hegewisch Baptist Church, which was located in a breakdown Indiana town off the freeway between Gary and Chicago.

"This guy was a member of the Hegewisch congregation, and one day he came to work with a book he'd picked up at church that dealt with world conspiracy—you know, the UN, Freemasons, the Vatican, that sort of thing. I was a bit of a conspiracy buff myself, and I was intrigued. I thought, What kind of a church would have such a book? So I went."

Pastor Mike had no idea what he was getting himself into.

"The pastor of Hegewisch was a huge man, a transplanted Texan named Win Worley," he told me. "Pastor Worley specialized in deliverance, but I had no idea what this was. My first visit, a guy threw himself on the floor, spinning around, crying out, 'Hail Satan! Hail Satan!' It freaked me out. I said, 'Good God. What is this?' I ran home and told my friend across the street, 'You've got to come and see this. You won't believe it.' "

Pastor Mike returned to Hegewisch the next week and the week after that, and before long he was undergoing deliverance himself.

"I received massive deliverance for several years, very violent, with four or five men holding me down," he said. "I was completely infested with demons, demons of drug addiction, demons of degeneracy—you name it. I went through at least a hundred very heavy sessions. There were lots of manifestations. I would attack the workers. I remember everything vividly. Along the way I was saved, and the real heavy deliverance ended in 1984."

Along the way he also married Joy Worley, the pastor's elder daughter, and became a mainstay of the Hegewisch congregation. And in 1996, three years after Win Worley's death, Pastor Mike was called by the congregation to take over the ministry.

"Win Worley was a huge man in every respect," he said. "He was a pioneer. People don't realize it, but before Win there were only a few charismatics and Pentecostals involved in deliverance. Win got the word out to a much broader Protestant audience. I know there's no way I can fill his shoes. I can just try to do my best."

———

P astor Mike is right: Although now largely forgotten, Win Worley was once a force to be reckoned with in American Protestant deliverance ministry. A hulking man, easily over four hundred pounds, Worley was born in Tyler, Texas, in 1925, and ordained as a Southern Baptist minister in 1947. After preaching for twenty-five years in Texas and Oklahoma on what he sometimes referred to as the "cornbread and turnips circuit," he moved north in 1962 to take over the pastorship of Hegewisch Baptist, a tiny interracial church then located on the South Side of Chicago. Worley's first eight years at Hegewisch passed unremarkably, but in late 1970 he began performing exorcisms, wild, rambunctious affairs that sometimes raged on well past midnight. At first most of those on the receiving end were members of the Hegewisch congregation, and Worley himself, showing that even the pastor was capable of getting down and dirty, led the way by getting exorcised of three nasty, snarling demons that identified themselves as Religion, Wounded Love, and Lust. Before long, however, visitors from as far away as Florida and California were streaming into the small South Side church looking for treatment, and in 1978, desperately needing a bigger space, Worley moved his operations to their current location in Highland, Indiana.

Throughout his tenure at Hegewisch, Win Worley was fiercely independent, a tough man to pin down. A Baptist fundamentalist by background and training, he was perpetually rankled that Baptists in general refused to accept the legitimacy of his exorcism ministry. And although he claimed to have received the gift of tongues in the early seventies, he was contemptuous of the charismatic renewal movement, not least because of its openness to Roman Catholics. A strange kind of theological hybrid, a Baptist preacher who cast out devils and spoke in tongues and who liked to refer to himself as a "Baptecostal," Worley answered to no one's bell but his own. Not even the demons seemed capable of fazing him. "You're just a fat man from Texas," a devil he was casting out of a woman once taunted him. Worley shot back, "Yes, but you're rubbing your nose in the dirt with the fat man from Texas."

With Pastor Mike now running the show, Hegewisch Baptist remains as busy as ever: twice-weekly deliverance services and a three-

day summer workshop where participants learn how to perform deliverance while also getting the chance to undergo deliverance themselves. Besides this, Hegewisch is the leading link in a network of
like-minded churches in the Midwest and Great Lakes regions that
also offer deliverance workshops, quite often with Pastor Mike as a
featured guest. (It was at just such a workshop, held in the Buffalo
area in the summer of 1997, that I witnessed Pastor Mike battling
Brian from Long Island's demons to a standstill.)

The Hegewisch church building, a solid, redbrick structure
erected in 1949, is nestled in a mostly white, middle-class neighborhood on the outskirts of Highland, a scrawny scratch of town a short
spin from Gary. When I visited the church for the first time, on an
early Sunday morning in May 1997, the neighborhood was already
buzzing, people tending lawns, kids riding bikes along shaded walks.
Inside, everything was stark, primed for battle. Simple wooden pews,
the whitewashed walls screaming out biblical quotations in black,
hand-painted letters. About ninety people were there for the morning
service, a working- to lower-middle-class crowd, the men in plaid
shirts, jeans, sports jackets, the women in long skirts and long-sleeved
blouses.

First, twenty minutes of lackluster hymn-singing, with Win
Worley's widow accompanying on piano and, on fiddle, a big fiftyish
man wearing blue jeans. Then testimonial time, and Pastor Mike's
message: anti-Catholic boilerplate . . . Roman Catholicism a fallen
church, its sale of indulgences tantamount to mob protection money.

Finally, three hours of semiscripted mayhem. Paper towels were
handed out, and at Pastor Mike's invitation a dozen people came to the
front of the church for deliverance. A young black man threw himself
to the floor, sobbing, arms upraised mournfully. A middle-aged white
woman broke into a spasm of twitching and coughing. Seated at the
front pew, an obese, chalk-faced lay minister prayed over a thin,
growling, purple-lipped man in his mid-thirties. All the while, people
not immediately involved milled about, kibitzing, catching up on the
latest gossip. Two men and a woman standing in the center aisle

swapped tips on septic tanks. A tussle of young boys play-wrestled in the vestibule.

During a lull in the action, Pastor Mike joined me in my pew, friendly, solicitous, asking what I was doing at Hegewisch. I said that I was doing research on exorcism, and when he asked whom I'd spoken to about the subject so far, I mentioned Malachi Martin. Pastor Mike was impressed, said that he greatly admired Malachi, even though he was Catholic, and that no one was a bigger authority on the subject. Said he'd be happy to help out with my research and escorted me out of the main auditorium, along an adjoining wing to the church's book room.

A feast of materials. Everything for sale. Win Worley's very own "Hosts of Hell" series, five noisy paperbacks bursting with exorcism tales, Win Worley triumph tales, Roman Catholic atrocity tales. Dozens of two-dollar pamphlets: *Deliverance: The Forbidden Ministry, Proper Names of Demons, Is It Mental Illness or Demons?* And another dozen titles from Hegewisch's conspiracy sideline: *Invisible Government, Occult Theocracy, Death of a Nation—None Dare Call It Treason.* I scooped up some material and took it to a sullen young woman standing behind the sales desk.

She seemed unimpressed by my selection. "Well, you can always come back later for some of the better stuff," she said.[2]

12.

carolina blues

Most conservative Protestants involved with deliverance these days have probably never heard of Hegewisch Baptist. And most of those who have don't want to be reminded of it. Hegewisch is an embarrassment to them: its steamy anti-Catholicism, its marathon puke-and-rebuke sessions—something out of the fever swamps. And let there be no mistake. The vast majority of Protestant deliverance ministries on the scene today bear little resemblance to Hegewisch. They're not in the business, by and large, of expelling Roman Catholic demons wholesale, engaging demons in midnight wrestling matches, or tearing up the scenery at suburban auditoriums.

Embarrassment or not, however, Hegewisch must be given its due. In the United States today there are hundreds of conservative Protestant deliverance ministries, but during the 1970s Win Worley's operation was just about the only show in town. If you were an evangelical or fundamentalist desperately seeking an exorcism at the time, and unwilling to settle for an expressly Pentecostal or charismatic one, chances were you'd find your way to Hegewisch. You might find some of the shenanigans distasteful, you might think twice about returning a second time, but you'd almost certainly be taken care of by Win Worley or one of his assistants. Regardless of what you might think of him, the "fat man from Texas" was definitely on the case.

As it turns out, there are a number of other deliverance ministries on the scene today, besides Hegewisch, that also make their living on the seamier side of town. Taken together, these ministries constitute what may be termed the rough-and-ready school of exorcism in contemporary America. They're committed to a highly combustible form of demon-expulsion, and also to a cartoonishly crude anti-Catholicism—cartoonish almost to the point of inoffensiveness. In their theology and institutional identity they tend, like Hegewisch, to be fiercely independent—self-professedly evangelical, but not wanting anything to do with evangelicals outside of their own orbit; open to speaking in tongues, but deeply suspicious of more mainstream charismatics and Pentecostals.

Hegewisch Baptist, in fact, isn't even the best-known member of the rough-and-ready school. This distinction probably goes to the Word of Faith Fellowship, a network of churches based in Spindale, North Carolina, and headed by the husband-and-wife team of Jane and Sam Whaley. On February 28, 1995, the Whaleys were thrust into the national spotlight when their ministry was featured on the tabloid television show *Inside Edition,* preceding a segment on O. J. Simpson. (O.J. came off looking almost sympathetic in comparison.) There was hidden-camera footage of frenzied exorcisms at the Whaleys' flagship church in Spindale: men, women, and children stomping the floor and pounding the air with clenched fists, wailing and screaming, faces scrunched into masks of fury. There were interviews with former church members, who sounded like recently tunneled-out POWs, accusing the Whaleys and their henchmen of child abuse, mind control, and other crimes against humanity. There was footage of the televangelist Robert Tilton, a fellow traveler of the Whaleys', practically foaming at the mouth while remonstrating, "In the name of Jesus, loose those foul devils!"

At roughly the same time as the airing of the *Inside Edition* exposé, the print media were also hot on the trail. In newspapers throughout the South and Southwest, the atrocity stories multiplied. The Whaleys and their followers, it was claimed, regularly conducted earsplitting exorcisms they referred to as "blasting" prayer, with maniacal shouting and screaming and mandatory vomiting. They strapped preschoolers into chairs for hours at a time during church services, and any children adjudged less than fully cooperative were blitzed by screaming exorcism chants. They sometimes put adult churchgoers under house detention, once tying a fifty-four-year-old woman to a bed for thirteen days while trying to expel her demons. They separated children from their parents, husbands from their wives, in bizarre experiments in communal living. And Jane Whaley, the real spiritual muscle of the operation, insisted that church members, on pain of damnation, seek her approval on everything from the choice of a dating partner to the purchase of a home appliance.[1]

As so often happens in these affairs, the Whaleys came to their position of spiritual power unexpectedly and unannounced. They were married in the early 1970s, and in 1975, after undergoing a spiritual awakening of sorts, Sam spent a year in Tulsa, Oklahoma, studying at the Rhema Bible Training Center, a fast-track institution that had been founded the previous year by a Texas-born evangelist named Kenneth Hagin. With his preacher's certificate in hand, Sam hooked up with Jane back in North Carolina, and the couple soon became something of a hit on the local salvation-and-miracle circuit. They were fervent and dedicated, they were supremely ambitious, and, most important of all, they were solidly plugged in to one of the trendiest and most audacious religious movements of the day: the Faith Movement.

Every so often in the United States one comes up against something so deliciously American, so perfectly in tune with the times, that taking it literally seems almost a failure of the imagination. One can think, in this connection, of the tabloid television business, with its mock seriousness, its weepy sensationalism, its celebrity fawning — soul food for the bloated and the brokenhearted. Or the suburban shopping mall, with its faux promenades and giddy consumerism and manufactured sociability—community without contact, community contrived precisely to avoid contact. Stuff of this sort is too good to be true; it's living, strutting, pulsating caricature: One almost expects it at any moment to break into a Bugs Bunny cartoon.

The Faith Movement is something of this sort. Only more so. To the uninitiated it seems like something that must have sprung, half-baked, from the mind of an Andy Warhol—a collage of American clichés. The preacher as snake oil salesman or used car salesman; the preacher as Vegas showman. Miracle-workers in pink Cadillacs and pinkie rings, soul-savers in three-piece glitter suits and sixty-dollar haircuts. This is the world of the Faith Movement. Gushing emotionalism, grasping materialism, tears on demand, hustles blessed with a thousand "Amens." The product of old-fashioned hucksterism, New Thought optimism, and Southern-fried born-againism, the Faith Movement is one of the fastest-growing enterprises on the American religious scene today—and also one of the most wildly controversial.

By most accounts the granddaddy of the movement is the evangelist Kenneth Hagin—the same Kenneth Hagin who founded the Tulsa-based Bible institute attended by Sam Whaley. During the late 1960s word began to get out that Hagin was a preacher with a special message. Stripped to essentials, the message was tantalizingly simple: True Bible-believing Christians had the blessings of the world at their beck and call. There was nothing, save lack of faith, to prevent them from enjoying unlimited good fortune. Health, wealth, and prosperity were theirs for the taking. All they needed to do was master the art of positive confession, harness the force of faith, and tell God what they wanted. Not ask God, or plead with God, or cajole God; simply tell God, and the desired blessings would pour forth. This was their birthright as Christians; this was what had been wrought for them through Christ's atonement. Their wish was God's command. *Name-it-and-claim-it*. Christians who were poor, or in bad health, had only themselves to blame. Their faith was deficient, they had surrendered authority to Satan and his demons, and they were almost certainly in need of exorcism. Health and prosperity were godly; poverty and sickness were demonic. It was as simple as that.

There was more to it than this, to be sure, but the health and prosperity angle was the come-on, the righteous sizzle, that made Kenneth Hagin's message the hottest theological property of the day. Throughout the seventies and eighties it was picked up and given an added twist here, a nip and tuck there, by many of the leading preachers in what is sometimes referred to as the independent charismatic movement. Kenneth Copeland, Benny Hinn, Robert Tilton, Jerry Savelle—these (and dozens more) were preachers who spoke in tongues and claimed the gift of miraculous healing, but who mostly kept their distance from more mainstream charismatics and Pentecostals. They tended to be leery of theological labels, but if push came to shove, they'd likely as not define themselves as charismatic evangelicals. Denominationally non-aligned, they operated their own ministries—big-time, lucrative ministries, for the most part—and were sometimes seen by their followers as prophetic figures with direct pipelines to heaven. This was the world in which Kenneth Hagin's Gospel of Health and Wealth flourished, and in which Jane and Sam Whaley and others of their ilk made a regular practice of blasting demons to smithereens.[2]

A ll of my sources said I'd be wasting my time. The Whaleys had always run a closed shop, outsiders strictly forbidden, and they had clamped down even tighter in the wake of the *Inside Edition* exposé. Their ministry, they believed, was under siege, persecuted by the media, demonic forces massing outside the gates. If I took the trouble of visiting Spindale, my sources said, there'd be no chance of my setting foot inside the Word of Faith church, let alone witnessing a full-blown exorcism.

In a sense I couldn't fault the Whaleys for being defensive. They had been burned badly by the *Inside Edition* business—more badly, in fact, than most viewers of the show could have realized. For their exposé the producers of *Inside Edition* had used hidden-camera footage provided them by a young man working undercover for a Dallas-based evangelical watchdog outfit called the Trinity Foundation. The young man, Pete Evans, was a licensed PI from Texas, and for four months beginning in September 1994 he had attended the church, posing as a true believer, without anyone's catching on to the deception. When they did finally catch on, the damage already done, the Whaleys felt stabbed in the back. Whom now could they trust? Their enemies seemed everywhere.

When I spoke with him, several years after the fact, Pete Evans expressed no regrets. He was just doing his job, he said. There were a number of reports of physical and emotional abuse coming out of Spindale, and the Trinity Foundation (with whom he's still associated) sent him to investigate. He moved to town and lived in a tent for a while before getting an apartment, and eventually he worked his way into the Word of Faith congregation. It was a tough gig. During his four months undercover, he personally submitted to deliverance eleven times.

"Anywhere from six to twelve people would form a circle around you and scream the devils out of you at the top of their lungs," he said. "They wanted you to vomit the devils out in plastic buckets they put in front of you. Sometimes people complained about being spit on during deliverance. So Jane made everybody practice screaming in front of a mirror without getting spit on it. The screaming was so intense that some people suffered hearing damage or damage to their vocal cords. When you join up, you're asked to sign a waiver releasing the church from liability for injury. What kind of a church is that?"

I had heard about the waiver; I had seen excerpts printed in an Oklahoma newspaper:

> The Word of Faith Fellowship Inc. [and its ministers and members] do speak in tongues, do have deliverance, do have healing services, do have casting out devils services and most of the usual and normal services as are carried on in charismatic evangelical churches. . . . I hereby release the pastors and other persons connected with The Word of Faith Fellowship Inc., severally

and individually, from any and all liability of any nature or kind, for whatever injury or harm or complication of any kind . . .³

Despite what my sources said, I thought I'd give it a shot. From New York, I tried phoning a man named Ray Farmer, who was, I'd been told, a prominent minister in the Spindale church, a kind of point man for the Whaleys, someone who might be able to get me through the door. I phoned a dozen times, leaving messages, once having an agreeable chat with Farmer's son, Joshua, but Farmer himself was always just now away on business, or just now entertaining guests, or just now otherwise occupied. I tried calling several other numbers, with no better luck, and then, having other business to attend to in North Carolina anyway, I decided to drive to Spindale on the chance of finding out something, anything, worthwhile.

The city of Spindale has more serious things to worry about these days than the Whaleys. Once a busy textile center on the far fringes of the Great Smoky Mountains, the city has been ravaged of late by plant closings. Almost two thousand manufacturing jobs were lost in the first half of 1999 alone, and the city's longtime biggest employer, a textile company called Stonecutters, was on the verge of shutting down altogether the week I arrived. The main street had a disheartened and bedraggled look about it, most of its older businesses sucked to shriveling by vampire malls on the city outskirts. Even many of the local churches seemed dusty and unkempt, as if hunkered down for last call.

Just beyond the city limits, on a tiny dead-end street, I found the Word of Faith church complex. It seemed a different world. The main church building, a big windowless sanctuary connected to a handsome office wing, was surrounded by green, freshly mown lawns, and standing at opposite ends of the property were a trim elementary school and a newly constructed high school.

It was a late Saturday afternoon, and I turned into the empty parking lot with the thought of taking a brief reconnaissance swing around the property. All at once the church's internal security system sprang into action. A family that had been playing baseball on the front lawn of the house across the road dropped their bats and balls, the woman ran into the house, and the man headed for the parking lot and intercepted me at the entranceway.

"Can we help you?" he said.

I introduced myself and said that I was hopeful of learning more about exorcism at Word of Faith for a book I was writing.

By this point there was a parade of minivans on the narrow street, people driving back and forth checking me out. A middle-aged couple pulled up beside me and said that Ray Farmer was on his way. I got out of my car and chatted with them for a bit—the weather, the local scenery, nothing too serious—and then Farmer drove up in a minivan with his son, Joshua.

Ray walked up to me, smiling, amiable, a big, smooth-complexioned guy in his forties, and shook my hand.

"Michael, it's so nice to meet you," he said.

I also shook hands with Joshua, who was tall and fair, somewhere in his early twenties. We made some small talk, and then Ray Farmer took charge, saying he knew I was there to find out about exorcism, but they wouldn't be able to help me; they had a training session going that weekend and were just "too maxed out," he said.

I asked if I could meet briefly with Pastor Jane Whaley or perhaps sit in on part of the training session or attend one of their Sunday services.

No, all of this was impossible, he said. The best they could do was possibly get back to me if I mailed a list of questions to the pastor.

I said I could understand why they'd be leery, considering the *Inside Edition* business and all their other troubles.

Ray, now forcing a smile, asked how he could be sure I myself wasn't wired for sound or pictures.

I opened my jacket and made a show of patting myself down. "I'm clean," I said.

Ray laughed and said he was just kidding. He told Joshua to fire up a golf cart, and we rode about the property for a short while, talking mainly about my work (Joshua had done a background check on me), Ray's cell phone ringing every few minutes with various church people wanting to know if everything was under control. Finally another minivanned minister arrived on the scene, and after conferring briefly with him, Ray said to me, "Sorry, but there's nothing else we'll be able to do for you now."

Walking around town a bit later, I struck up a conversation with a young cop who was hosing down his cruiser and spitting tobacco juice on the sidewalk outside the local police station. He said he didn't know much about the Word of Faith church beyond what had been reported in the media, but he'd heard rumors that Pastor Jane Whaley possessed extraordinary powers.

"If you ever get a chance to meet her, just be careful she doesn't get her eyes fixed on you," he said. "I've heard she can take a man down."

At about ten o'clock the next morning I drove over to the church again, thinking I might at the very least check out the action in the parking lot for the nine-thirty Sunday service. I went past the church, turned around at the dead end, then reversed direction for fifty yards and pulled up on the shoulder opposite the jam-packed parking lot. The entire operation couldn't have taken more than thirty seconds, but Ray Farmer, in an immaculate blue suit, was already striding across the lot, waving his arms, Joshua close behind.

I got out of my car, half expecting to be chased away, but instead Ray called out, "Michael, a couple of our people spotted you. Why don't you come on in and join us for worship?"

I said thanks very much, adding that maybe I should put on a shirt and tie from my traveling bag in the trunk.

Ray said that I could change inside, and he led me to a washroom down the corridor from the sanctuary. He said that he'd wait in the corridor for me, but a minute later, while I was in the midst of changing, he ducked in for a few seconds, apparently satisfying himself that it wasn't anything more than a fresh shirt and tie I was putting on.

Ray and Joshua escorted me, conspicuously, through a door that opened onto the front of the sanctuary and directed me to a spot in one of the front pews. The service was in full tilt, the congregation loudly singing hymns whose words were projected by an overhead onto the front wall above the stage. Half an hour more of singing, and then

Pastor Jane Whaley asked a young man named Michael to share his testimony.

Standing on the stage, he said that his mother had died recently and his siblings had given her a Catholic funeral. They'd asked him to attend, pleaded with him to attend, but he'd stood his ground. He told them that he no longer had room in his life for Catholic falsehood, and attending the funeral would be a breach of religious principle. They said they respected his decision but couldn't fully understand it. It was his mother's funeral, they said. Michael told the congregation that this had been a difficult time for him, and he wanted to thank Pastor Jane for guiding him through it. The congregation applauded.

Immediately after the service Pastor Jane walked over to my pew, followed closely by her husband, Sam, and five or six other Word of Faith ministers. She was an attractive middle-aged woman of medium height, with an uncreased helmet of shoulder-length blond hair—and large, piercing eyes that now fastened on me and remained fastened for the next thirty minutes.

She said that I'd been much on her mind since I first tried calling Ray Farmer, and she knew that I was down from New York hoping to sit in on some of her exorcisms. But there was absolutely no way she could permit this, she said. She performed exorcisms for the glory of God, whereas my interest was merely intellectual. Was there really any chance I'd appreciate what was involved?

Nevertheless, Pastor Jane wasn't entirely closed to discussing her ministry with me. Just about everyone, she said, was demonically afflicted in some way or another. Just about everyone needed ministry. She herself had received exorcism, and so had her husband. Sam had been afflicted by spirits of lust and fornication, and she had ministered to him personally.

"That's right," said Sam, a stocky, gravel-voiced man about ten years his wife's senior. "I was in rough shape before Jane got in there and cleaned everything out."

Did everyone who joined her church receive exorcism? I asked.

She said that they did, often involving multiple sessions. Her exorcism ministry was a special gift from God, and she wasn't stingy with it. And contrary to how it had been portrayed in the media, it wasn't a screaming ministry. It was a wailing, groaning, and travailing ministry. This was the gift that God had given her: exorcism through wailing, groaning, and travailing.

And then, suddenly, the tears. Clasping my arm and sobbing, Pastor Jane said she was deeply concerned about my doing research on exorcism. "And do you know why?" she asked. "It's because you don't know Jesus. Just standing here with you, I just know that you don't know Jesus. And it just breaks my heart." Still weeping, she said she knew that I worked at a Jesuit university, and she worried that I was caught up in "that whole Roman Catholic thing." She promised that she'd pray for me, and that was that.

Although I didn't have an opportunity to sit in on a Word of Faith exorcism while visiting Spindale, I was pretty certain I came away with the basic idea. And the more I thought about it, Pastor Mike of Hegewisch Baptist came out looking quite the better in comparison. Next to the Word of Faith operation, Pastor Mike's ministry seemed marked by a kind of proletarian honesty: no health and prosperity mumbo jumbo, no manipulative weeping, no pressure to submit to an authoritarian leader. With Pastor Mike it was a grapple on the floor, a slap on the back, a regurgitation, perhaps, into a paper towel— no questions asked, no strings attached, take it or leave it. In the exorcism business one could do worse.

In any event I wouldn't want to give the rough-and-ready school an importance it really doesn't deserve. Far removed from the worlds of Hegewisch and Spindale, there is another kind of exorcism being practiced in the United States that over the past fifteen years or so has been of far greater cultural consequence.

Part Five

The Rise of
Evangelical
Deliverance

13.

satanic
conspiracies

Have you had a chance to talk with Hannah?" the woman sitting across the table, a Christian psychotherapist named Catherine, asked me. All seven of my tablemates were Christian psychotherapists, and we were just now being served coffee and dessert at the opening-night banquet of a 1998 conference on deliverance and spiritual warfare in Sioux City, Iowa. I said that I hadn't yet spoken with Hannah, and I wasn't sure who she was. "After coffee I'll go see if I can find her and bring her over," Catherine said. "You really should hear her story. It will help you make sense of what we're up against."

A bit later, after everyone else had dispersed to adjoining rooms at the downtown convention center for talks and seminars, Catherine returned to the table with a pale, thin woman in her forties, lank blond hair parted in the middle. "This is Hannah," she said. "I'll leave you two to talk."

I told Hannah something about my research and said I understood she had an interesting story to tell. Yes, she did, she said, and then proceeded to tell it, speaking so softly, and matter-of-factly, that I was forced to move my chair just inches from hers to hear what she was saying.

She said that her people had emigrated from Scandinavia to America in the late nineteenth century and settled in the hardscrabble plains of North Dakota, where they scraped by repairing railroad tracks and farming. Most of the women in the family, and some of the men, were deeply involved in traditional Scandinavian spiritism. Her maternal grandmother was a witch, one of her aunts was a necromancer who became quite famous locally for her colorful séances, and another aunt earned extra money as a "spiritualist finder," using her telepathic gifts to help neighbors locate mislaid items. Shortly before Hannah was born, the extended family moved from North Dakota to a small town in the Great Lakes region, without any alteration in their religious lifestyle. Indeed, while she was growing up, and even into her early adulthood, Hannah said, her family's spiritism was part of her taken-for-granted reality. She never questioned it, never considered it odd. Levitation, séances, psychic communications—this, quite simply, was the world she knew, enchanted, uncomplicated in its own way, a world that wrapped its arms around you.

As it turns out, however, this was just one side of Hannah's world. There was another side, so horrible, so painful, that she was forced to banish it from her conscious awareness while growing up. Only in recent years, closing in on middle age, had she finally been able to come to terms with it. When she was six years old, she told me, her father, her paternal grandfather, and an uncle joined a satanic cult that was operating secretly in their small town, and over the next twelve years, until she finally left home for college, she was subjected to hideous abuse. She was regularly raped and tortured by her grandfather, her uncle, and their cult cronies. Her father twice impregnated her during satanic orgies, and in both cases the babies were taken from her at birth and then sacrificed before her eyes. She saw many other babies murdered the same way, and she was routinely forced to have sex with cult members during the sacrificial rituals. One summer morning, the first morning of her summer vacation, her father and two other cult members raped her in the family kitchen while one of her older brothers sat just ten feet away eating a bowl of cereal. She cried out to him for help, but he ignored her and continued with his breakfast. He, too, had suffered relentless abuse at the hands of the cult, and scenes of this sort were nothing new to him, nothing worth getting excited over.

As for Hannah, this scene and dozens like it were too horrifying to face up to. For survival's sake she was forced to drive virtually all memory of them into hiding. While she was away at college, and for years afterward, the savagery committed against her as a child was little more than a smudge on her consciousness. She was able to recall exquisite details of her girlhood—the blue ribbon around the neck of a favorite stuffed animal, the crunch of November leaves in the playground down the street—but the satanic abuse occupied a blank space in her personal history. It was a lost continent, uninhabitable, a place too terrifying to register. Yet, as the years passed, there were grim intimations of something gone wrong, distress signals from the past, which confused and frightened her: the nightmares that left her drenched and trembling, the mistrust and anxiety that short-circuited potential romance, the chronic insecurity and bouts of self-loathing. Convinced that something was wrong, but without any idea what it might be, Hannah, by now a born-again Christian and a tenured professor at a small liberal arts college, decided to discuss her situation with her pastor. He said that her symptoms, the nightmares and so forth, were indications, quite possibly, that something terrible had happened in her past—something so terrible that she had blotted out all memory of it. He raised the possibility of satanic ritual abuse. Hannah was nonplussed. Nothing of this sort, she was quite sure, had ever happened to her. Nevertheless, she agreed to undergo deliverance, a procedure she hadn't previously heard of, just in case there was something from her childhood still haunting her. The deliverance proved a highly dramatic affair, with lots of weeping and wailing, leaving her pastor to think that she had in fact been victimized as a child by the occult. He set her up for counseling with a Christian psychotherapist, and over the next several years she gradually ("bit by bit") recovered memories of her abuse. The process of retrieving these fragmentary memories and assembling them into a coherent picture was unspeakably painful, Hannah told me, but toward the end she finally began to feel like a whole person.

As part of her healing process she also sought out members of her family who had been party, in one way or another, to her childhood trauma. Her two brothers, when she finally tracked them down, were like crippled ghosts. One was drug-addled and suicidal, and the other had just been released from prison and was living out of his car, winding down the hours. She went to see her father, who was now a widower, sick, dying, and emotionally broken. She didn't confront him with her recovered memories, though she was convinced he knew what he had done, but instead took him into her home out of state, where he lived out his last days.

Hannah recounted all of this in a flat, uninflected voice—no self-dramatizing, no tears of bitter remembrance. This was her story, she fully believed it, and she didn't seem overly concerned whether I did or not. She thanked me for listening and encouraged me to catch as much of the conference as I possibly could.[1]

The three-day conference was sponsored by the International Center for Biblical Counseling (ICBC), a Sioux City–based outfit founded in 1987 for the purpose of advancing the cause of deliverance and spiritual warfare among American evangelicals. The ICBC had been running biannual gatherings of this sort since 1990, and this year's edition was the biggest yet, with more than eight hundred people forking out the ninety-five-dollar registration fee and, in many cases, upward of a thousand dollars more for travel and accommodation and the privilege of rubbing shoulders with some of evangelical Protestantism's leading experts on deliverance and the demonic. It was a broadly middle-class crowd, clean-cut and smooth-faced, overwhelmingly white, with a sizable contingent of pastors and psychotherapists. I rather doubted that very many of them would be complaining about not getting their money's worth. Compared with similar events I'd attended, the conference was a well-oiled machine: The headline speakers were witty and engaging (if not always entirely lucid), the workshops were rich with practical advice on demon-expulsion, the coffee was hot, the trains ran on time.

The affair was also, I thought, pervaded by an air of civility. The conference organizers knew who I was, that I worked at a Jesuit university and was open-mindedly skeptical, but I didn't encounter so much as a twinge of anti-Catholicism. There were no hard theological sells, no convert-or-be-damned jeremiads. And something else: Unlike many of the charismatic gatherings I'd attended, here there were no displays of emotional fervor. Indeed, most of the people here were insistently and adamantly noncharismatic. They were old-style evangelicals who looked upon tongue-speaking and Spirit-baptism with considerable suspicion and, in some cases, outright contempt. The only thing most of them shared with the charismatics I'd encountered was a strong belief in the value of exorcism.[2]

The spirit of civility was such that even a contrary point of view was slotted into the program. During the second day of the conference a seminarian and author named David Powlison took to the podium and spent thirty vigorous minutes slamming evangelical exorcism for being unbiblical and unedifying and just plain unseemly. Powlison probably didn't succeed in convincing anyone, but he was permitted his say, and just about everyone in the audience listened respectfully.[3]

There seemed, in fact, no limit to the respectful listening. The same day as Powlison's futile protest, I attended a workshop in which a dapper, middle-aged deliverance minister talked about some of his recent experiences in the field. Several years back, he said, while waiting for his flight in the airport of a faraway city, he found himself irresistibly drawn to a rack of porn magazines. He struggled mightily against the temptation to leaf through them, but he felt himself the pawn of some awful and overpowering lust. Then, finally, it dawned on him: On the ride out to the airport, his cabdriver—a rather sinister-looking fellow, to be sure—must have somehow demonized him. Now knowing the cause of his plight, he performed a discreet act of self-deliverance and succeeded in boarding his plane with no further damage done.

I was half expecting some nervous coughing, some embarrassed shifting of seats, but just about everyone, so far as I could tell, found the anecdote inspiring. The deliverance minister was a man of God, after all, someone on the front lines of the battle against demonic evil, and it was only to be expected that Satan would single him out for special torment. And in the end, the man of God had emerged victorious.

The final talk of the conference, by a Christian psychotherapist named Ed Smith, wasn't nearly so upbeat. Smith said that his practice was dedicated almost exclusively to counseling victims of satanic ritual abuse—SRA—and he asked how many people in attendance had also encountered genuine cases of SRA. About two-thirds of the audience raised their hands. Smith nodded grimly and said that he had some disturbing news to report on the ritual abuse front. In recent years he had discovered that some of the most ghastly groundwork for SRA was routinely being conducted in hospitals throughout the country. High-level satanists in the medical professions were administering sophisticated electric shock to infants and even fetuses as a way of priming them for ritual torture and demonization later down the road. This may sound unbelievable, Smith told his audience, but it's really happening. It's just one indication of what we're up against. (His audience gave no indication of finding any of it difficult to believe.)

While the headline speakers performed admirably, the unofficial stars of the conference were people such as Hannah. She was part of a small company of ritual abuse survivors on hand for the occasion, and without her story (and stories like hers) there likely wouldn't have been a conference in the first place. Hannah and the other survivors were living proof that satanism was a terrible scourge in contemporary America, and living proof also that exorcism was a ministry that evangelicals in the United States could ill afford to be without.[4]

The Sioux City conference was a sign of the changing times. As recently as the late 1970s exorcism was virtually a taboo subject among evangelical Protestants in the United States. It was rarely discussed, at least not publicly and approvingly, and even more rarely was it actually put into practice. During the early eighties, however, all hell seemed to break loose. Suddenly, after decades of neglect, exorcism and demonism became major concerns for significant numbers of American evangelicals. Dozens of new evangelical deliverance ministries sprang into being, evangelical Bible colleges that previously wouldn't have touched the subject began offering courses in demon-expulsion, and the evangelical publishing industry couldn't churn out new titles on exorcism and spiritual warfare fast enough.[5]

So what was going on here? Why, seemingly out of the blue, this sudden interest in exorcism on the part of so many evangelicals?

Well, for starters, it wasn't entirely out of the blue. During the 1970s there were several developments that helped set the stage. One of these, not surprisingly, was the release of *The Exorcist*, whose enormous suggestive powers clearly weren't limited to just nonevangelical segments of the population. Another was the publication, in 1972, of Hal Lindsey's *Satan Is Alive and Well on Planet Earth*, a book that enjoyed a vast readership among conservative Protestants in the United States. Still another was the provocative about-face of the respected evangelical biblical scholar Merrill Unger, who published two books in the 1970s arguing that true born-again Christians could in fact fall victim to demonization, after previously arguing that they couldn't. No less significant were the efforts of an evangelical theologian from Germany named Kurt Koch, who reached a substantial American audience during the seventies through his extensive writings on demonism and deliverance.[6]

During the 1970s, moreover, there were a small number of American evangelicals besides Win Worley of Hegewisch Baptist actually performing exorcisms—though not nearly on so flamboyant a scale. The most important of these was a Kansas-based preacher named Ernest Rockstad, whose series of teaching tapes on exorcism would prove a valuable resource for evangelicals who took up deliverance ministry in the early eighties. Dean Hochstetler, a Mennonite from Indiana, was also ahead of his time in actively promoting evangelical deliverance, and so, too, was the Baptist pastor-author Mark Bubeck, whose 1975 book *The Adversary* has garnered sales in the hun-

dreds of thousands. (A decade later the hugely popular novels of
Frank Peretti would also help fuel interest among evangelicals in exorcism and demonization.)[7]

Far more important than these scattered efforts, however, were
several interrelated developments that took place during the 1980s.
The first involved a talented preacher and onetime Vegas showman
named John Wimber. In the early eighties, while serving as an adjunct
faculty member at Fuller Theological Seminary in Pasadena, California, Wimber argued that evangelicals in the United States had been
far too genteel over the years in championing the Christian Gospel.
During His own earthly ministry, Jesus had demonstrated the power
of the Gospel by regularly healing the sick and casting out demons,
and in more recent years Pentecostals and charismatics had attempted
to do the same. Now was as good a time as any, Wimber said, for evangelicals to follow suit.

Wimber developed these ideas in a rambunctious course called
"Signs, Wonders, and Church Growth" that he team-taught with two
Fuller professors named C. Peter Wagner and Charles Kraft from
1982 to 1985. By its third semester the course was enrolling upward
of three hundred students, making it the most popular draw on the
Fuller campus. Not everyone at the staunchly Calvinistic seminary,
however, was pleased with Wimber's efforts. More than just a few
professors claimed that he was promoting a fanatical and magicalized
kind of Christianity. Demon-expulsion, miraculous healing, and other
signs and wonders, they insisted, had ended with the apostolic age.
The church today possessed the Scriptures; nothing more was
needed.[8] Faculty opposition eventually grew so intense that the Fuller
administration canceled "Signs, Wonders, and Church Growth" and,
effectively, sent Wimber packing. Much to the displeasure of some of
their colleagues, Wagner and Kraft continued teaching the course on
a noncredit basis in the basement of a church across the street from
the seminary. Wimber, for his part, went on to considerable fame as
leader of the Vineyard Christian Fellowship, a fast-growing evangelical movement distinguished by its openness to miraculous healing,
demon-expulsion, and other extraordinary phenomena.[9]

As Wimber's story indicates, something rather unexpected was taking place in American evangelicalism during the early eighties. Across the country many evangelicals (quite often to the chagrin of some of their co-religionists) were moving to a more charismatic style of belief and worship. Adapting a phrase from Alvin Toffler, C. Peter Wagner christened these evangelicals the "third wave of the Holy Spirit"—the Pentecostal and charismatic movements representing the first and second waves. While relatively few third-wavers went so far (at least publicly) as to speak in tongues, most were interested in cultivating a more emotional and experiential piety than evangelicalism at the time was generally noted for. They tended, moreover, to be receptive to a wide range of so-called spiritual gifts, including the gifts of discernment and exorcism. Not all evangelicals who became committed to exorcism during the 1980s, it must be emphasized, were part of this third-wave movement. Nevertheless, the movement's rise helped make exorcism a more attractive (and more feasible) proposition within evangelicalism than might otherwise have been the case.[10]

In a related development, the early eighties were also a time of enormous growth for psychotherapy within American evangelicalism. Throughout the country new evangelical counseling ministries were launched at an unprecedented rate, and evangelical psychotherapists soon found themselves one of the hottest new professional groupings on the American religious scene. More to the point, many of these freshly minted psychotherapists were perfectly willing to incorporate exorcism into their therapeutic practice, and some would play a critical role in inflaming the satanism scares that broke out in the United States during the 1980s.[11]

It was the satanism scares, above all else, that constituted the real breakthrough for exorcism within American evangelicalism. Throughout the eighties and nineties, as I pointed out earlier, significant numbers of Americans, evangelical and otherwise, became convinced that a clandestine cult of satan-worshippers was spreading menace across the land. Cleverly disguised as teachers, doctors, and other paragons of middle-class respectability, satanic cultists were presumably torturing, brainwashing, and demonizing countless innocents, when they weren't occupied, in their less incendiary moments, with plotting world domination. Within certain evangelical circles this threat of satanic conspiracy was taken deadly seriously, and exorcism was embraced as a spiritual weapon of utmost urgency.

satanic panics revisited

If any one event can be credited with setting off the recent satanism scares, it was the publication in 1980 of *Michelle Remembers,* a silly and tedious testimonial of satanic ritual abuse written by a Canadian woman named Michelle Smith with her psychiatrist, Lawrence Pazder. Smith initially went to see Pazder complaining of mild depression following a miscarriage, but in the course of her treatment she miraculously recovered long-repressed memories of horrific abuse she had presumably suffered at the hands of satanists in British Columbia more than twenty years earlier, when she was just five years old. Lying on Pazder's couch, she conjured up vivid images of being tortured in cemeteries and locked up in snake-filled cages, of being raped and sodomized with candles, of being forced to witness the mutilation of dead babies, of having a devil's tail and horns surgically grafted to her, and of being forced to confront Satan himself in an orgiastic ritual. Read this tale of woe now and almost nothing rings true; it makes *Hostage to the Devil* look like a textbook study in fact-based reporting. Never mind the cameo appearance of Satan or the two-decade-long memory blackout. All of this abuse apparently took place without leaving any significant physical traces, without Michelle's sisters having the slightest hint of it, and without Michelle herself having to miss any time at school. None of these implausibilities prevented *Michelle Remembers* from striking it rich, however, or prevented its authors (who eventually divorced their respective spouses and married each other) from being regaled as folk heroes on the ritual abuse lecture circuit.

The book succeeded, moreover, in setting the tone for the chorus of ritual abuse allegations that would fill the air over the next fifteen years. First there were the day care scandals, with young children, often under the relentless badgering of prosecutors and child-protection advocates, recounting scenes of horror strikingly similar to those described by Michelle Smith. And then, on a much broader scale, there was the recovered memory frenzy, with thousands of adults, mostly women, digging into their deepest past for long-buried memories of hideous abuse suffered at the hands of parents and other family members. About 15 percent of the recovered memory cases involved explicit allegations of satanic ritual abuse, and just about all of these shook out the same way.

A young woman, usually in her twenties or thirties, would turn to a psychotherapist for help dealing with depression or poor self-image or some other problem of daily living. During the course of treatment, which typically involved hypnosis, guided imagery, or a related technique, the client would gradually develop memories of having been incestuously abused as a young girl, perhaps even as an infant. She might reject these memories at first, she might even find them preposterous, but the therapist would advise her to trust the process and dig even deeper into her past. In time the memories would become increasingly intense and painful, graduating beyond incest to monstrous scenes of satanic ritual abuse—the flaying and sacrifice of infants, the forced ingestion of feces and urine, unspeakable privations and torture. As often as not, the client would be encouraged by her therapist to "relive" these memories while in hypnotic trance. During these emotionally excruciating reenactments (or "abreactions"), she might engage in "switching behavior," shifting in and out of various personalities, resulting in a diagnosis of multiple personality disorder (MPD). After months or even years of therapy, she might be functionally worse off than when first starting out, but both she and her therapist would be sold on the recovered memories. The memories, in their view, were absolutely true, not true in just some narrative or metaphoric sense, but historically and literally true. The scenes and events underlying them had really happened. Armed with this conviction, the client would confront her supposed abusers, often by letter, and perhaps initiate legal proceedings against them.[12]

So what's the verdict here? Were all the recovered memories of this sort actually true? The best guess is that some of them (or parts of some of them) may have been true, but most were elaborate fictions. To believe that all of them were true would entail believing in a vast conspiracy of satanists around the country responsible for murdering thousands of infants and abducting thousands of children and young adults, all the while eluding police detection and never leaving behind a shred of forensic evidence. Hardly a likely scenario.

It's far more likely that many of these memories were the product, at least in part, of the therapeutic process itself. For one thing, there seems little question that many of the psychotherapists who succeeded during the 1980s and 1990s in eliciting memories of ritual abuse had strong ideological incentive for doing so. Some were evangelicals who fully believed, in the wake of *Michelle Remembers* and its inevitable imitators, that a satanic cult was wreaking havoc throughout the land, and who wanted nothing more than to expose it and bring it down. Others were a curious assortment of feminists, hypnotherapists, and MPD enthusiasts who were out to prove that women and children in contemporary America were routinely being subjected to secret atrocities, as often as not in the presumed sanctity of their own homes. If satanic ritual abuse, the worst atrocity imaginable, could be shown to take place, was there anything that couldn't (or didn't) take place? Recovered memories of ritual abuse addressed the ideological need of the hour, and some therapists resorted to everything short of bribery to ensure that the need was met. Through subtle cuing, hypnotic suggestion, and other therapeutic equivalents of "leading the witness," clients were often provoked into producing precisely the material their therapists were looking for. And if any additional pump-priming was required, they were given copies of such heavy-breathers as *Michelle Remembers, Satan's Underground,* and *The Courage to Heal* to read and reflect on between sessions.

Not that all clients necessarily required much in the way of therapeutic inducement to deliver the desired goods. By the late 1980s the ritual abuse issue had caught fire in the popular media, and it was virtually impossible to pass a week in America without encountering yet another story of sacrificial infanticide, satanic breeding, and ghoulish torture. Ritual abuse "survivors" were frequent guests on tabloid television shows, and even mainstream publications such as *Ms.* magazine were more than willing to take their testimonies at face value. It wouldn't be much of a stretch to suggest that at least some of the people claiming recovered memories at the time were taking their cues directly from the popular culture.[13]

There were also undeniable benefits to "coming out" as a ritual abuse survivor. Within evangelical circles especially, survivors were lavished with attention and prestige. They were invited to tell their stories at conferences, where they were often treated as martyr-saint figures, and they were afforded ample opportunity to meet and befriend other survivors from around the country. For some people, arguably, survivorship may have been a role well worth cultivating.

Remarkably, the ritual abuse allegation mill encountered very little public skepticism during the 1980s. Eventually, however, the entire business started to come undone, not least of all due to its own escalating weirdness. In 1992, for example, a Utah-based psychologist named Cory Hammond, an expert on hypnotherapy and a heavyweight in the recovered memory field, told a gathering of his peers that the satanic cult that was making so much trouble in the United States had been started after the Second World War by Nazi brainwashing specialists working in cahoots with the CIA and an evil Jewish scientist who went by the code name Green. For decades now, according to Hammond, the cult had been programming people with electrodes and electric shock treatment to carry out its dirty work. The psychiatrist Colin Ross, a former president of the International Society for the Study of Multiple Personality Disorder, made similar claims, and Dr. Bennett Braun, director of the Dissociative Disorders Program at Rush Presbyterian–St. Luke's Medical Center in Chicago, warned that satanists were organized in impenetrable cell structures throughout the country and that tens of thousands of Americans had already fallen victim to their machinations.[14]

Nuttiness of this sort was bad enough; disclosures of outright fraud proved even more damaging. One of the biggest celebrities of the recovered memory/ritual abuse movement during the late eighties was a woman named Laurel Willson, whose 1988 book *Satan's Underground*, written under the pseudonym Lauren Stratford, garnered almost as much publicity as *Michelle Remembers*. Stifling sobs, Willson informed her readers that she had been thrust into a vile nightmare of prostitution and brainwashing after being sold into a satanic cult as a teenager by her mother. She said that she gave birth to three children while serving as a breeder for the cult, at least one of whom was sacrificed before her eyes. Absolutely no one, she wrote, should have to suffer such agony. This is obviously true, and one person who seems not to have suffered it is Laurel Willson. In a 1990 article, investigative reporters for the evangelical magazine *Cornerstone* unearthed some irksome details. During the years when she was purportedly bearing babies for the cult, a number of Willson's friends and relatives saw her quite regularly, but not one of these people could remember ever seeing her pregnant. What they did remember was that Willson was a troubled young woman with a penchant for concocting attention-seeking fantasies. Muttering apologies, her publisher withdrew the book from the market.[15]

Worse blows were still to come. In 1992 the False Memory Syndrome Foundation was founded in Philadelphia, a tiny organization at first but before long a real powerhouse, with a blue-ribbon advisory board of academics and medical professionals and a grassroots membership of several thousand. Most of its members were parents who had been accused by an adult child, on the basis of memories recovered in therapy, of performing horrible abuse years and sometimes decades earlier—including, in some cases, satanic ritual abuse. The foundation was committed to discrediting the techniques and theoretical underpinnings of recovered memory therapy, and by the mid-nineties it had succeeded in swinging public opinion to its side. Helping out in this regard was a troop of hard-hitting academics and journalists, including Debbie Nathan, Richard Ofshe, Frederick Crews, and Elizabeth Loftus, who turned out high-profile books during the decade decrying recovered memory therapy as a feckless pseudoscience and satanic ritual abuse as its lunatic offspring.[16]

By the mid-nineties the fuss had died down. Most of the magazines and television shows and child-protection groups that had been so worked up over satanism just a few years earlier now seemed to have forgotten all about it. The thrill was gone, the story grown stale. But evangelicals hadn't forgotten. During the height of the satanism scares they had created their own structures and ministries for waging battle against demonic forces in America, and they saw no reason to call off the fight until it was clearly won. Just because the popular media had stopped talking about it didn't mean satanism was dead. It was still alive, still cunningly organized, and just as dangerous as ever.

Battling the Demonic

In waging battle against supernatural evil in America, evangelicals have pursued two distinct strategies. One of these, which doesn't directly concern us here, the third-wave theologian C. Peter Wagner has termed "Strategic-Level Spiritual Warfare." Its operating assumption is that the nation as a whole is positively churning with demonic activity: Battalions of evil spirits, with their own distinctive marching orders and chains of command, have been assigned to various cities and regions throughout the country. The idea is to smoke out these territorial spirits, ascertain their missions and regimental ranks, and then defeat them through aggressive "warfare prayer."[17]

The second strategy, of course, is exorcism or deliverance—working directly on behalf of individuals who have somehow fallen prey to evil spirits. By conservative estimates there are at least five or six hundred evangelical exorcism ministries in operation today, and quite possibly two or three times this many. Some, such as the International Center for Biblical Counseling in Sioux City and Neil Anderson's Freedom in Christ Ministries in La Habra, California, are significant concerns, with full-time counseling staffs and separate media divisions. The vast majority, however, are considerably more modest, centered on an individual pastor or psychotherapist and taking on clients on a word-of-mouth basis.

In a sense these are days of reckoning for evangelical deliverance. Most ministries sprang into being during the height of the satanism scares, and many remain committed to the belief that a satanic cult is secretly brainwashing and demonizing people across America. The existence of such a cult remains their primary justification for being in business. More than just a few ministries, in fact, have staked their credibility on it. It would be a harsh blow, ironically, if such a cult, as seems likely, turned out not to exist, or if most of the claims of ritual abuse at its hands turned out to be fabrications.

This point isn't lost on Clinton Arnold, a bright, soft-spoken, handsome man in his mid-forties who must be counted the preeminent theologian of exorcism and demonism in evangelical Protestantism today. Arnold was raised in a farming community twenty miles outside of Bakersfield, California, he went on to earn a doctorate in New Testament exegesis at the University of Aberdeen in Scotland, and since 1987 he's been on the faculty of Biola University's Talbot School of Theology in La Mirada, California. In 1997 Arnold published a lucid and impressively nuanced book on exorcism and spiritual warfare, and for a number of years now he's been personally involved in a small deliverance ministry at his local church in Southern California. When we met in his office at Biola recently, I suggested that evangelical deliverance in the United States had been living, to a large extent, off counterfeit currency.

"Yes, I agree with this," Arnold said. "All the claims of satanic ritual abuse in the popular media have had a tremendous influence on evangelical deliverance. We've used these claims to promote deliverance. And so many of them have been fraudulent. Our ministries have uncritically embraced so much of this stuff. We allowed ourselves to get caught up in the media frenzy. This is a major black eye for evangelical deliverance. It's damaging to our credibility. I'm convinced that demonization does sometimes take place and that there's a legitimate place for deliverance, but we haven't helped the cause in believing everything that's been thrown our way by the media."

John Kelley, in his late forties and as tall as a basketball forward, is a colleague of Clinton Arnold's at Biola, and every bit as bright. He received a doctorate in clinical psychology from the University of Arizona in 1974, and he's currently director of the Biola Counseling Center. Kelley first became interested in deliverance and demonization in the late seventies through the writings of Merrill Unger and Kurt Koch, and in more recent years he has counseled quite a few people claiming to be survivors of satanic ritual abuse. At first he took these claims at face value, trusting in their historical truthfulness, but as time went on, he found himself becoming increasingly skeptical.

"In 1992 or '93 — I forget the exact year — I started doing considerable work with ritual abuse survivors," Kelley told me. "I had a sizable caseload — six or seven cases all at once when I first went into it, and the number grew every year. The cases were referred to me by Christian psychotherapists, and just about all of them involved people who had presumably recovered memories in therapy of having been brainwashed and demonized by a satanic cult. I'm talking about people who were convinced they had been victimized by a cult. The clients fully believed this, and so did their spouses."

I asked Kelley whether he himself believed in the existence of such a cult.

"No, I don't believe in it. Not now, at least. At first I probably wanted to believe in it, but the whole idea is pretty incredible. There's simply no evidence of such a perfect conspiratorial cult that's operating covertly throughout the country. Of course, there's no way you can absolutely prove such a cult doesn't exist. It's all nonfalsifiable stuff, these allegations of a supercult."

What, then, did Kelley make of his clients' recovered "memories" of satanic ritual abuse?

"I think that in some cases these memories might be empirically or factually based," he said. "But this would be just a small minority. I think that in most cases the literal components of the memories are factually false. But this doesn't mean the memories are necessarily worthless. In some cases they may constitute a fictitious reality that gives the person some motivation for changing or improving her life. Even though they're not true, in other words, the memories might convey a potentially helpful therapeutic message to the person. But the bottom line is, most of them probably aren't true in any factual sense. I became convinced of this while I was counseling these people. It put me in a very tough spot. I didn't believe in the literal validity of the memories. I thought they were a reflection of pervasive and enduring psychological problems that hadn't been adequately dealt with. So I was extremely skeptical, but I also wanted to play a constructive therapeutic role in helping these people."

Despite his good intentions, Kelley soon found himself persona non grata in ritual abuse circles.

"Many of my ritual abuse clients were also convinced they were suffering from multiple personality disorder. I'm not particularly proud to admit it, but I was specializing in MPD at the time, and this was one of the main reasons they were referred to me in the first place. It got to the point where I found the whole MPD/ritual abuse scene tough to take. It was a real tight network of therapists and clients. I was surprised to find how many people knew one another. There was terrific pressure in the scene for therapists to validate the memories of their MPD/ritual abuse victims. Victims would make a sharp distinction between good therapists or doctors and dirty ones. The dirty doctors were those who were skeptical of the abuse memories and the MPD diagnoses. So I gained a reputation of being a dirty doctor. All of this nonsense has been very damaging to evangelical deliverance. It's a shame, because I think demonization does sometimes take place. There's an important place for deliverance. But we have to move beyond this satanic cult business."[18]

For some time now, evangelical deliverance ministry has in fact been moving beyond the satanic cult business, though perhaps not quite in the direction John Kelley would hope. While continuing to handle a fair share of ritual abuse cases, quite a few ministries today offer full-service deliverance, expelling demons of every imaginable kind, for every imaginable reason. The message broadcast by these ministries is alarmingly clear: Demonic evil lurks everywhere in contemporary America, not just in the machinations of satanic cults but in the everyday affairs of the heart and the mind. If one is struggling with sexual temptation or burdened with anxiety or self-doubt, the chances are good that demons are on the scene. Problems of daily living that evangelicals might previously have ascribed to the failings of the flesh and sought to resolve through prayerful resolution and self-discipline are now ascribed to the workings of evil spirits. It's not just survivors of satanic ritual abuse who require exorcism; today, it would seem, almost everyone does.

There's something more than just vaguely familiar about all this. As much as its practitioners might want to deny it, evangelical deliverance of this sort is very much in tune with the therapeutic fashions of the age. It seems inspired less by the Christian Scriptures than by the recovery or codependency movement, that dizzying array of twelve-step groups and self-help literature that has become a ubiquitous feature of suburban life in America over the past two decades. No less than the secular recovery movement, many evangelical deliverance ministries today preach an ethic of unvarnished victimization. The addictive behaviors and stubborn disappointments of life, in their view, are due primarily not to moral failing but rather to some external force beyond one's control. (Here, of course, evangelical deliverance substitutes the demonic for the dysfunctional family, the preferred bogeyman of the secular recovery movement, but the effect is much the same.) People are hapless sufferers, locked into conditions not of their own choosing. To get back on track, to win liberation, the psychologically oppressed, the emotionally afflicted, the guilt-ridden innocents—and this includes potentially just about everyone—must submit to a therapeutic program, apprentice themselves to a technique. Evangelical deliverance (or at least a great deal of it) is such a technique; it's a recovery program with a supernaturalist twist.

On this same point, much of the literature of evangelical deliverance closely echoes that of the secular recovery movement, especially in its overweening confessionalism and its penchant for reducing just about everything to handy twelve-step or eight-point or just-about-any-number-will-do formats. Take, for example, *The Bondage Breaker* by Neil Anderson, currently one of the hottest books in the deliverance field. A former theology professor and the founding president of Freedom in Christ Ministries in La Habra, California, Neil Anderson is best known for championing a kinder, gentler approach to deliverance, which he defines in *The Bondage Breaker* and elsewhere as a "truth encounter." Here the deliverance minister doesn't confront evil spirits head-on but rather helps his clients reach the point where they can take personal responsibility for winning freedom from demonic oppression.

Judging from the letters of simpering gratitude that stud the pages of *The Bondage Breaker,* Anderson himself must be counted an especially skilled practitioner of this approach. "Dear Dr. Anderson, I will always remember the day I came to you for counsel and prayer. Ever since that day I have felt such freedom. There are no more voices or feelings of heaviness in my brain. I'm even enjoying a physical sense of release. Satan has returned many times trying to clobber me with those old thoughts, but his hold on me has been broken." "Dear Neil, I want to thank you again for being so gracious and available to counsel me a few weeks ago . . . After several hours of reliving the horrors of my past and forgiving the 22 people who had sexually abused me, I was finally free from Satan's bondage."

Lost-but-now-found testimonials of this sort, which seem an almost obligatory feature of evangelical deliverance books, also figure prominently in the literature of the secular recovery movement. Besides serving as a running advertisement for the therapeutic technique du jour, they seem calculated to break down the average reader's resistance. If all of these seemingly normal (and exceedingly grateful) people were able to find strength and peace, why not the rest of us? Aren't we all suffering from some impediment to happiness? Isn't some affliction standing in the way of complete self-realization? Why settle for just half a life when the possibility of fullness beckons? Why not join the program? True destiny awaits.

In the secular recovery movement the program inevitably consists of graduated steps and numbered checklists. In a very real sense the steps and the lists *are* the program; they're its magical substance. Evangelical deliverance isn't much different.

In *The Bondage Breaker,* Neil Anderson gets rolling with a stern warning. "The [worldwide] Satanist organization is massive and extremely secretive," he writes. "I have counseled enough victims of Satanism to know that there are breeders (producing children expressly for sacrifice or for development into leaders) and infiltrators committed to infiltrating and disrupting Christian ministry." As if this weren't bad enough, Christians must also contend with the harassment of demons, which are mysterious spiritual beings bent on evil, but not so mysterious, apparently, as to prevent Anderson from enumerating their eight vital characteristics. Demons, we're told, are able to travel at will, to communicate with one another, to evaluate and make decisions, and to combine forces. Such, at any rate, is the short list.

Anderson also claims that there are three levels of demonic bondage to which Christians may fall victim, the third the most severe. "At the third level of conflict, the individual has lost control and hears voices inside his mind which tell him what to think, say, and do. These people stay at home, wander the streets talking to imaginary people, or occupy beds in mental institutions or rehab units. Sadly, about 5 percent of the Christian community falls victim to this level of deception and control." For the record, "about 65 percent of all Christians" are trapped at the first level of bondage and 15 percent at the second; more than enough work, it would seem, for an army of deliverance ministers. (Somewhat incongruously, Anderson laments that "some Christians are a little paranoid about evil powers, suspecting that demons lurk around every corner just waiting to possess them." Reading this stuff, there's little wonder.)

But the news isn't all bleak. Toward the end of *The Bondage Breaker,* Anderson unveils his seven-step program for attaining spiritual freedom. Not five steps or nine steps, but seven; seven steps precisely. The first involves renouncing any previous or current entanglement with "satanically inspired occultic practices or false religions," which in-

cludes not just outright satanism but also New Age spirituality,
Mormonism, and Buddhism. Other steps include making a personal
decision for truth over deception, for forgiveness over bitterness, and
submission over rebellion. The process culminates with the renuncia-
tion of "the sins of your ancestors and any curses which may have
been placed on you."[19]

I'm not suggesting that people such as Neil Anderson have inten-
tionally lifted their therapeutic riffs from the secular recovery movement. Rather than plagiarism, it's a question of influence through
cultural osmosis. While evangelical deliverance is relatively new, the
themes and impulses that animate it are deeply embedded in the
American cultural soil. It isn't accidental that *The Bondage Breaker* is
subtitled "Overcoming Negative Thoughts, Irrational Feelings, and
Habitual Sins." For generations now, Americans have been trying to
overcome these things. It's the perfectionist strain of the national her-
itage. Evangelical deliverance isn't nearly so singular or countercul-
tural as its advocates would have us believe. It's merely the latest
installment in a long American line of sacred nostrums and self-
improvement techniques, which includes everything from New
Thought to Alcoholics Anonymous, the Human Potential Movement
to the kinds of charismatic exorcism explored here in previous chapters.

14.

on the front

The first evangelical exorcism I personally attended took place in the cozy basement lounge of a snowbound seminary in the Midwest. Excluding myself, six people were present for the occasion: three female divinity students who had previously undergone deliverance themselves and were now hoping to learn more about the procedure from a pastoral counseling standpoint; a young man from Montreal named Jean-Guy, who was the subject of the evening's session, and Jean-Guy's wife, Sheila, both of whom were also divinity students; and a fifty-five-year-old theology professor named Dr. Donald Graves.

The session opened with some hymn-singing and Bible-reading, and then Dr. Graves asked Jean-Guy to discuss as frankly as possible why he thought he might be demonized. Jean-Guy, trim and handsome and soft-spoken, said that he had converted to evangelical Christianity just two years earlier through a chance encounter with Sheila, who had been visiting Montreal with a church group. After getting married, the couple decided to attend seminary together, but for several months now Jean-Guy had been experiencing difficulty fully committing his life to Christ. He sometimes felt there was something inside him holding him back. At the same time, he had also been experiencing periodic anger and resentment toward Sheila. He would sometimes yell at her when things didn't run smoothly in their student apartment or when he was struggling with an overdue course paper. It was after one of his more recent outbursts of temper that Sheila suggested he might need deliverance.

Dr. Graves told Jean-Guy that we were now ready for the testing, or diagnostic, phase of the procedure. Lowering his head, he prayed that God would permit Jean-Guy to serve as a reporter or voice box for any evil spirits that might be residing in him.

Dr. Graves: I command you in the name of Jesus Christ, and by the authority of the Lord Jesus, any spirits in Jean-Guy, identify yourselves.

Jean-Guy: [silence]

Dr. Graves: By the authority of the Lord Jesus, identify yourselves.

Jean-Guy: Clare.

Dr. Graves: Clare. Is that the name of an evil spirit? Truth before God.

Jean-Guy: Yes.

Dr. Graves: Are there any others?

Jean-Guy: Yes. Pom.

Dr. Graves: Pom, are you an evil spirit? Tell me, truth before God.

Jean-Guy: Yes.

Dr. Graves: Clare, when did you enter Jean-Guy? I command you by the authority of the Lord Jesus Christ, tell me.

Jean-Guy: When he was fifteen years old.

Dr. Graves: Fifteen years old? You entered him then? Tell me, truth before God.

Jean-Guy: Yes.

Dr. Graves: Clare, tell me, truth before God, who is your leader? Is there someone over you?

Jean-Guy: Yes.

Dr. Graves: Who is it?

Jean-Guy: [silence]

Dr. Graves: Clare, truth before God, what hold do you have over Jean-Guy?

Jean-Guy: I provide him comfort.

Dr. Graves: But hasn't Jean-Guy been renouncing you?

Jean-Guy: He's too weak. I'm still here in him.

Dr. Graves: What other hold do you have over Jean-Guy?

Jean-Guy: Lustness.

Dr. Graves: Clare, are there any other spirits with you?

At this point Jean-Guy (or Clare) identified four additional evil spirits that had entered Jean-Guy at various stages of his life. Dr. Graves calmly interrogated each one ("Truth before God; by the authority of Jesus Christ"), trying to get a fix on their distinctive missions and rankings. The spirits generally responded in Jean-Guy's natural voice, though sometimes their timbre shifted somewhat, becoming slightly higher.

Dr. Graves called for a short break and invited everyone to help themselves to hot chocolate, cookies, and potato chips. He told me that he personally prefers a low-key approach to deliverance.

"A lot of evangelicals go in for a blast-'em method, but I don't think this really works," he said. "You have to take your time and find the grounds for why the demons are there. You have to eliminate these grounds, the hold they have on the person, before you can cast them out. Otherwise they'll stay. This is the case even for someone such as Jean-Guy, who seems definitely to be demonized, but not to a very great extent—about a two, I'd say, on a demonization scale of ten."

I asked Jean-Guy how he was feeling. He said that so far he'd found the process "physically and spiritually exhausting." He added that he was fully aware of the spirits speaking through him, and that they tended to communicate "in broken phrases and verbal gestures."

Dr. Graves requested that we take our seats so we could get started on the second major phase of the deliverance, the identification phase, which involved ascertaining the precise names, points of entry, and purposes of all of Jean-Guy's indwelling demons. He said that we had already gotten a good start on this prior to the break and that he anticipated a pretty smooth ride.

Just as calmly as before, without the least hint of theatrics, Dr. Graves asked the demons individually whom they served, how they had infiltrated Jean-Guy, and what their intentions were. Jean-Guy sat motionless, eyes shut tightly, his face wrapped in a grimace of concentration. After fifteen minutes of question and response, Dr. Graves broke off the interrogation and said that Jean-Guy was afflicted by four separate demons. One of these was an ancestral spirit that had entered Jean-Guy before he was born through a curse placed on him by his paternal grandfather. The others had gained entry through Jean-Guy's intermittent anger, laziness, and frustration, his sexual vanity, and his jealousy of his wife's superior course grades.

Dr. Graves told Jean-Guy that it was now time for him to renounce his indwelling demons and to ask Jesus Christ to reclaim those areas of his life that had been taken over by them. "By the authority of Jesus Christ, I command you to come to attention," Dr. Graves said to the demons. Then he instructed Jean-Guy to renounce each individual demon and command them "in the name of Jesus Christ to depart his life and never return."

This accomplished, Dr. Graves asked the spirits individually whether they had "any grounds for staying in Jean-Guy." Each spirit answered no. He then said to Jean-Guy, "Do you think that was the full complement? Did we miss any?"

"I think we got them all," Jean-Guy said.

Dr. Graves checked that the door was locked and pulled the drapes shut on the basement room's lone window. He said that the time had arrived to expel Jean-Guy's demons once and for all.

"By the authority of Jesus Christ, I cast you out," he said in a loud and forceful voice to each demon by name. "By the authority of Jesus Christ, I cast you into the abyss. I expel you."

He asked Jean-Guy how he felt. Jean-Guy said that he felt fine and that he'd had a vision of the demons leaving him.

The actual deliverance was now concluded, but Dr. Graves still had stern words of advice for Jean-Guy.

Okay, Jean-Guy, he said, these demons are now expelled. They are out of your life. They no longer have grounds for infesting you. But your attitudes of anger and resentment and vanity are long-standing. They have become habitual. So you still have a lot of work to do. You could easily fall back into these habitual patterns of behavior. But this wouldn't be the work of evil spirits; it would be sinful habit. Remember that Satan and his demons are masters of the lie. If you find yourself falling back into this rut, you may be tempted by Satan to believe that the demons weren't expelled tonight and that you're still enslaved to them. But this would be a satanic deception. You have been freed, but now you have to work on this habitual behavior. You need the help of a supportive Christian community and a regular prayer group. It could take a long while.[1]

W as Jean-Guy demonized? Needless to say, I'm not able to answer this definitively. From my limited perspective, however, there seemed nothing much wrong with him. Throughout the course of the evening he struck me as alert and charming and self-confident. The mixture of petty resentments that he and Sheila were complaining of seemed nothing more than the stuff of ordinary adjustment. In the space of less than two years Jean-Guy had undergone a religious conversion, gotten married, and enrolled in a faraway seminary, where he was taking courses in his second language. It's quite possible that he needed some psychological fine-tuning, but why on earth bring demons into the equation?

These reservations aside, the deliverance itself was an impressively civilized affair. Dr. Graves—cool, unflappable, a seasoned pro—ran things very much like a college seminar, occasionally pausing to field questions and jot notes on a legal pad. Even if demons weren't involved, there's a good chance Jean-Guy benefited from undergoing the procedure. In psychodynamic terms the deliverance may have been a galvanizing event, helping him clarify some of his personal anxieties and confusions and prodding him into more constructive behavior.

Afterward Dr. Graves told me that he's been conducting weekly deliverance sessions at the seminary for several years, but lately he's been having trouble keeping up with the demand.

"I've got a big backlog," he said. "I might have to go to twice a week for a while just to catch up. This is something that a lot of our students really want."

I didn't find this especially surprising. Deliverance ministries such as Dr. Graves's, which aren't uncommon in evangelical colleges and seminaries these days, provide a relatively safe and nonjudgmental forum for students to sort out difficult (and potentially embarrassing) problems that might otherwise be left to fester. Sexual anxiety, suicidal ideation, marital conflict — no problem is too sensitive or too personal to be given a full airing. After all, it isn't the students themselves but rather their indwelling demons that stand in need of correction. In the hands of someone as pastorally adroit as Dr. Graves, moreover, deliverance may serve as a kind of functional equivalent to the Roman Catholic sacrament of confession, providing relief not only from tension and anxiety but also from an accumulated sense of personal guilt.

All told, I sat in on about a dozen evangelical exorcisms during my research, and virtually all of them were as restrained and low-key as Dr. Graves's. The only outright exception, in fact, wasn't an evangelical exorcism in the strict sense. It was a hybrid affair, a public deliverance conducted during a conference at Wheaton College in Illinois for the benefit of several hundred charismatics and evangelicals (third-wave and otherwise) who were seeking liberation from demons of sexual perversity. (If conclusive evidence of the recent blurring of boundaries between evangelicalism and the charismatic movement were ever needed, this would surely be it.)

The weeklong conference, which was sponsored by an organization called Pastoral Care Ministries, took place in Wheaton's main chapel, a beautiful facility with pale blue walls located at the heart of the college campus. The crowd of six hundred or so was overwhelmingly white, clean-cut, and middle-class, the women dressed casually in simple summer frocks or shorts and T-shirts, the men in slacks and sports shirts. The bookstalls that had been set up in the chapel's spacious vestibule were doing a brisk business. In addition to the usual pop psychology suspects (M. Scott Peck's *People of the Lie*, Melodie Beattie's *Codependent No More*, and so forth), there was a fair amount of explicitly Christian literature for sale, including half a dozen titles apiece by G. K. Chesterton and C. S. Lewis.

The first evening Leanne Payne, the founder of Pastoral Care Ministries, addressed the conference participants in gushing, grandmotherly tones, frequently referring to her audience as "my little ones" and "my dear ones." She said that too many people today had been "indoctrinated into the false doctrines of this evil age" and that she herself was "one who had had to learn through great adversity to hear God." She asked all those who were seeking healing from sexual and emotional sickness to stand. Roughly two-thirds of the audience rose to their feet, many with arms upraised and hands extended, charismatic style. Payne prayed briefly in tongues, and then resumed her talk, which dealt mostly with the spiritual and emotional tribulations of homosexuality. At the end of the evening she invited the audience to confess their sins to lay ministers who were stationed along the side walls of the chapel.

To my mind Leanne Payne's opening-night talk seemed meandering and repetitious, a vague circling back and forth rather than a sustained argument. In the context, however, this was rather beside the point. Payne wasn't interested in winning a debate; she was there to bring sight to the blind, healing to the afflicted. As if to underscore the point, she noted at one juncture, "There are intellectuals who spend almost their entire lives writing papers that are entirely worthless, that are simply dialogues with darkness. Why? Why would anyone do this?" While I was struggling to make intellectual sense of her talk, most of those in attendance seemed spellbound. This small, gray-haired woman, wearing a simple purple dress with a cross around her neck, was promising precisely the kind of healing for which many of them had been desperately looking.

There are a growing number of Christian ministries in America today that specialize in "healing" or "curing" people of homosexuality through prayer and counseling. Leanne Payne's is one of the very few that also deploys exorcism toward this end. Payne believes that homosexuality is caused primarily by torturous emotional conflicts that occur during childhood, and secondarily by a pathological culture that has "reconciled good and evil" and lost sight of the "idea of normality." She also believes that people suffering from "sexual perversions and neuroses" are oftentimes afflicted by demons. In a recent book entitled *Restoring the Christian Soul,* for example, she writes of ministering to a demonized woman whose head was "spinning around as if it would swing off her neck" and to a young man who was "frothing at the mouth and in agony of the demons" until she thrust a crucifix into his hands and exorcised him.[2]

The next evening's talk was given by an associate of Leanne Payne's named Mario Bergner, an Episcopal minister in his late thirties with dark curly hair and a soft, soothing delivery. Bergner informed his audience that although homosexuality was a neurosis, it was an eminently curable one. He himself had received sexual healing a number of years ago, he said, and he was now dedicated to providing similar help for others.

At Bergner's invitation several hundred people stood up to receive healing prayer. Standing on the stage with his arms extended, occasionally breaking into a lyrical glossolalia, Bergner prayed softly and insistently that everyone present might be "delivered of their painful memories, their stored-up hurts, their loss of attachment to their mothers, and, most of all, their sexual perversions, their shames, their self-hating."

Almost at once a number of people started whimpering, and as Bergner continued praying, the sound of wretched sobbing filled the air. Then several people began howling and screaming, and within minutes the crowd was utterly transformed. The auditorium was filled with howling and thrashing, incessant braying, ejaculations of profanity, and primal shouts. Most of the really hot action took place up front, close to the stage. A primly dressed brown-haired woman who looked to be in her mid-thirties threw herself to the ground and began pummeling her genital area. A slim, tanned guy in his forties (an insurance executive from the West Coast, I would find out later) sank to his knees and went into a prolonged fit of screaming and thrashing. Dozens of people who just half an hour earlier had seemed models of middle-class decorum were suddenly clutching their groins, shaking ferociously, and moaning. Three or four people within my view were simulating masturbation. Up onstage Mario Bergner was joined by five women gently singing *"Ave Maria,"* lending a spectral feel to the proceedings. Then, at ten o'clock sharp, forty-five minutes after it had started, Bergner called a halt to the action. He instructed the audience to leave the auditorium and retire for the evening. All at once, with the flick of a switch, the shaking and groaning and moaning came to a stop. People embraced, some sobbing quietly, and everyone filed out of the chapel into the night.

The next morning, before a public (or mass) deliverance that was scheduled in the chapel for nine o'clock, I struck up a conversation with the insurance executive I'd seen writhing in his pew the previous evening. He told me that he was married with children and a born-again evangelical, and that he'd been struggling with homosexual impulses for most of his adult life. He said that he found the conference "a bit too charismatic" for his liking, but quite a few evangelicals he knew had assured him it would be "just the ticket" to solving his problems.

Once again Mario Bergner took the stage, and after praying alternately in English and in tongues for several minutes, he called on everyone in the chapel who was suffering from sexual perversion "to renounce Baal." This seemed the moment many of those in attendance had been waiting for. All at once, or nearly so, the place was utter pandemonium, making the action of the night before look like a mere walk-through by comparison. About fifteen minutes into the screaming and pummeling I spotted my insurance man, eight aisles away, howling like a werewolf, his face hideously contorted, one hand shaking wildly, the other clutching his genitals.[3]

A ll description, of course, is a matter of perspective, and my description of the Wheaton conference, written from the perspective of an outsider, runs the risk of caricature. I was present merely as an observer, without any emotional investment in the proceedings, and armored with a fair measure of skepticism. The lectures, which most conference participants seemed to find deeply meaningful, struck me as a curious (and tedious) hodgepodge of New Age psychobabble, charismatic crackerjackism, and old-style revival preaching. And the healing and deliverance was like stumbling across some exotic middle-class tribe reenacting childhood temper tantrums.

An insider's perspective, a description written by someone personally connected to the proceedings, would read quite differently. Several months afterward, quite by accident, I bumped into a young man in New York who had attended the same conference. He told me that it had been the most moving and transformative experience of his life. Thanks to the healing and deliverance sessions, he said, he had conquered "a lifelong addiction to sleazy porn and nowhere one-night stands." Prior to the conference he didn't think he was demonized, but he had decided to give deliverance a shot. And why not? he told me. Nothing else had worked. He went to Wheaton, sat through Leanne Payne's lectures, which he found "beautiful and stirring," and when the time came for deliverance, he threw himself into the action.

Did he now believe that he'd been demonized? I asked.

"I'm still not sure," he said. "But I acted as if I was, almost willed myself to believe I was, and then something happened at the conference, and I've never felt better."

So here's the other side of the coin. This positive report (and I suspect it wouldn't be difficult digging up others no less positive) made my own reactions to the conference seem downright misanthropic.

And it also brings out yet another angle to deliverance in contemporary America. In a sense, deliverance (or exorcism) is perfectly consistent with good old-fashioned Yankee pragmatism. In trying to solve personal problems, why not try anything, at least once, that might stand a chance of working? And if it works, why waste time worrying about the reasons?

εvαngelicαl Deliverαnce ministers

During my research I occasionally heard horror stories about evangelical deliverance ministers who had done great damage to their subjects or clients, bullying them into exorcisms and then accusing them of cowardice and lack of faith when the exorcisms didn't deliver instant results. I don't doubt that such people exist, but I personally didn't cross their paths. The ministers I met, almost without exception, went about their work with genuine humility and compassion, very rarely drawing attention to themselves or laying guilt trips on their clients.

Oddly enough, the most assertive, and flamboyant, evangelical exorcist I encountered was a Mennonite—probably the first Mennonite in America, in fact, actually to be ordained to the office of exorcist. I had heard rumors of Dean Hochstetler practically from the start of my research. Some people said that he was an intimidating, almost fearsome presence, known for rambunctious, blast-'em-out exorcisms that were guaranteed to leave even the most cynical of onlookers quivering with goose bumps. Others said that he had taught them more about casting out demons than they had ever wanted to learn. Practically everyone said that I'd be seriously remiss not to take time to meet him.

Hochstetler was born near Napanee, Indiana, in 1928. He was trained as a carpenter, spent two years in Puerto Rico during his early twenties working as a maintenance engineer at a church hospital, and then returned to Indiana and went into farm machinery sales. He became interested in deliverance during the early to mid-sixties when he read *Blumhardt's Battle,* an exorcism tale set in nineteenth-century Germany, and Jessie Penn Lewis's *War on the Saints,* regarded by many evangelicals as one of the classic books on spiritual warfare. His interest intensified in 1968 when he heard the German Lutheran theologian Kurt Koch preach at a church in Chicago. By this time Koch was already well known for his writings on exorcism and spiritual warfare, and the two men struck up a fast friendship. For five weeks in late 1968, in what he describes as his "apprenticeship period," Hochstetler traveled with Koch throughout the Caribbean, watching the German theologian perform deliverance and soaking up his knowledge of the demonic. Upon returning home, Hochstetler started up a deliverance ministry of his own, making him one of the very first noncharismatic evangelicals in the United States in recent decades to do so. His specialty was "freeing people from the bondage of the occult," and he made a point of never turning anyone down who showed up on his doorstep looking for help. On May 25, 1986, his local Mennonite conference, in recognition of his years of service and not quite knowing what else to do with him, formally ordained Hochstetler to the deliverance ministry.

Today Hochstetler lives with his wife, Edna, in an attractive bungalow with an attached double garage on the outskirts of Napanee. With his gravel-pitched voice and straight-backed demeanor, he certainly has the capacity to strike an intimidating pose, but I found him, off-duty at least, an immensely likable man, with an easy charm and a mischievous sense of humor. He chided his fellow Mennonites for being "the loudest at preaching love and the worst at getting along with each other." He said that he has the flexibility, as an Anabaptist, to plug in to both the Roman Catholic and the Protestant traditions of demon-expulsion, and that he's been particularly impressed by the writings of Malachi Martin and Francis MacNutt. He also said that while Win Worley must be counted an important pioneer in evangelical deliverance ministry in the United States, he has personally visited Hegewisch Baptist several times and thought that "it sounded worse than a hog pen."

Hochstetler told me that he has been overwhelmed by requests for help since the mid-eighties, but not all of the cases that have come his way have required deliverance.

"This is where I'm different from a lot of evangelical deliverance ministers," he said. "They think it's always about demons, but it's not. A lot of the people who come to see me have issues of sin and guilt they haven't dealt with. They think they're demonized, but they're not. You just can't go blasting demons out of people as soon as you see them. You've got to get to the root of their problems. I have serious theological objections to Roman Catholicism, but the Catholics have the sacrament of confession. This allows them to deal with their sin and guilt, and it also explains why Catholics have fewer problems with mental illness than Protestants."

And what about the cases where he has performed deliverance? I asked.

"I've found that one of the biggest factors in demonization is generational bondage," he said. "Many of the people I've worked with are paying the price for an ancestor's involvement with the demonic. This might sound bizarre if you're not in the business, but it's true. What our ancestors do has consequences for us genetically and environmentally. Why not also spiritually? If you don't believe me, go look at Matthew 23:29–33. It's very simple—if you don't deal with generational issues, you don't get people free.[4]

"The other really big factor is when people have a background in the occult. You have no idea how many people are stuck in psychiatric wards in this country because they've messed around with the occult. Secular psychiatry can't help these people because it doesn't address spiritual issues or the demonic realm. These people are the rejects of secular psychiatry. One of the biggest reasons I was ordained to the deliverance ministry was to make it easier for me to visit psychiatric wards and work with demonized people. The other big reason, I guess, was that I was so controversial some people in my conference figured ordination was one way of gaining control over me. But it doesn't matter. The fact is, I'm the first and only Mennonite to be ordained to cast out demons. And I'm proud to say that Tim Warner preached at the ordination service. You tell me, is there anyone in deliverance more qualified than Tim Warner?"

I 'll say this: There may not be anyone in deliverance more widely respected than Tim Warner. I first met Warner in the fall of 1997 at a conference on spiritual warfare in Gettysburg, and then I visited him and his wife, Eleanor, at their home in Fort Wayne the following spring. Tall, gray-haired, and scholarly, with a Bible Belt certitude and down-home geniality, he's a grandfatherly figure in evangelical deliverance circles, looked up to by just about everyone and frequently turned to for advice. In a field where rivalries often run deep and personal animosities linger, it would be tough to find anyone with a negative word to say about Tim Warner.

Warner was born in 1924 and raised in Davenport, Iowa, as the fifth of eight children. After a stint in World War II as a chaplain's assistant, he studied at Taylor University in Upland, Indiana, and then at the Biblical Seminary in New York. In 1953, the same year he was ordained, he married Eleanor, and the couple went off to do missionary work in Sierra Leone.[5] (This was the second marriage for both of them. Tim's first wife died of liver disease while he was still an undergraduate at Taylor; Eleanor's husband of nine years was struck dead by lightning on a golf course a couple of years before she met Tim.) Upon returning home, Warner taught at Fort Wayne Bible College, where he eventually took over as president, and along the way he also found time to earn a doctorate in education at Indiana University. In 1980 he became director of the School of Mission at Trinity International University in Deerfield, Illinois, and three years later he and Eleanor started up a deliverance ministry that would soon become one of the best known in the country.

"There were only a few isolated evangelicals performing deliverance before the eighties, and they were considered a bit weird," Warner told me. "Ernest Rockstad was doing it in the seventies, and so was Victor Matthews, who taught at Grand Rapids Baptist Seminary. Dean Hochstetler was also involved, and Dean knew more about dealing with wicked spirits than anyone else. But the biggest impact on us was Kurt Koch. We cut our eyeteeth on his books. Pretty well all of us were influenced by Koch."

Was charismatic deliverance also a significant influence? I asked.

"Maybe for third-wave evangelicals such as John Wimber and Chuck Kraft, but for most of us definitely not," Warner said. "A lot of us remain deeply suspicious of the charismatic renewal movement, especially the practice of speaking in tongues. You can put tongue-speaking to a spiritual test, and we've found that more often than not it's a demonic phenomenon. The first Sioux City [International Center for Biblical Counseling] meeting took place in 1988. This was the first national meeting of evangelical deliverance ministers, and charismatics weren't invited. Mark Bubeck was president of ICBC at the time, and he was adamantly opposed to the charismatic movement."

I asked where Malachi Martin's *Hostage to the Devil* factored in to the equation.

"Well, Malachi Martin's certainly a huge name, but we found *Hostage* very weird," Eleanor said. "We also think that M. Scott Peck was led astray by it. The confrontational approach in *Hostage* is unnecessary and unedifying. You don't need marathon exorcisms lasting eighteen hours to get rid of a demon. In general we've got kind of mixed feelings about the Roman Catholic exorcism ritual. The truth is incorporated in it, but the danger is it can be treated as magical. All of that holy water, for example."

I asked the Warners where they personally stood on the satanism scares that erupted throughout the country during the 1980s.

"This is pretty complex," Eleanor said. "We realize there have been fraudulent claims, and deliverance ministry runs the risk of being discredited if we're not careful here. But you have to realize that satanism is a very powerful and very secretive force in the United States. Sometimes the satanic cult has sent agents with false claims of ritual abuse to Christian counselors for the very purpose of subverting de-

liverance ministry. The false claims don't disprove the existence of satanism. If anything, they show how insidious a force it really is."

"The situation is much worse than is generally recognized," her
husband added. "Satanic ritual abuse is just the tip of the iceberg.
Satanists fully expect to take over the federal government in the near
future. We shouldn't be fooled into thinking they're not capable of doing it."

B ob Mueller, a middle-aged man of quiet intensity and unremark-
able appearance, is pastor of Zion Lutheran Church, a rambling
wood-framed structure located in a lush Indiana farming belt about an
hour's drive out of Fort Wayne. He's also about as decent a person as
one could hope to meet. A native of the South Bronx, where his father
raised four kids driving cab by day and waiting tables by night,
Mueller earned his B.A. at Concordia College in Fort Wayne (where
he also met his wife, Barbara) and then went on to a Master's of
Divinity at Concordia Seminary in St. Louis. In the early seventies,
with three children in tow, the Muellers moved east when Bob was offered a job in Christian deaf ministry in Washington, D.C. ("Barbara
and myself had seen someone signing in college and thought it was utterly beautiful, so we learned it ourselves," Mueller told me.) Over the
next seven years, despite straitened financial circumstances, the couple legally adopted three handicapped children and opened their home
to a number of others for months at a time on a per-need basis.
("While working in deaf ministry, we kept finding children who were
being misdiagnosed, treated as retarded, and then hung out to dry in
warehouses, so we felt we had to do something," he said.) In 1981 one
of their adoptive daughters, Tabatha, perished and Barbara herself
suffered terrible burns in a house fire that was apparently set by an ar-
sonist. Seven years later tragedy struck again when another adoptive
child, a young man named Al who was a severe hemophiliac, con-
tracted full-blown AIDS and died.

Several months after Al's death, Mueller accepted the call to become pastor of Zion Lutheran in rural Indiana. The job proved considerably more than he had bargained for.

"I'd only been here six months when a family in the parish called," he told me. "They said they'd experienced a frightening poltergeist phenomenon in their house that morning. Their nine-year-old daughter had somehow been picked up and levitated. These people seemed sane and sensible; I couldn't write them off as lunatics. I told them I'd never run across anything like this before, but I'd try to get someone to help them. I contacted a guy I knew from seminary who was an expert on the occult, and he sent me several books by Kurt Koch. Then I prayed deliverance, which seemed to solve the problem, but I found the whole process sickening. I couldn't believe it.

"About a year later, in June of 1990, I was counseling a young woman from the parish who had been horribly abused as a child and was now filled with incredible hate. One day I asked her whether she'd ever considered that her hatred might be demonic. Right then, right here in my office, she went catatonic. Her skin complexion turned gray, her eyes beaded, her irises — I'll never forget her irises — they seemed to narrow or tighten and the inner parts glowed red. This lasted for two or three minutes. I was paralyzed with fear. I had no idea what was happening. Then she snapped out of it, and I escorted her out of the office and phoned my seminary friend and said I'd unwittingly caught a demon and it had manifested. I didn't know where else to turn. I wanted to remain a pastor, and I figured people would think I was crazy. My friend gave me the name of a Lutheran missionary to call, and then the missionary gave me Dean Hochstetler's name. I didn't know anything about Dean Hochstetler, but I remembered hearing about Tim Warner, so I phoned him and then I phoned a Lutheran couple in California who I'd heard had a deliverance ministry, and all these people also recommended that I get in touch with Dean Hochstetler. I phoned Dean, and he invited Barbara and myself to his house. We thought we were going over to talk, but when we got there, Dean and some other people were performing an exorcism on a young girl. I was terrified, sheet-white scared, and I sat there praying that these people weren't crazy, because if they were crazy, the poor girl was in deep trouble. It was a good old-fashioned power encounter, lots of frightening manifestations, but Dean pulled it off. He exorcised the girl. It was the most amazing thing we'd ever seen.

"Anyway, Barbara and myself prayed over it, and we said, 'Yes, this is something I should learn to do.' Over the next eighteen months Dean served as a mentor to me. I saw incredible, unnerving stuff. One night Dean had a Japanese woman visiting him while he was exorcising a teenage girl. He told the woman to speak to the demon in Japanese. The demon became enraged and spoke back in Japanese. Then Dean spoke in German, and the demon barked back in German. The teenage girl didn't know these languages. Finally Dean said he'd taught me all he could, and I started doing deliverance myself. At the beginning my elders in the parish weren't in the least supportive. They thought it was insane. But eventually they came around. We studied Scripture together, and they read my case studies. It also helped that I was developing a reputation as someone who could deal with tough cases. I don't have any formal training in counseling, but people from all over the area who needed help with deliverance were contacting me. Occasionally I was even forced to perform deliverance in potentially violent situations—once when a guy had a gun at his wife's head."

Mueller estimates that he's performed somewhere in the vicinity of a hundred exorcisms over the past five or six years. Most required no more than one or two sessions, but a dozen or so ("mainly multiple personality cases") went on for several weeks. About 80 percent of his exorcisms have involved women ("Men are much less in tune with their spirituality," he said), and his youngest subject was a three-year-old girl who had alarmed her parents by scrunching into a ball and screaming whenever they tried to pray with her.

Like most other evangelical deliverance ministers these days, Mueller frowns on the high-octane, pulverizing approach to exorcism that was popularized by William Peter Blatty and Malachi Martin more than twenty years ago. He discourages dramatic manifestations during deliverance and tries to keep the procedure as low-key as possible.

"The power-encounter approach, where you directly confront the demons, is something a lot of us have shied away from," he said. "Neil Anderson's truth encounter has been a big influence on me and a lot of other evangelicals. Even Dean Hochstetler is much gentler than he used to be. But I'm not doctrinaire about this. Sometimes, especially in really tough cases, you have to do a kind of testing to make sure you've gotten all the demons. At the end of every one of my deliverances I say the following prayer: 'In the name of the Lord Jesus Christ, I bind every evil spirit who finds its ground in these issues we have here confessed, and I command you to depart. Go to the Lord Jesus, and from there go to wherever He sends you.' If there are still demons present at this point, they'll manifest. And this lets me know there's still more work to be done."

Deliverance and
Its Discontents

Despite its spectacular rise over the past two decades, deliverance still has a long way to go in American evangelicalism before its future is assured. Many evangelicals, seeing it as not much more than a passing fad, have thus far been content simply to ignore the ritual. Others have been actively opposed to it, on the grounds, not least of all, that it constitutes a threat to time-honored ways of thinking about sin and evil.

Evangelical Protestantism has traditionally held that there are three sources of evil, three avenues of perfidy, against which Christians must perpetually be on guard: the *world*, which refers to ungodly cultural and social influences; the *flesh*, or the cravings of our sinful nature; and the *devil*. With evangelical deliverance, however, the flesh and the world have been reduced practically to bit players, virtually crowded off the stage. It has been left almost entirely to the devil and his demons to carry the show. In seeing demons everywhere, in blaming virtually everything on the activity of demons, deliverance

ministers (or at least a good many of them) have thrown the entire system out of whack. The sins of the flesh, worldly temptation, the lusts
of both the groin and the pocketbook—all of this, as often as not, is
now attributed to the workings of evil spirits.[6]

The criticism, baldly stated, isn't altogether fair. Individual deliverance ministers such as Dean Hochstetler, Tim Warner, and C. Peter
Wagner have tried their hardest to maintain a balance in the calculus
of evil, and evangelical deliverance books invariably include a warning against blaming everything on demons. For every Tim Warner or
C. Peter Wagner, however, there are half a dozen others who aren't
nearly so prudent. And as for the books, it's a question of too little, too
late. After scaring the pants off readers for two hundred pages, an
obligatory paragraph or two cautioning them against imagining
demons behind every bush seems rather a hollow gesture.

There is, finally, a strong element of futility to the entire business.
Evangelical deliverance ministers are convinced that contemporary
America is ruled by a secularist mind-set and that the concept of demonic evil, even among most self-professed Christians in the country,
isn't given anything close to its proper due. They see themselves as
agents of countersecularization, righting the record, bringing demons
back into the equation. The problem, however, is that most of them far
exceed the call of duty. In their eagerness to find demonic evil in
places most people wouldn't even think of looking, they run the risk
of trivializing the concept, neutralizing it, robbing it of real bite. If
everything's demonic, after all, nothing is.

Part Six

ROMAN
CATHOLIC
EXORCISM

15.

A DAY AT
the office

The exorcist was late.

Seven people were waiting for him, four women and three men. I saw them when I pulled into the weed-choked parking lot alongside the defunct office building where their exorcisms were supposed to take place. They were standing in the baking Midwestern sun, heads lowered, bodies stiff, arms hanging like dead weights.

I had met all seven the previous evening at a special Mass the exorcist had arranged, and now, seeing me approach, one of the women raised a hand in silent greeting.

"Father Jack's not here yet?" I asked. She shook her head.

I didn't know what else to say. We stood together for fifteen minutes, no one speaking, before I went off to inspect the building. I found a rear door unlocked, and inside it was dusty and damp, small offices with green metal chairs and desks and filing cabinets along a narrow corridor.

When I went back outside, the group of seven had disappeared. I found them at a restaurant across the street, staring into cups of coffee, two or three of them bravely chatting. A thin, middle-aged woman clutching rosary beads in one hand, tissues in the other, gestured me over.

"Where is he?" she whispered.

"Who knows?" I shrugged. I said I'd go watch for him.

I took my coffee in a cardboard cup back to the office building and sat on the front steps. Just when I was thinking about looking for a pay phone, Father Jack pulled up in a dented Ford with his two assistants, Father Peter and Father Joseph. A blunt, burly, balding man in his mid-fifties, Father Jack eased out of the car and asked where everybody was.

"They're across the street having coffee," I said. "They've been waiting for you."

Car trouble, Father Jack muttered. His entire schedule was thrown off. He asked me to tell the group to come back over.

I didn't have to. Someone from the restaurant must have spotted him. The entire company was already headed across the road.

Father Jack unlocked the front door, and everybody followed him in. He turned on a big industrial fan that was standing in the foyer, then placed a sheaf of papers on a small table. These were release forms, he explained, exempting the local Catholic diocese from any legal liability stemming from the exorcisms.

While the group of seven took turns signing, the exorcist huddled in a corner with Dr. Joan Smith, a psychiatrist from a nearby teaching hospital, who had just arrived. Dr. Smith had been working with Father Jack for about a year, reviewing some of his cases and suggesting which ones might be suited for exorcism. Just suggesting, she had stressed to me in our previous meetings. The final call was always Father Jack's.

She waved me over, and Father Jack moved off to confer with his assistants.

"So here's the story," she said, extending a hand and smiling, always the laid-back professional. "We're going to break things up. We'll do two exorcisms now and the rest after lunch. Father Jack is asking the afternoon people to come back later. He wants you and Father Peter to go into the basement with Warren. You remember Warren? We're not expecting anything dramatic."

Dr. Smith had mentioned Warren to me over lunch several weeks earlier, and I'd been introduced to him by Father Jack after Mass the night before. He was a big, good-looking guy in his forties, a computer technician, who was convinced that he was afflicted by demons. Father Jack and Dr. Smith were pretty certain that he wasn't, but they'd agreed to go ahead with an exorcism anyway. If he wasn't demonized, the exorcism would at least clear his head and allow him to get on with dealing with his real problems. And if it turned out that he was, in fact, demonized . . . well, it was a "win-win proposition," Dr. Smith had told me.

"It looks like we're going into the basement," I said to Father Peter, who was now standing off to the side, holding a shopping bag from a discount department store.

"Yes," he said, "it looks like this is it."

Tall and gentle and unassuming, Father Peter was a latecomer to the Catholic priesthood after an earlier career as a Methodist minister. This was to be his first exorcism. The idea, I had learned from Father Jack, was to set him up with an easy case to start off, so he could build up confidence and gain some experience.

Father Peter told Warren that we should get started, and the three of us gingerly made our way down a flight of stairs leading off the foyer. The windowless basement was pitch-black. Father Peter and I ran our hands across the walls at the foot of the stairs, but we couldn't find a light switch. I tripped over a chair, then lit a match and groped along the side walls, but still no luck. We fumbled around in the dark for a good ten minutes, lighting matches, burning our fingers, before Warren suggested that he go to his car for a flashlight. He came back with one, and with its help I finally found the switch, buried in a recess along a wall by the back stairway.

The basement looked as if it had once been used as a recreation and meeting area. There were stacks of metal folding chairs, a sagging pinball table, an old television set lying on its side in a corner. Not much else.

Father Peter arranged three chairs in a semicircle in the middle of the cement floor and opened with a brief prayer asking for guidance and protection. He told Warren that Father Jack had briefed him on certain aspects of his case, but he'd like to hear more about it from Warren himself.

Warren, speaking softly and looking directly into Father Peter's eyes, said that he was raised an only child in Los Angeles where his parents, devout Catholics, ran a successful retail business. After graduating college, he took a series of white-collar jobs, all of which he found tedious and unfulfilling. During his early thirties he stopped attending Mass, and out of "boredom and curiosity" threw himself into a "life of debauchery." Boozy one-night stands. A constant stream of women. Lunchtime hangovers. He moved to the Midwest, thinking a change of scenery might help him settle down, but it proved more of the same. Perhaps even worse. He had sex wherever he could, with whomever he could. He masturbated compulsively, sometimes inserting objects into his anus for enhanced pleasure. He was consumed by guilt, but felt a total prisoner of his lifestyle. There was no breaking free.

And what then? Father Peter asked.

What then, apparently, was a descent into the macabre. While trying to sleep, Warren said, he was often kept awake by hectoring voices, voices taunting him for his sexual misdeeds. At least once or twice a week a repulsive, leering face appeared out of nowhere on his bedroom wall. Frightened and miserable, he sought refuge in religion, the sure, certain, and innocent faith of his boyhood. He became an intensely committed Catholic, a scrupulously observant Catholic—daily Mass, weekly confession, the rosary and retreats, scraped knees and signs of the cross. He became closely involved with a small circle of theologically conservative parishioners at his church, and every Saturday he joined them in protesting outside local abortion clinics. He married a woman from the circle, and for a while he was hopeful that he had everything under control.

Just three months into his marriage, however, the old torments returned—the overpowering sexual temptation, the boozing, the nocturnal voices and visions. Only now there was an added twist. Almost nightly, for periods lasting from five to fifteen minutes, to the accompaniment of cackling laughter, he felt unbearable pressure on his chest and shoulders. It was at this point, Warren said, that he began to suspect he needed an exorcism.

But why an exorcism? Father Peter asked. Why not seek out professional psychiatric help? Was there anything in particular that caused him to think he needed an exorcism?

The television show, Warren said. The *20/20* show in which a Catholic priest had expelled demons from a teenage girl named Gina. A friend had taped the show and given him a copy. After watching it, he contacted his pastor and six months later was put in touch with Father Jack.

Father Peter nodded and said okay. He stood up and put on a surplice and purple stole from his shopping bag, then unfolded a Xeroxed copy of the Roman Ritual of Exorcism and positioned himself directly in front of Warren.

"All-powerful God," he said, making the sign of the cross and sprinkling all three of us with holy water from a small plastic bottle, "pardon all the sins of your unworthy servant. Give me constant faith and power so that, armed with the power of Your holy strength, I can attack this cruel evil spirit in confidence and security. Through You, Jesus Christ, Our Lord God, Who will come to judge the living and the dead and the world by fire."

Warren sat perfectly still, head bowed, hands clenched. Father Peter made the sign of the cross again and, stepping closer, placed his right hand on Warren's head.

"I exorcise you, Most Unclean Spirit! All Spirits! Every one of you! In the name of Our Lord Jesus Christ: Be uprooted and expelled from this Creature of God. He who commands you is He who ordered you to be thrown down from the highest Heaven into the depths of Hell."

Warren remained as still as ice. But from upstairs, where Father Jack was working with Dr. Smith and Father Joseph, there was a loud thud, then a scuffling and scurrying across the floor. Father Peter made the sign of the cross on Warren's forehead and pressed a relic, a tiny splinter of wood encased in plastic, against his chest.

"I enjoin you under penalty, Ancient Serpent! In the name of the

Judge of the Living and the Dead! In the name of the Creator of the world! In the name of Him who has power to send you into Hell! Depart from this servant of God who has had recourse to the Church. Cease to inspire your terror in him."

More thuds from upstairs, and loud moaning, sobbing and moaning.

"God the Father commands you. God the Son commands you. God the Holy Spirit commands you. The faith of the Holy Apostles, Peter and Paul, and the other saints commands you. The blood of Martyrs commands you."

Now piercing screams. And crashing noises. Things being smashed against walls. The stomp, stomp, stomp of someone jumping. Warren wiped tears from his eyes with the back of his hand and hunched forward, elbows on knees, palms pressed against his brow. Father Peter coughed into his fist. He turned his page, then turned it back again, momentarily losing his place.

"God of Heaven! God of Earth! God of Angels! God of Archangels! God of Prophets! God of Apostles! God of Martyrs! There is no god but You. Creator of Heaven and Earth. Your kingdom is without end. Humbly, I supplicate Your majesty and Your glory: that You deign to free this Your servant from unclean servants."

Through the ceiling, shrill wildlife sounds. *Yip Yip Yip Yip. Ka-ka-ka. Yip Yip Yip Yip.* Father Peter caught my eye. He reached under his surplice for a handkerchief and mopped his forehead.

"I enjoin every unclean spirit, each devil, each part of Satan: in the name of Jesus Christ of Nazareth."

Yip Yip Yip Yip. Ka-ka-ka. Woo-Woo-Woo-Woo-Woo-Woo.

"Desist from attacking this man whom Jesus formed from matter for His honor and His glory. Shake with fear, not at the human fragility of a miserable man, but at the image of the all-powerful God."

Ka-ka-ka. No No No No No No No No Nooooo.

"Death is your lot, Impious One! And for your angels there is an endless death. For you and for your angels the unquenchable flame is prepared, because you are the prince of cursed homicides, the author of incest, the head of all the sacrilegious, master of the most evil actions, the teacher of heretics, the inventor of all obscenity."

Again, crashing noises. Shouts of *No! No! No! No!*

"Go out, therefore, Impious One. Go out, Criminal! Go out with all your falsehoods! God has willed man to be his temple."

No! No! No! No! A two-beat pause. Then one last resounding *Nooooooo!* Then quiet.

"Go away, Seducer! The desert is your home. The serpent is your dwelling. Be humiliated and cast down. For even though you have deceived men, you cannot make a mockery of God. From His eyes nothing is hidden: He has ejected you. All things are subject to His power: He has expelled you. The living and the dead and the world will be judged by Him with complete discernment. He has prepared Hell for you and your angels."

Father Peter led Warren through a profession of faith and several closing prayers, the Our Father, the Hail Mary, a reading from the Psalms. He asked Warren how he was feeling.

Peaceful, Warren said, but also a bit confused. He thought he'd felt something leaving him during the exorcism, but he wasn't sure.

Father Peter said that was fine, perhaps all that could be expected right now. He said we should go upstairs so Warren could make arrangements with Father Jack and Dr. Smith for counseling.

Upstairs, Father Peter beckoned me into a vacant office. He sat on the edge of a desk and lit a cigarette.

"So what did you make of it?" he said.

"You mean the basement? Or the commotion up here?"

"Maybe we were in the wrong place. It would have been nice to see what was going on."[1]

A t the restaurant across the street we're forced to split up. It's lunch-hour rush. Father Jack and his assistants take a small table at the back. Dr. Smith and I grab a couple of spots at the counter.

Several stools down, by the cash register, Warren is sitting by himself, drinking coffee and smoking. Father Peter goes up behind him, squeezes his shoulders, and whispers something into his ear. Dr. Smith tells me that she's already set up an appointment for Warren. Now that he's gone through an exorcism, she hopes he still won't be blaming his problems on demons.

I ask her about the ruckus upstairs.

"Oh, that was mostly theatrics," she says, a dismissive flick of her hand. "It was Louise carrying on. I hope it wasn't too much of a distraction for you guys in the basement."

Louise was the middle-aged woman with rosary beads with whom I'd spoken in the restaurant several hours earlier. I'd already been given a brief rundown on her case. She was single and self-employed, and she lived with her elderly mother in a fancy suburb of a nearby city. Shortly after her fiftieth birthday, apparently, she began getting vivid nighttime visions of various Catholic churchmen engaged in homosexual acts. Sometimes it was the Pope with the local bishop, sometimes the Pope with the local pastor, or the pastor with the assistant pastor. Sometimes it was three or four churchmen together, busily swapping positions. Louise told her pastor about the visions, but he offended her by asking whether she found them sexually titillating. Two weeks later she went back to him with even more disturbing news. Almost every night now, she said, her legs were pried apart by some mysterious force, which then proceeded to rape her. She was convinced that she was under serious demonic attack and desperately in need of an exorcism. The pastor recommended that she seek professional counseling. The next week a prominent parishioner who was a close friend of Louise's visited the pastor. She told him that the night before, in response to a frantic call from Louise's mother, she had gone to see Louise and had found her levitating six inches above her bed, thrashing violently, her nightgown pulled up to her waist. The pastor was still skeptical, but he agreed to inquire about the possibility of an exorcism. Three months later, after an exchange of letters and a brief phone conversation, Louise was sent by Father Jack to one of the psychiatrists on his team for evaluation. The psychiatrist reported back that something preternatural might be involved in the case, and that exorcism might be worth a shot.

So what was Father Jack's take on the exorcism? I ask.

"We both thought it a waste of time," Dr. Smith says. "Louise was acting out demonic possession, screaming and sobbing, throwing chairs, making animal noises, jumping around. A real performance. She's got problems that need attending to, but the problems aren't demonic. Father Jack thinks she's seen too many movies."

The difficulty here, of course, is that we've all seen too many movies, read too many books. People who believe that they're diabolically possessed, and who want to deliver a convincing rendition of such, have almost nothing but the popular media's depictions of possession to go by. Hollywood sets the scripts, and with very few exceptions (Warren was an exception) people undergoing exorcism fall into line.

Much the same is also true for the priests conducting exorcisms. The Roman Catholic Church in the United States offers no formal preparation for the job: There's no curriculum, no fail-safe manual, no sustained seminary training in demonology. So how is the priest-exorcist supposed to behave while in the line of duty? What, exactly, are the parameters of his performance? The actual Rite of Exorcism provides some useful stage directions (the holy oil, the signs of the cross, and so forth), but for the rest the priest is thrown back on his own devices. Yet not entirely so. Although he might not care to admit it, the priest-exorcist is also operating in the shadow of the popular media. Those sacrificial Jesuits immortalized by William Peter Blatty, those embattled hero-priests risking life and limb and dignity in Malachi Martin's *Hostage to the Devil*—these are the mythic figures, the pop cult icons that real-life priest-exorcists are forced to contend with. Their stories, their fictionalized narratives, constitute the inevitable standard against which men such as Father Jack and Father Peter, at some level, sooner or later, measure their own performances.

"Do you think I was forceful enough down there with Warren?" Father Peter asks me outside, waiting for Father Jack to take care of the check.

"Forceful? I think so. What do you mean?"

"You know, everything we've seen and heard about exorcism. I just thought maybe I was too laid-back."

F ather Jack is forceful.

Janice, a twenty-five-year-old woman who has flown in from San Francisco for the occasion, is the prize subject of the day, the only one of the seven Father Jack suspects of being seriously demonized, and he wastes no time taking command. His face and hair glistening with sweat, his feet planted, a bulky heavyweight primed for action, he rips into the exorcism with the swaggering confidence of someone who knows he can't lose. And for Father Jack it's really that simple. He has his faith, he has his church's authority and his church's ritual, he has the mysterious powers conferred on him by ordination. And the demons? The demons have nothing; the demons stand no chance.

But something's wrong. Things aren't proceeding quite as Father Jack had anticipated. He thrusts and he jabs, he presses a crucifix against Janice's face, sprinkles holy water on the top of her head, but nothing happens. There's no response; the demons aren't cooperating. Janice sits absolutely still, stone-faced, staring straight ahead, not so much as a quiver. Father Jack thunders through the ritual, but the only response he elicits from Janice, toward the very end, is a slight crinkle of a smile and a slow, don't-waste-my-time shake of the head.

Father Jack returns the smile. He asks Janice to stay put for a moment, then goes to the rear of the small office to confer with Dr. Smith, who's standing, arms folded, with her back to the wall.

It's an awkward moment. This was supposed to be the main event, but the demons (so far) are a no-show. I had met Father Jack a couple of months earlier and told him I was writing a book on exorcism. After several conversations he had invited me to sit in on today's sessions, suggesting, hopefully, that Janice's case promised real fireworks. In the jargon of the trade, "fireworks" refers to dramatic demonic manifestations—if not spinning heads and navel-licking tongues, at least something comparably spine-shivering, something chillingly not of this world, a howling from hell.

And here's the thing: While priest-exorcists as a rule don't actively seek out demonic fireworks, they can't live indefinitely without them. They need them the same way a pathologist needs disease or a coroner homicide—as a validation of purpose, a confirmation of actually being in the game. They're an occupational necessity. This is why Father Peter seemed almost envious not being part of the action upstairs before lunch. And it's also why Father Jack, who's certainly no ambulance-chaser, was hoping that at least one of today's cases would deliver the goods. Without the occasional hell-blasting, even the most stalwart exorcist can begin to doubt the relevance of his work.

Janice's case had come Father Jack's way several months earlier through a chance circumstance. One of his old seminary buddies, who was now pastor of a church in the Bay Area, had phoned to tell him about a shy, petite, young woman who had dropped by his rectory looking for help. The young woman—Janice—was attending college part-time, and she lived with her mother, who was an aspiring artist, in a government-subsidized apartment. Her most recent boyfriend had been deeply involved in the occult, and following their breakup she became convinced that she was demon-possessed. She was tormented by graphic visions of mutilated bodies and by sinister, snarling voices urging her to murder her mother and then commit suicide. Two or three times a week she also experienced a painful sensation of some snakelike entity working its way into her abdomen. Janice had sought relief through a variety of New Age therapies, but as her fantasies of death and violence grew increasingly intense, she decided to try the Roman Catholic Church.

The Bay Area pastor had heard that Father Jack had been appointed to the office of exorcist, and he asked him if he was interested in Janice's case. Father Jack already had more cases in the works than he knew what to do with, but he agreed to send Father Joseph, his most experienced assistant, to San Francisco to undertake a preliminary investigation. After interviewing Janice, Father Joseph performed a diagnostic procedure sometimes referred to in exorcism circles as a "provocation." He prayed over her, pressed a crucifix against her cheek, and sprinkled her with holy water. If demons were present, there was a good chance this would draw them out. The provocation, apparently, created quite a stir. As soon as he sprinkled her with holy water, according to Father Joseph, Janice underwent a drastic transformation. She blistered the air with profanity and threatened him with disembowelment; she tore open her dress, then threw herself to the floor and slithered around the room. Upon hearing from Father Joseph, Father Jack arranged an appointment for Janice with a psychiatrist he knew in the area. The psychiatrist told Father Jack that Janice was suffering from mild neurosis, but that he couldn't rule out the possibility that she was also demonized.

Father Jack confers briefly with Dr. Smith at the back of the small office. Then, a reassuring wink my way, he positions himself in front of Janice again.

He wants to go through the ritual a second time, he tells her. Sometimes it has to be repeated to get the desired results.

Once again the exorcist puts on a rousing show. His voice hoarse, his face soaked with sweat, he gestures emphatically, commanding the demons to reveal themselves. But it's the same scene as before. Janice sits still as a statue, impervious, looking slightly bemused. Then, just as the ritual is drawing to a close, she flops out of her chair and starts slithering across the room. She bumps her head gently against the door, then reverses herself and slithers and squirms underneath the desk by the window.

From my vantage this seems nothing more than a courtesy flop, an obliging slither. It's almost as if Janice felt compelled to do something to salvage the performance. The exorcist was working his heart out, but she hadn't been holding up her end of the bargain. She wanted to reward him with at least some token gesture.

The point isn't lost on Father Jack. He asks Dr. Smith to help Janice up before she hurts herself, then advises Janice he'll be in touch soon to talk about follow-up treatment. He tells Father Joseph, who's just wrapped up an exorcism with Father Peter in the basement, to take Janice outside and help her get a taxi back to her hotel.

Dr. Smith asks the exorcist what he thinks. The slithering routine was probably for his benefit, he says. Janice saw how hard he was trying and didn't want to disappoint him. He hadn't meant to put any pressure on her.

Father Peter says the exorcism in the basement, which involved a young man who felt oppressed by demons every day at his job in a brokerage, was mostly uneventful. Plenty of scowling and cursing, but nothing serious. Father Jack shrugs. Pretty much what he had anticipated, he says.

The last two subjects of the day are waiting in the foyer. (One of the original seven, a heavyset, middle-aged woman whom I saw earlier in the day, twitching and scratching her forearms while waiting outside for Father Jack, hasn't returned for the afternoon sessions.) Dr. Smith and Father Peter head downstairs with an alarmingly pale woman in her thirties, who's hiccuping nervously. Father Joseph escorts a fortyish, working-class man named Frank to an office at the far end of the corridor.

The exorcist, chewing on a toothpick, tells me that we'll be joining Father Joseph once he's had a chance to run through the preliminaries with Frank. But don't expect much excitement, he says. He's convinced that Frank isn't demonized.

This puzzles me. I could see why Father Jack had agreed to go ahead with an exorcism for, say, Warren. While he didn't think Warren was demonized, he hadn't completely ruled out the possibility. Doing the exorcism was a way of testing the supernatural waters, so to speak, and also settling the issue once and for all in Warren's mind. But why in this case? I ask. Why an exorcism for Frank?

For strictly pastoral reasons, Father Jack answers. Frank had contacted him through the local chancery a few months ago. He'd just lost his job, his marriage was on the rocks, he was estranged from his kids. And he was convinced that all of this was the result of his being possessed. Dr. Smith examined him and told him that he needed psychiatric help. Father Joseph saw him and said the same thing. There was no budging him, however. Frank felt certain that he had fallen prey to satanic forces, and this was preventing him from putting his life in order. He was paralyzed by imaginary demons. In cases of this sort, Father Jack tells me, exorcism may sometimes be an appropriate response. You do the exorcism and then say to the person, Look, we've tried this. Now you can be quite certain that your problems aren't demon-related. So let's figure out what we need to do next.

Father Joseph gets started. He's a tall, pleasant-featured man, thirty years a priest, decent and unpretentious. He proceeds through the exorcism softly and slowly, caressing each phrase, gesturing with the avuncular ease of an umpire at a parish softball game. About halfway through, Frank tenses up and makes a loud gargling noise, as if trying to force phlegm into his throat. Then, lurching forward, his head between his knees, his arms hanging straight down, he begins growling, quietly at first, then louder and louder, until, just as the exorcism nears the end, he breaks down sobbing.

Father Jack, who had been standing by the back wall, pulls up a chair and puts a hand on Frank's shoulder.

Frank calms down and says he's pretty certain the exorcism didn't do the trick. He needs another one, he says, this time from Father Jack himself.

Father Jack tells him that the exorcism he just received was perfectly fine. Father Joseph is authorized by his bishop to perform exorcisms, he says, and this is the only thing that matters.

Frank is adamant. He wants another exorcism, he says, and it has to be from the main guy.

What he really needs, Father Jack says, is professional psychiatric help. That way he can begin to get his life back on track.

Now Frank becomes agitated. Raising his voice and waving his arms, he demands an exorcism from Father Jack. It's the only chance he's got, he says.

Father Jack tells Frank that he'll help set him up with counseling. He'll even see about finding him a job. But no more exorcisms.

And so it goes. For a solid twenty minutes Frank pleads for another exorcism while Father Jack, showing reserves of patience I didn't realize he possessed, tries talking him into a more practical course of action.

Finally Frank says okay, he'll take Father Jack's advice. Father Peter walks him outside to the parking lot.

I ask Father Jack if he thinks he got through.

He says he's not sure. Only time will tell.

The exorcist suggests we grab some supper at a beer and burger joint across town. I drive over with Dr. Smith. She asks my impressions of the day.

"Pretty grueling," I say. "You guys have impressive stamina."

"Do you think you saw any evidence of the demonic?"

"I don't think so."

"Well, if you hang around with Father Jack long enough, you're bound to see some strange stuff. He's got a tough job."

Not much tougher, it strikes me, than Dr. Smith's. She's one of about a dozen psychiatrists around the country today who are evaluating cases of suspected demonization on a pro bono basis for the Catholic Church. It's a job, needless to say, loaded with potential conflict. As a committed Catholic, with conservative theological leanings, Dr. Smith is quite open to the possibility of demonization, and only too happy to lend her expertise to the church. As a medical professional, however, with justifiable concerns for her reputation and livelihood, the last thing she wants is to be publicly associated with scenes such as today's.

Dr. Smith has reviewed approximately sixty cases for Father Jack and one or two other exorcists she knows. To help determine whether any particular case might be worthy of exorcism, she goes through several diagnostic stages, first ruling out organic disorder, then the two major functional psychoses—schizophrenia and manic depression—and then, finally, any emotional disturbances that may have given rise to more transient psychoses. Of the cases she's looked at so far, about twenty involved what she describes as inexplicable phenomena—symptoms and behaviors that don't seem to fit any recognized psychiatric syndrome. Some of these have gone on to exorcism, and some others, which she thought explainable in psychiatric terms, have also gone on for pastoral reasons.

The beer and burger place is crowded and noisy, a television set perched above the bar tuned to an extra-inning baseball game. All five of us jam into a wooden booth near the back. Father Jack and his assistants seem subdued, almost dejected, a combination, perhaps, of fatigue and frustration. In the dim light they look pale and fragile, black shirts rumpled, faces lined with worry. I have to remind myself that these men are ordinary parish priests. Father Jack has a funeral Mass the next morning; Father Peter is gearing up for a retreat. They didn't campaign to become exorcists. Father Jack was asked by his bishop to take on the job; then he in turn asked Father Peter and Father Joseph, two men he knew and trusted, if they'd be willing to be appointed as his assistants. They're not theological stars or academic schmoozers. They're decent men of sturdy, unassuming faith who took on a ministry they were asked to take on, did something they thought needed doing. They hadn't anticipated there'd be so many people clamoring for their services.

Father Peter is anxious to hear my take on the day's events. He knows that I've been doing research on various kinds of exorcism in the United States and that this was my first exposure to the official Roman Catholic variety.

I say that it will probably take some time for my thoughts to settle, but that the day seemed to go quite well. I found the ritual itself beautiful and moving, and I felt that the individual cases were handled with care and sensitivity. It seemed to me that no harm had been done; if anything, something good may have come out of the day. This is how I honestly feel.

"But what about supernatural evil?" Father Peter asks. "Do you think you saw anything?"

"Nothing that reared up and jumped me. But I'm certainly not the best judge of such matters."

We sit without speaking for a minute or two. Then Father Peter says that he didn't see any clear-cut evidence of the demonic either.

"Maybe it's because I'm new at this, but it would be nice to see something," he says. "I don't necessarily mean the complete package, but something definite."

By the "complete package" Father Peter means total diabolical possession—the thoroughgoing domination of an individual by demonic forces. Possible indications of total possession, according to Catholic exorcism lore, would include an intense aversion to sacred symbols, a sudden fluency in previously unfamiliar languages, prodigious physical powers, and knowledge of hidden or distant things. Just about all Catholic authorities on the subject agree that total possession is an exceedingly rare phenomenon. An exorcist could practice his craft for a lifetime without ever encountering it.

Rather less rare, presumably, are more moderate forms of demonization—referred to variously as obsession, oppression, or infestation—in which an individual is harassed or tormented by supernatural evil without falling entirely under its sway. Father Jack had suspected that several of today's cases, Janice's in particular, involved demonization of this sort, and he says that he has quite a few additional cases, at various stages of investigation, that seem likely to fit the bill.

It shouldn't be long, he tells Father Peter, before he has an opportunity to see something definite.

There's some brief shouting and cheering from the people gathered around the TV by the bar. Someone's just delivered the game-winning hit.

I raise an obvious philosophical point with Father Jack—nothing, I'm quite sure, he hasn't already raised himself. If supernatural evil is truly an active force in the modern world, why should we think it would be bothering poor souls such as Warren and Janice? Aren't there plenty of other places it might more plausibly be found? Other more likely spheres of influence? Ethnic cleansing in the Balkans, for example? Or crushing poverty in the Bronx?

Father Jack nods in agreement. It's quite possible, he says, that much of the structural evil in the world—the poverty, the warfare, the materialism, and so forth—possesses a demonic dimension. And fighting evil of this sort should be a top priority for the Catholic Church. But demonic evil can also infiltrate the lives of ordinary people. Why does this happen in any particular case? It's a mystery, he says. You certainly don't go looking for it, but when the problem comes knocking at your door, you've got to deal with it. This is why the Catholic Church has a rite of exorcism.

D r. Smith drops me off at the parking lot where I left my car earlier in the day. The street is empty, the night air heavy with humidity. The restaurant across the road has closed for the evening, metal shutters pulled down over its windows and door.

From the front of the building beside the lot I catch the flare of a match. It's Warren, sitting on the steps and lighting a cigarette. I walk over and ask if he needs a ride.

It's okay, he says. He's staying at a motel not too far away, and it's not too bad a night for a walk. Besides, he adds, he's still got a lot of thinking to do.

16.

official, unofficial, quasi-official

This was my first direct exposure to Catholic exorcism—official, fully credentialed Catholic exorcism, that is. I'm not sure exactly what I expected, but it was something rather different from what I got. The proceedings had an improvised, patchwork, here's-what-we-do-now feel to them. There was no scene of shuddering finality, no soul-piercing moment of truth. Everything seemed drawn out and inconclusive—seemed somehow too human. Partly this was because Father Jack and his assistants were relatively new to the job, feeling their way, ironing out the kinks as they went along. Partly it was because they had stretched themselves thin by scheduling half a dozen exorcisms for the same day. Mainly, however, it was because this is how exorcisms tend to go. Whatever else they might be, they're resoundingly human affairs, with all of the faltering unremarkability this implies.

The truly remarkable thing is that the exorcisms took place at all. As recently as the mid-nineties there was only one officially appointed priest-exorcist in the entire country—approximately one more, it might be added, than even most bishops were probably aware of. It wasn't, of course, that there weren't plenty of people looking for

Catholic exorcisms at the time, but actually getting one was about as easy as booking a midnight flight to Mars.

Not long after I first met with Father James LeBar at the Hudson River Psychiatric Center, however, the wheels began to turn. Over an eighteen-month period, beginning in the fall of 1996, ten Catholic priests in the United States were appointed to the office of exorcist. Father Jack was one of the first out of the blocks; so, too, was Father LeBar, who was named head exorcist of the Archdiocese of New York. Ten exorcists might not seem like many, especially in a country with a Catholic population of sixty million. Compared with the recent past, however, it was an outright bonanza. There are no official statistics on such matters, but American Catholicism probably has more bona fide exorcists at its disposal today than at any given time since the invention of color TV.[1]

If the appointment of ten new exorcists signaled a new moment for American Catholicism, it was only fitting that the moment should be sealed by the popular entertainment industry. On April 22, 1998, ABC aired a segment on its newsmagazine show *PrimeTime Live* entitled "The Devil Within." Off the top, opposite some opening shots of a teenage girl writhing and screaming while a priest thrust a crucifix up against her, anchorwoman Diane Sawyer, hitting just the right note of calculated credulity, announced that "you may have seen it in the movies, but this is terrifyingly real. What you are watching is an exorcism."

What we weren't watching, however, was a Roman Catholic exorcism—at least not in the strict sense. Desperate to get its cameras into a Catholic exorcism, *any* Catholic exorcism, ABC was forced to settle for a wannabe one. As further proof that the cheesiest acts live longest, the teenage girl was being worked on by none other than Father Robert McKenna, the traditionalist priest-exorcist of Ed and Lorraine Warren fame. For this performance, however, Father McKenna wasn't being assisted by Ed and Lorraine but rather by a certain Dr. Joseph Klimek, who was advertised as an infectious-disease specialist and chief of medicine at Hartford Hospital, and also by a registered nurse named Jennifer Banever. As so often happens with these affairs, the performance couldn't live up to the hype. Father McKenna blustered, the teenage girl moaned and screamed, and Dr. Klimek and Nurse Banever stood around looking concerned. There may have been demons present, but who could tell? What it looked like — well, there's no getting around it — what it looked like was a few concerned-looking adults hanging about watching a teenage girl moan and scream.

The segment wasn't a complete loss, however. ABC managed to score a brief interview with Father James LeBar, which was spliced, incongruously, between shots of Father McKenna's wayward performance. *PrimeTime Live* correspondent Cynthia McFadden identified LeBar as "an exorcist for the New York Archdiocese," thus making him the first Catholic exorcist in the United States ever to be outed on network television. "Last year alone," McFadden gushed, "[LeBar] performed twenty exorcisms."

So there we have it. Twenty-five years after William Peter Blatty, things have changed somewhat, but mostly they've remained the same. Fully official and authentic Catholic exorcisms are somewhat easier to come by these days, but you wouldn't want to hold your breath waiting on one. Renegade priest-exorcists such as Father McKenna are still in business, with the demand for their services as great as ever. And the biggest promoter of Catholic exorcism (official? unofficial? It doesn't matter; we'll take what we can get) remains the popular entertainment industry.

The situation, actually, is a bit more complicated than this. Besides official and unofficial Catholic exorcisms, there are also quasi-official ones. In what must be counted a kind of gray area, some Catholic dioceses around the country have made provisions for exorcism without actually appointing anyone to the office of exorcist. Until very recently, for example, if you were a Catholic living in the Chicago area, you wouldn't have been able to get a fully accredited exorcism, regardless of how demonized you thought you were. The Archdiocese of Chicago didn't have an officially appointed exorcist on call until September 2000 (at which point this book was in press). This didn't mean, however, that you would be denied help altogether. For more than a decade, the Chicago Archdiocese had been referring cases of suspected demonization to a small deliverance team of charismatic Catholics. The two leaders of the team were a Jesuit priest and a married laywoman who was a practicing psychotherapist, both of whom had been involved with charismatic deliverance for more than fifteen years. The drill worked as follows: If a particularly troubling case came to their attention, archdiocesan officials would forward it to a liaison officer connected with the chancery office, who would get in touch with the deliverance team.

"About ten cases on average are referred to us a year," the Jesuit team-leader told me in 1998. "The vast majority of them involve women—why? I'm not entirely sure—and to this point they've all been lesser forms of demonization, demonic oppression rather than outright possession. I don't know if I'd even recognize outright possession if I saw it, but it might actually be easier to deal with than these subtler cases. The issues would be more clear-cut."

For a rather different shade of gray there are also a number of priests around the country (exactly how many, it's hard to say) who claim to have received general permission from their bishops to cast out demons without actually being appointed to the office of exorcist. In some cases such claims appear to have merit. For almost two decades, for example, until his death several years ago, a New Orleans–based priest named Father Emile LeFranz served as a kind of exorcist-without-portfolio for the Catholic Church in southern Louisiana.

In other cases it's tough to tell. Not long ago I visited with a priest I'll call Father X in a large Eastern Seaboard city. Father X assured me that he was authorized by his bishop to perform discretionary exorcisms for cases of demonic oppression or affliction and was required to seek explicit approval only for cases of full-fledged possession. My subsequent efforts at checking this out came to naught, but during my visit Father X invited me to assist with an exorcism that was scheduled later the same week. He had asked several priests he knows if they'd agree to help out, but they'd apparently turned him down.

("Most priests are simply too afraid, too lacking in faith, to go anywhere near an exorcism," Father X told me.)

The exorcism took place in a convent chapel and involved a
teenage boy whose parents were prominent members of Father X's
parish. A couple of years earlier, apparently, the teenager had fallen in
with a heavy metal clique at his high school. His grades declined, he
quit the varsity football team, and he became sullen and withdrawn at
home. One day his mother discovered occultic paraphernalia in his
room, and she also suspected that he was experimenting with drugs.
His parents insisted that he attend Mass with them one Sunday morning, but during the consecration (according to Father X) the teenager
began "howling like a wolf."

I told Father X that from my point of view nothing in this short
case history suggested the need for an exorcism. He said that he'd
helped arrange several psychiatric appointments for the teenager, and
the psychiatrist ("a good Catholic doctor") had concluded that there
was "no natural explanation" for the misbehavior at Mass.

Anyway, the exorcism went ahead. There was the usual screaming
and blaspheming—not much else. By now I was a bit of an old hand
at events of this sort, and more than just a bit jaded. It was almost like
viewing stock footage. Father X declared the procedure a success and
told the teenager's parents to check back with him in a week or so.

Father X might very well have consulted with a psychiatrist on this
case, but I'm not sure it really matters. There are plenty of sympathetic medical professionals in the United States willing to give the
go-ahead for an exorcism. It doesn't take much shopping around to
come up with one.

To some extent this is true even of official Catholic exorcisms carried out by fully accredited priest-exorcists. In theory a priest-exorcist
isn't supposed to assume diabolical possession in any particular case.
Quite the opposite, in fact. According to the revised Roman Ritual of

1952, whose instructions for exorcism were in effect throughout most of my research, the priest-exorcist should always approach his work from a posture of incredulity. Rather than assuming that certain tell-tale symptoms (an aversion to sacred symbols, extraordinary physical strength, and so forth) are of diabolical provenance, he should first consider and, if possible, rule out other alternatives, including fraud, organic disorder, and psychological disturbance.[2]

The reality, however, is quite a bit different from the theory. For one thing, it would be too much to expect an exorcist—even the most scrupulous and incredulous of exorcists—to consult with a psychiatrist who's hostile to the idea of demonization. By virtue of being an exorcist, he himself will quite obviously be open to the idea and will choose to work with psychiatrists who are similarly inclined. And the psychiatrists he works with, just as obviously, will not in every case definitively rule out demonization. As part of the exorcist's team, they, too, have a vested interest in encountering, if only occasionally, pre-ternatural symptoms. Otherwise why would they have signed on in the first place? They know, moreover, that the exorcist is expecting some action, they too wouldn't mind seeing some, and hence they have little interest in shutting down the show time and again by turning in strictly secular diagnoses.

The point here isn't that the psychiatrists who work with exorcists are somehow incompetent or given to slipshod diagnoses. Far from it—most of those I've met have top-flight professional training and are highly regarded by their peers. The point, rather, is that the human dynamic in the exorcist/psychiatrist relationship, and the demands of role, virtually ensures that at least some cases will proceed to exor-cism. Dr. Smith knew without having to be explicitly told that Father Jack was anxious to try his hand on a case or two, and she certainly didn't want to be the one person standing in the way. What's more, she herself didn't have a clear diagnostic fix on some of the cases she'd been asked to evaluate. So why not give exorcism a shot?

If an exorcist is appointed, in other words, and if he's afforded a supervisory role in the investigative process, exorcisms will take place. This is virtually a given, a propositional inevitability. One of the reasons there were so few official Catholic exorcisms in the United States until quite recently (besides the fact there were so few exorcists) was that the investigation of suspected cases of demonization was overseen by someone who wasn't himself an exorcist. During the seventies and eighties this job was filled informally by Father John Nicola, whom we encountered briefly in an earlier chapter.

Nicola seems to have been an ideal man for the job. A lifelong student of the paranormal and the mystical, he put in several stints during the 1960s working in Durham, North Carolina, with the pioneering parapsychologist Dr. Joseph B. Rhine, and he eventually went on to earn a doctorate in theology at the Pontifical Gregorian University in Rome. After serving as technical adviser to Blatty and Friedkin during the filming of *The Exorcist,* he became the person most often turned to by American Catholic bishops seeking advice on suspected cases of demonization.

It wasn't easy getting a case past Father Nicola. Although he believed in the possibility of diabolical possession, he approached his work with a hard-nosed skepticism.

"The watchwords are caution and circumspection," he told me recently at his home in North Carolina. "You should never proceed with an exorcism without ruling out natural causation. When I was actively investigating cases, I operated under the assumption that exorcism should be used only as a last resort."

Some might argue that Nicola sometimes took caution and circumspection to unnecessary lengths. In 1970, for example, he assisted the then official exorcist of Rome, a Passionist monk named Candido Amantini, in examining a young Spanish nun who was suspected of being possessed. One afternoon, while Amantini was interviewing the bedridden nun in the presence of Nicola and three other witnesses, she appeared to rise six feet in the air and remain suspended for thirty seconds or longer. This episode eventually came to serve as the inspiration for the famous levitation scene in *The Exorcist,* but to this day Nicola is disinclined to believe the testimony of his own eyes.

"Everyone in the room saw her body levitate," he told me. "At least this was our experience. We saw it, but I'm *not* saying the body levitated. Quite frankly, I don't believe it actually did levitate. We may have been involved in a situation of mutual hypnosis. Or, from my researches in parapsychology, I'd propose it might have been psychokinesis. The point is, you can't jump to conclusions. You can't assume that the demonic is present. You have to rule out these other possibilities."

Tall and handsome and in his early seventies, Nicola still investigates the occasional case, but for the most part in recent years he's been out of the loop, a concerned outsider looking on. And he's not entirely certain he approves of what he's seen.

"I don't want to give the impression of knowing more than I really do," he said. "As Damien Karras said in the movie, 'There are no experts in this field.' This is one of the first things I told Blatty and Friedkin when they invited me up to New York for an interview. So I might be wrong, but I'm concerned about the direction things seem headed. The televised exorcism of that poor girl Gina on *20/20* some years back was utterly bizarre. She probably shouldn't have received an exorcism at all, let alone a televised one. From my vantage point, some of the priests doing exorcisms these days are too rash, too loose and easy with their investigations. Why do we have all these exorcisms? Are they all absolutely necessary? Somehow I doubt they are."

O ver a two-year period I personally sat in on about a dozen Catholic exorcisms. Unlike Father Nicola, I never personally witnessed levitation or any other spectacular effects—demonic or otherwise. I did, however, hear reports of such effects taking place at exorcisms I was unable to attend—a middle-aged man rising four feet in the air during the preliminary stages of an exorcism conducted on the East Coast; a hugely obese woman in the Midwest levitating in her chair, despite the efforts of three people to hold her down. I have no way of vouching for the historical truthfulness of reports such as these, which were relayed to me by people of considerable intelligence and integrity, if not exactly sterling impartiality. When I asked why these effects always seemed to occur at exorcisms I had just missed or was prevented from attending, but never at ones where I was present, my informants answered in one of two ways. Some said it was probably just the luck of the draw. Others suggested it was because Satan, knowing I was a writer and not wanting to blow his cover, was deliberately keeping me in the dark about his very real powers to possess people.

If Satan really was concerned with avoiding publicity, I should have been the least of his worries. In January of 1999 the news media were gift-wrapped another cycle of stories on satanic possession when the Vatican published a revised version of the Roman Catholic rite of exorcism. (The exorcisms I attended for this research were among the last in the United States conducted according to the older rite, which had stood substantially unchanged since its publication by Pope Paul V in 1614.) The new rite dispenses with most of the baroque epithets (Prince of Darkness, Accursed Dragon, and so forth) that figured prominently in the older one, and it underlines the importance of subjecting all cases of suspected demonization to intensive psychiatric examination. For the most part, however, the media weren't interested in the theological niceties of the new exorcism rite. What they wanted were the spinning heads. New rite? Old rite? What's the difference? Just bring on the exorcisms. Where were they taking place? And who was performing them?[3]

The truth is, officially sanctioned Catholic exorcisms are being performed today in practically every country in the world with a significant Catholic population. Some of these countries are more exorcism-intensive than others. Italy in particular is a hot spot (several exorcists were appointed in the diocese of Turin alone during the late eighties), and the United States seems on its way to becoming one. Theologically conservative bishops are far more inclined to appoint exorcists than are more liberal bishops, and the exorcists they appoint tend to share their theological conservatism. There are very few liberals, it would seem, in demonic foxholes.[4]

It's difficult to say how many officially appointed Catholic exorcists there are worldwide today, but it's almost certainly more than a hundred and fifty and probably somewhere less than three hundred. This is a significant increase over just six or seven years ago, but hardly a staggering number. Even today the Catholic exorcist remains something of a rare breed.

As their numbers have grown in recent years, Catholic exorcists have started communicating with one another across national boundaries and even taken an initial stab at forming their own guild of sorts. In the summer of 1992 the International Association of Exorcists held its first biannual meeting in Rome, and at the meeting two years later the eighty-three exorcists and medical professionals in attendance elected Father Gabriele Amorth, the chief exorcist of Rome, as their first president. They couldn't have made a better choice. Urbane, tough, pious, and self-deprecating, Amorth is regarded by many of his peers as an exorcist's exorcist, and under his stewardship the association has rapidly taken on shape and purpose. For an annual dues the equivalent of thirty dollars, members receive a quarterly newsletter and are entitled to participate in both the biannual international conference and occasional national or regional conferences.

The newsletter alone is worth the price of admission. Exorcists talking shop, writing about their more challenging cases, swapping tips on technique, occasionally taking issue with one another over questions of theology and psychology—there's probably never been anything quite like it.

There's something else that comes out in the pages of the newsletter, besides the friendly jousting and news-from-the-front features. Catholic exorcists, apparently, aren't entirely happy with their status in the contemporary church. They feel underappreciated; they believe they're not always accorded the respect they deserve. They want to be recognized as true professionals—professionals of an unusual stripe, to be sure, but professionals nonetheless. Starting their own association was an important step in this direction. Setting stringent membership requirements was another. Only priests specifically authorized by their bishops to perform exorcisms, and so-called auxiliaries—medical professionals who assist duly authorized exorcists— are entitled to join. Charismatics, self-styled exorcists, half-baked exorcists, and anyone else not duly appointed needn't apply. As with any fledgling, status-seeking professional group, who's kept out is just as crucial as who's let in.

Another step that might be on the horizon, and that's discussed here and there in the newsletter, involves setting up a training program for exorcists, a concentrated course of study in demonology and demon-expulsion. In setting standards for treatment and precisely defining the field of specialization, such a program would be another way, as one exorcist put it to me, of separating "the real pros from the fakes and pretenders."

It's difficult to say what will come of initiatives such as these. For the moment, however, there's little question that Catholic exorcists (especially in the United States) suffer from a strange kind of status discrepancy. In the news and entertainment media they're generally portrayed as pop idols, dark-side warriors, the last of the lonesome gunfighters. In an age accustomed to finding its answers through yet another planning committee, yet another over-the-counter drug, exorcists stand defiantly apart, throwing everything on the line in midnight showdowns with grimacing, demonic evil. This isn't to say that the popular media necessarily take demonic possession and exorcism seriously, but it's fun and titillating and endlessly profitable to cavort with the possibility. In the irony-begetting-irony fashion of the day, the media create the myth of the sacrificial priest-exorcist out of scraps of truth and snatches of fiction, and then wind up half believing in their own creation.

When it comes to their own church, however, Catholic exorcists in the United States don't fare nearly so well. Mention the idea of demonic possession and exorcism to a gathering of Catholic academics, and you'll likely as not be rewarded with knowing snickers or mutterings of disbelief. The priest-exorcist as hero? Try again. Among the intellectual and leadership elites of American Catholicism, it's more likely the priest-exorcist as yesterday's man, the priest-exorcist as flake, the priest-exorcist as benighted loser. It's no accident that so few Catholic exorcists have been appointed in the United States over the past several decades. In the view of many of those calling the shots, the job probably isn't worth filling, and anyone willing to fill it probably isn't the kind of person you'd want anyway.

I certainly wouldn't characterize the Catholic exorcists I've met as flakes or losers. On the whole, they're solid, earnest, unpretentious men, trying to do their best in a strange business in which no one, as Father Nicola pointed out, can rightly claim expertise. I'm not sure, however, that all of them are ideally suited for the job. In my view the ideal Catholic exorcist is someone who, paradoxically, doesn't want to be an exorcist, someone who takes on the job with utmost reluctance and without any real expectation of encountering demonic evil. He is skeptical to a fault, perfectly willing—if confronted with something that tastes and sounds and feels like the demonic—to disbelieve the evidence of his own senses. The ideal exorcist is someone who'd just as soon not see any live action; he'd much rather keep his guns holstered.

The ideal Catholic exorcist, as I've described him here, sounds suspiciously like Damien Karras. And why not? In its first and most memorable crack at the subject, Hollywood actually got it right. William Peter Blatty's fictional exorcist is precisely the sort of person you'd want on the job. Karras certainly had no ambition to become an exorcist, and he initially dismissed the idea that Regan, the young girl he'd been asked to help, might actually be possessed. Even while investigating her case, he seemed determined to deliver a straightforwardly secular verdict. Regan was obviously suffering from some horrible affliction, but demonic possession was just about the last thing Karras wanted (or expected) to find. Only at the very end, when Regan's demons revealed themselves to monstrous effect, was he forced to concede that the unthinkable had really happened.

This as much as anything else, Karras's hard-boiled skepticism, his refusal to resort to exorcism until all the evidence was in, accounts for his enduring appeal in American popular culture. Americans want their exorcisms, but they don't always want them cheap and easy. Karras paid the price; he took his investigation to the limit and went ahead with an exorcism for Regan only when he was convinced there was no other recourse.

Damien Karras has proven a tough act to follow. Next to him, some of the real-life Catholic exorcists I've met seem a bit overeager, a bit too quick on the draw. They sometimes proceed to exorcism without exhausting all other options, and without the not-on-my-watch circumspection that seems so indispensable to the exorcist's role. Let there be no mistake: It is still exceedingly more difficult to obtain an official Catholic exorcism in the United States than it is virtually any other kind of exorcism. But it isn't as difficult as it probably should be. Catholic exorcism is a rarity among religious rituals. It seems actually to lose value unless it is performed only under the most extraordinary circumstances—or not at all. Those who perform it more often than is absolutely necessary run the risk of trivializing both the ritual and the evil it is designed to combat.

They also run the risk of frittering away the cinematic legacy of Damien Karras. This is no small thing. Without Damien Karras, Catholic exorcism in the United States might very well have been dead and buried a long time ago.

conclusion

I f you believe you're demonized, and you want something done about it, there's no shortage of people in the United States these days willing to help out. Where you live—East Coast, West Coast, anywhere in between—how you make your living, your skin color, your bank account—none of this really matters. If you're determined to get an exorcism, chances are you'll succeed in getting one. It might not be your exorcism of first choice, it might not get the job done to your complete satisfaction, but it'll at least be a start. And if you're not satisfied with the results, there's no reason you couldn't shop around for a second or even a third exorcism somewhere down the line.

Because here's the thing: Exorcism is more readily available today in the United States than perhaps ever before. It's not a procedure you'd necessarily brag about undergoing. It's not something that's generally spoken of in polite company. But it's most certainly available, and within certain sectors of the population it's in hot demand.

This, of course, isn't the way things were supposed to play out. For some time now, academics have been declaring that Satan was all but dead and buried in the United States.[1] In the brave new world of CNN, online wish fulfillment, and professional spin-doctoring, there was supposed to be no space, no elbow room, no room whatsoever, for belief in a personal agent of supernatural evil—let alone one who routinely sends out spiritual underlings to take care of some of his nastier business. Satan's day, we were assured, had come and gone.

Well, not yet anyway—maybe sometime later, but not just yet. For a significant minority of Americans, Satan and his henchmen are still very much alive, working double-time spreading misery and menace across the land. It's among Americans such as these that exorcism is most commonly practiced, and in their hands the ritual isn't just some medieval hand-me-down, or a scream-in-the-dark B-movie contrivance. Rather, it's a spiritual weapon of utmost, life-and-death importance.

Many of these true believers in exorcism are Christians of various persuasions, and they justify their convictions regarding demons and demon-expulsion by invoking the traditional teachings and practices of the Christian church. Didn't Jesus Himself regularly perform exorcisms during His earthly ministry? And didn't Jesus explicitly commission His followers to take up His ministry of demon-expulsion and spiritual warfare? Hasn't the Roman Catholic Church, through its forbidding rite of exorcism, always conceded the possibility of demonic possession? And haven't the major Protestant denominations, at least until relatively recently, recognized the pervasive threat of malevolent spiritual forces? In combating demonic powers through exorcism, true believers claim, they are standing faithfully (and defiantly) within a two-thousand-year-old religious tradition.

This may be so—but they are also standing within another, far more recent tradition. While true believers may be reluctant to admit it, the practice of exorcism in contemporary America has also been deeply influenced by the popular entertainment industry. Just consider. During the mid-seventies, after decades of neglect, decades of near-invisibility, exorcism suddenly became a raging concern. Almost overnight, untold numbers of people were complaining of being afflicted by demons, and new exorcism ministries couldn't spring up fast enough to meet the soaring demand. So how can we account for this? Was there really—*really and truly*—a sudden onslaught of demonism in America at the time? Did evil spirits, perhaps awakening from a

decades-long slumber, suddenly begin infesting people as never before? Well, this may have been what happened—we wouldn't want to
rule out the possibility—but we don't know for sure.

There is, however, something we do know for sure. Exorcism became a raging concern in the United States only when the popular entertainment industry jacked up the heat. Only with the release of *The
Exorcist* and the publication of *Hostage to the Devil* and all the rest of it
did fears of demonization become widespread. This we do know for
sure. And the inference seems clear. The dramatically increased market for exorcism that surfaced in the United States during the 1970s
was generated—there's no way around it—it was generated in large
measure by the mesmer-minds of the entertainment business.
Exorcism—contemporary American-style exorcism—was a box-office
smash, practically speaking, before it was anything else. Hollywood
and New York City called the shot; a highly suggestible public took
care of the rest.

But can this be true? Am I really suggesting that the popular entertainment industry, with all its dreck and drivel, is capable of manipulating—actually *manipulating*—religious beliefs and behavior?
Indeed, this is one of the main contentions of the present study, and
there seems nothing (to my mind) especially far-fetched about it. Like
it or not, the products of Hollywood and the tabloid media are an inescapable fact of life in contemporary America. Taken together, they
constitute the inevitable background buzz of daily existence, the lin-
gua franca of the nation's nervously jostling tribes. No less (and probably quite a bit more) than the religious sermon or town hall meeting
of yesteryear, they play a crucial role in shaping public sentiment and
engaging the national psyche. Why should religiously inclined
Americans be less susceptible to their charms than anyone else? When
Hollywood or Oprah or Madison Avenue advertises the existence of
demons and satanic cults, it is hardly surprising that at least some
Americans will comport themselves accordingly. The only surprise, in
my view, is that scholars of religion in the United States have been so
slow to make this connection.

Let me be perfectly clear. In making the connection here, I am not suggesting that everyone who encounters demons and exorcism at the movie theater or on television will automatically jump off the deep end. In the suggestibility department, not all women and men are created equal. For many Americans (and here I merely state the obvious), Hollywood shock-pieties such as *The Exorcist* are little more than disposable commodities, morsels of amusement for after-hours consumption. It's only among people who are already disposed, for one reason or another, to believe in demons and exorcism that they may sometimes amount to more than this. You have to want to believe, or need to believe, before you take the plunge. Not everyone, needless to say, takes the plunge.

But plenty of people have taken it. Over the past thirty years plenty of people have needed or wanted an exorcism badly enough to go looking for one. They've gone looking for exorcisms not just because of the hypnotic powers of Hollywood, not just because of a personal belief in demons, but also because they've lived in a culture where getting an exorcism makes a certain kind of sense. Exorcism may be a strange therapy, it may be the crazy uncle of therapies, but it's a therapy nonetheless. And no less than any of the countless other therapies in the therapy-mad culture of post-sixties America, it promises liberation for the addicted, hope for the forlorn, solace for the brokenhearted. It promises a new and redeemed self, a self freed from the accumulated debris of a life badly lived or a life sadly endured.

But does it work? Does exorcism, when all is said and done, actually deliver on its promises? Does it bring relief or freedom or wholeness? And—the million-dollar question—*does it really deliver people from demons?*

It's the demons I'm most often asked about. People who've heard I've been doing research on exorcism, their curiosity piqued, will usually sidle up to the topic.

So have you actually seen any exorcisms? they ask. Been right there while they're taking place?

Yes, I say. I've seen quite a few.

But what about Catholic exorcisms? Have you managed to see any Catholic exorcisms?

(Forget about any other kind of exorcism. Let's cut to the chase. Tell us about the real stuff, the righteous Hollywood stuff.)

So I tell them, yes, I have seen some Catholic exorcisms.

And then, invariably, an expectant pause, a hopeful pause, followed by the question, usually asked haltingly, often in a near-whisper.

So did you see anything . . . well, you know?

Sure, I know. No need to spell it out. Did I see anything . . . weird? bizarre? freakish? Did I see spinning heads . . . levitating bodies . . . prodigious vomiting . . . soft flesh tortured by blood-red letters? Did I see (taste? feel? hear?) . . . well, you know, demons? Did I find evidence of real, snarling, nasty supernatural evil?

I've had this conversation with a wide variety of people—some deeply religious, some not religious in the least. They all want to know about the demons. Some of them take up a tone of self-protective irony, but they still want to know. They're genuinely curious—and they're half hoping I'll confirm what they've heard only from Hollywood. They're half hoping I'll tell them something juicy, something outrageous, something they'd never admit to wanting to hear— something they'd certainly never admit to believing. Most of all, they want to know this: Does exorcism really work as it's advertised? Does it really succeed in driving out . . . *demons*?

The truth is, I don't know about the demons. I've personally witnessed more than fifty exorcisms—and this isn't even counting the occasions where I've seen dozens of people undergoing exorcism all at once. And I still don't know.

I started out this research with an attitude I'd characterize as "open-minded Canadian skepticism." I wasn't expecting to encounter demons—especially not the ripsnorting, mind-blowing demons of popular imagination—but I was entirely open to being surprised. If something happened during an exorcism that defied rational explanation, that seemed to reek of supernatural evil, I was committed to reporting it. Hell, I would have been happy reporting it. But nothing happened—at least nothing startling, nothing that reached out and grabbed me by the throat. At the exorcisms I attended, there were no spinning heads, no levitating bodies, no voices from beyond the grave. (There was plenty of vomiting, no question about it, but nothing more impressive than what you'd probably catch most Saturday nights out behind your local bar.) I wasn't counting on demonic fireworks, but neither was I counting them out. After all was said and done, more than fifty exorcisms—no fireworks, none at all.

At least none that I could make out. Occasionally I found myself in a situation where I was the odd man out, the party pooper of all party poopers. Just about everyone else on hand would claim to see something extraordinary, and they'd be disappointed—confused and disappointed—that I hadn't seen it also.

"But you must have seen the body rising. The rest of us saw it. It clearly rose two, maybe three feet off the chair. How could you not have seen it?"

"I'm sorry, but I didn't see it. I was looking as hard as I could, and I didn't see it."

No, I didn't see it, and the reason I didn't? There was nothing to be seen. People tend to be so keyed up during an exorcism, so eager to sink their fingers into something preternatural, that they easily convince themselves they're seeing, hearing, or feeling things that simply aren't there—not *really* there—to be seen, heard, or felt. As for myself, open-mindedly skeptical, skeptically open-minded, I was ready for any kind of action, but I was determined not to fall into the trap of conjuring things up just to suit the mood of the occasion. What I saw (I'm quite sure) was actually there to be seen; what I didn't see . . . well, I'm afraid not.

So what did I see? Some of the people who showed up for exorcisms seemed deeply troubled, some mildly troubled, and some hardly troubled at all. The symptoms they complained of—the addictions and compulsions, the violent mood swings, the blurred self-identities, the disturbing visions and somatic sensations—all of this seemed to me fully explainable in social, cultural, medical, and psychological terms. There seemed no compelling need, no need whatsoever, to bring demons into the equation. Bringing them in seemed superfluous, a matter of explanatory overkill.

The same with the antics I sometimes witnessed while the exorcisms were actually taking place, the flailing and slithering, the shrieking and moaning, the grimacing and growling—none of this, insofar as I could tell, suggested the presence of demons. It was sometimes an attempt (poignant? pathetic?) to satisfy the dramatic needs of the moment, it was sometimes an exercise in sheer self-indulgence, and it was sometimes an indication of profound personal distress. But demons? Here again, I saw no evidence of them; I saw nothing that had me itching to make a break for the door.

But I don't want to get too far ahead of myself. I don't want to make out that I know more than I really do. Let's consider a few possibilities. Maybe I was simply hitting the wrong exorcisms. Maybe the really hot action was always taking place just around the corner or the week just before I showed up. Maybe demons really were on the scene at some of the exorcisms I attended, but I was too spiritually obtuse to notice them. Maybe, to paraphrase Dr. John, I was looking in the right place at the wrong time, the wrong place at the right time.

There's something to be said for these possibilities. The mere fact that I didn't come across any spinning heads doesn't mean there haven't been spinning heads at exorcisms performed someplace else. And who says you need spinning heads anyway? Who says that demons always have to announce their presence by chewing up the scenery?

And who says, finally, that if you're suffering from some diagnosable psychiatric condition, you can't also be demonized? Why should the first diagnosis necessarily rule out the second? If demons actually exist, who can really claim to be an expert on their preferred modes of operation?

If demons exist . . . More than fifty exorcisms later I'm still in no position to pass judgment on this. All I can say is that my fifty-plus exorcisms turned up no definitive evidence of their existence. And right now this is all I have to go on.

But here's something else: Some of the people I met during my research claimed to have experienced significant improvement in their personal lives as a result of undergoing exorcism. Their depression lifted, their fears fled, their inner torments dissipated, their blues melted away. I have no way of knowing how extensive this improvement was, or how long-lived, or whether the people who told me about it were always telling the truth. But let's say, for the sake of argument, that they *were* telling the truth, and that their exorcisms really *did* have positive therapeutic impact. How can we account for this? How is it that exorcism works, unless it's by doing what it's supposed to do, namely, driving out demons?

Well, it's quite possible that exorcism sometimes works, but this need not have anything to do with the driving out of demons. What it has to do with, in all likelihood, is something I broached earlier in the chapter on charismatic exorcism: the placebo effect.

In psychotherapy—indeed, in virtually any medical procedure— the expectation of getting better may contribute a great deal to one's actually getting better. Simply receiving treatment—*any* kind of treatment, but especially treatment in a supportive healing environment— is the ticket at least partway home. The medical sciences have always strongly suspected as much, that suggestion and expectancy are powerful inducements to healing, and today only the most hardened scissors-and-scalpel skeptic would argue otherwise. Thanks to recent research on the subject, we now know for certain that the placebo effect is unquestionably real and sometimes quite powerful—so powerful, in fact, that some researchers have recommended that it actually be incorporated into clinical practice. If you're given pharmacologically inert drugs (dummy pills) for depression, food allergies, even heart problems, chances are your condition will improve. If you're given a bogus operation (*pretend* surgery!) for arthritic pain in the knees, chances are the pain will subside or disappear altogether. The placebo might not work (it doesn't work for everybody), its effects might not be long-lasting, but this shouldn't obscure the basic point. For many people the symbolic aspects of healing—the sympathetic attention of a therapist, the ministrations of a physician, the bolstered hope and renewed optimism that derive simply from *being* in a healing situation—for many people intangibles such as these may go a long way toward actually improving health.[2]

Now, if placebos can be effective when administered in the relatively antiseptic confines of a doctor's office or a consultation room, imagine the possibilities in the emotional swelter-box of an exorcism. Most people who seek out an exorcism are suffering from some psychological or emotional problem that they're convinced has been caused by demons. They believe that demons are just as real, if not quite so obvious, as anything else in the world and that only through an exorcism will their problem be eliminated and their circumstances improved. They anticipate walking away from the exorcism with a new lease on life. The person charged with performing the exorcism and the supporting cast of friends, family members, and assistants anticipate the same thing. All parties to the exorcism have an enormous investment in the affair: They want it to work, they expect it to work, they pray for it to work. The symbolic universe they inhabit, with its shared religious meanings and discourse, demands that it work. It doesn't always work, of course, but often enough (if only temporarily) it seems to. And little wonder—exorcism is a ritualized placebo, a placebo writ large, one that engages its participants on levels to which more conventional therapeutic procedures could scarcely aspire.

Here again, exorcism is more in tune with the Zeitgeist than one might imagine. In recent years increasing numbers of Americans have started experimenting with alternative medical therapies. Unhappy with the current state of the medical establishment—its impersonality, its technology, its bureaucratic chilliness—they've sought healing through the soothing, cottage-door remedies of a dizzying array of herbalists, homeopaths, acupuncturists, diet gurus—you name it. Though I wouldn't want to stretch the point too far, exorcism may be regarded as part of this scene, on its fringes perhaps, but part of it nonetheless. It, too, advertises a drug-free, X-ray-free, incision-free approach to restored health. It promises to mend not just the body and the mind but the soul as well. It's an alternative medical therapy for those who see demons, not cholesterol, not toxic particles, not environmental stress or genetic predisposition—no, not any of these, not primarily anyway—but rather demons, real glowering, hell-bent-on-evil demons as the major scourge of our time.

So exorcism, let's say, may sometimes work, though not most likely (or not very often) in precisely the way it's advertised. This is the positive side. But there's also a negative side. It doesn't always work, and in some cases it's downright detrimental. Some people, as we've seen, are bullied or badgered into undergoing exorcism. For others it's simply a cop-out or a means of self-glamorization. They want to avoid responsibility for their own shortcomings by blaming them on demons. Or they derive some perverse thrill from casting themselves in the role of demoniac. It's difficult to imagine anything good coming from exorcisms carried out under circumstances such as these. Emotional extortion, moral evasion, vainglory—this is what exorcism can sometimes amount to.

It can sometimes amount to even worse; sometimes exorcism can actually prove fatal. We've all heard the stories. In March 1995 a group of overzealous ministers connected to a tiny Pentecostal sect in the San Francisco Bay Area pummeled a woman to death while trying to evict her demons. Two years later a Korean Christian woman was stomped to death by a deacon and two missionaries operating out of a church in Glendale, California. The three men had gotten carried away trying to expel a demon they believed was lodged in the woman's chest. The same year, on the other side of the country, a five-year-old Bronx girl died after her mother and grandmother forced her to drink a lethal cocktail containing ammonia, vinegar, and olive oil and then bound and gagged her with duct tape. The two women claimed that they were merely trying to poison a demon that had infested the little girl several days earlier.[3]

There are other true stories of exorcisms gone horribly wrong, none more heartrending than Charity Miranda's. In 1998, on a cold Sunday afternoon in January, Charity Miranda spent her final hours undergoing exorcism at the hands of her mother, Vivian, and her sisters Serena and Elisabeth at their home in Sayville, Long Island. At one point, as fifteen-year-old Elisabeth subsequently informed the police, "Mom put her mouth to Charity's mouth and told her to blow the demon into her and she would try to kill it." When this didn't work, their mother said, "I'm sorry, girls, this isn't Charity. It's taken over her." She then tried to destroy the demon by smothering Charity with pillows. This also didn't work, so she picked up a plastic bag that was lying on the living room floor. Elisabeth Miranda told the police what happened next: "Mom placed the bag over Charity's head. Serena was holding Charity's body down because it was fighting. My mom told me to leave and I went into her bedroom." When Elisabeth, sometime later, came back into the living room, the job was finished. "Serena was pacing. Mom said don't be sad because that wasn't Charity, don't be attached to the body . . . The three of us went into my mom's room and she was saying don't cry because Charity left that body long before. We held hands on the bed and listened to my grandfather's favorite Frank Sinatra music."

Charity Miranda was seventeen years old and a cheerleader at Sayville High School. Her friends informed reporters that she'd been looking forward to starting college the next fall.[4]

Cases such as this, I should emphasize, are very much the exception. The vast majority of exorcisms are relatively innocuous affairs. They might not add up to much permanent good, but neither do they end in tragedy.

There is no evidence that Charity Miranda's mother and sisters, or Charity herself, got their beliefs about demons and exorcism from the popular entertainment industry.[5] But many Americans do. This is where many Americans, if only partially and indirectly, do in fact get such beliefs. And why not? At a time when traditional sources of religious authority have lost much of their previous prestige, it is little wonder that people should sometimes take their spiritual leads from the culturally sanctified products of Hollywood and the *Times* bestseller list. The cheesy scripts of *Star Trek* as Holy Writ? William Peter Blatty's *The Exorcist* as religious inspiration? More and more today, this is the climate in which we find ourselves.

One final note. In September 2000 a newly restored director's cut of *The Exorcist* was released to moviehouses around the country. It was the cinematic event of the season, inciting yet another jag of media-obsessed demon-and-exorcism blather. For a solid month, or so it seemed, you couldn't pick up a newspaper, flip through a magazine, or turn on the television without coming up against it. More than a quarter century after Damien Karras first smoldered across the screen, exorcism was still sexy, still very much in demand, still panted after. It hadn't lost a thing.

Exorcism in turn-of-the-century America may be regarded as a peculiarly modern-day religious syncretism. Drawing its inspiration from traditional religious symbolism, pop culture iconography, and current notions of psycho-spiritual healing, exorcism is a pastiche of curiously disjointed yet mutually enhancing elements. In this respect, understanding exorcism might very well be helpful toward understanding religion more generally at the dawn of the new millennium.

Notes

CHAPTER ONE

1. Bill Brinkley, "Priest Frees Mt. Rainier Boy Reported Held in Devil's Grip," *Washington Post* (August 20, 1949); quoted in William Peter Blatty, *William Peter Blatty on 'The Exorcist' from Novel to Film* (New York: Bantam Books, 1974), p. 4. For additional background on the Mount Rainier case, see Juan B. Cortés, S.J., and Florence M. Gatti, *The Case Against Possessions and Exorcisms* (New York: Vantage Press, 1975), pp. 70–84, 96.

2. This incident was ostensibly witnessed by a physics professor from Washington University, who later remarked that "there is much we have yet to discover concerning the nature of electromagnetism." See Blatty, *William Peter Blatty on 'The Exorcist' from Novel to Film*, pp. 23–24.

3. On reports that Regan's mother was modeled after Shirley MacLaine, see Blatty, *William Peter Blatty on 'The Exorcist' from Novel to Film*, pp. 25, 29.

4. Merrin is apparently based in part on Teilhard de Chardin. See Peter Travers and Stephanie Reiff, *The Story Behind 'The Exorcist'* (New York: Crown Publishers, 1974), p. 107.

5. William Peter Blatty, *The Exorcist* (New York: Harper & Row, 1971), p. 286.

6. Blatty, *The Exorcist*, p. 311.

7. Pauline Kael's review appeared in the January 7, 1974, issue of *The New Yorker.* For Canby's and Landau's review excerpts, see Travers and Reiff, *The Story Behind 'The Exorcist,'* pp. 150, 158–59.

8. See Travers and Reiff, *The Story Behind 'The Exorcist',* pp. 163–65, 176, 178–83; "Good, Evil and 'The Exorcist': A Discussion with a Theologian," *The*

Catholic News (February 14, 1974), pp. 1–11; and Colin L. Westerbeck, Jr., "The Banality of Good," *Commonweal* (March 1, 1974), pp. 532–33. The February 2, 1974, issue of *America* featured review essays by Donald R. Campion (p. 65), Richard A. Blake (pp. 66–68), Robert E. Lauder (pp. 68–70), Robert Boyle (pp. 70–72), and Moira Walsh (pp. 72–73).

9. Father Bermingham was cast in the movie as the president of Georgetown University. He passed away several months after our interview.

10. See Rev. John J. Nicola, *Diabolical Possession and Exorcism* (Rockford, Ill.: Tan Books, 1974); Cortés and Gatti, *The Case Against Possessions and Exorcisms;* Sybil Leek, *Driving Out the Devils* (New York: Putnam, 1975); Martin Ebon, *The Devil's Bride* (New York: Harper & Row, 1974); Travers and Reiff, *The Story Behind 'The Exorcist';* and Martin Ebon (ed.), *Exorcism: Fact, Not Fiction* (Bergenfield, N.J.: Signet, 1974).

CHAPTER TWO

1. For Malachi Martin's life and times, see Marian Christy, "The Freedom of Faith," *Boston Globe* (March 16, 1986); Lorenzo Carcaterra, "Malachi Martin: Going His Way," *Daily News* (March 16, 1986); and Tom Kelly, "'Jesuits' Stirs Papal Dispute," *Washington Times* (March 5, 1987). On the sexual-scandal front, see Peter Hebblethwaite, *Paul VI: The First Modern Pope* (Mahwah, N.J.: Paulist Press, 1993), p. 723.

2. *Hostage to the Devil* (New York: Reader's Digest Press/Thomas Y. Crowell Company, 1976).

3. The most famous of Martin's conspiracy tracts is *The Jesuits: The Society of Jesus and the Betrayal of the Roman Catholic Church* (New York: Simon and Schuster, 1987). For critical appraisals, see James M. Cameron, "Looking for Lucifer," *New York Review of Books* (June 25, 1987); and George G. Higgins, "Malachi Martin's 'The Jesuits,'" *America* (March 21, 1987).

4. Martin (p. 17) claims that these stages of exorcism were initially given to him by "one of the most experienced exorcists I have known." I have collapsed several of Martin's stages in order to arrive at this more schematic and analytically crisp formulation.

5. Francine du Plessix Gray, "Hostage to the Devil," *New York Times Book Review* (March 14, 1976); Peter S. Prescott, "The Possessed," *Newsweek* (March 8, 1976); Norris Merchant, "Hostage to the Devil," *Commonweal* (August 27, 1976); and John Nicola, "Sermon of Admonition," *National Review* (May 28, 1976).

6. Malachi Martin passed away on July 27, 1999.

CHAPTER THREE

1. Kaplan's odyssey is recounted in Stephen Kaplan and Roxanne Salch Kaplan, *The Amityville Horror Conspiracy* (Laceyville, Pa.: Belfry Books, 1995). The séance, which was the first of three in which the Warrens participated at 112 Ocean Avenue, was televised February 24, 1976, on Channel 5 (see Kaplan and Kaplan, p. 4). See also Jay Anson, *The Amityville Horror* (New York: Prentice-Hall, 1977), pp. 362–67.

2. Gerald Brittle, *The Demonologist: The True Story of Ed and Lorraine Warren, the World-Famous Exorcism Team* (New York: St. Martin's Press, 1980).

3. Ed and Lorraine Warren with Robert David Chase, *Ghost Hunters: True Stories from the World's Most Famous Demonologists* (New York: St. Martin's Press, 1989), p. 71.

4. Robert Curran (with Jack and Janet Smurl and Ed and Lorraine Warren), *The Haunted: One Family's Nightmare* (New York: St. Martin's Press, 1988), pp. 226–27.

5. *The Demon Murder Case* was a 1983 NBC television movie. For the Warrens' account of the case, see *Ghost Hunters*, pp. 87–97.

6. On Catholic traditionalism in the United States, see Michael W. Cuneo, *The Smoke of Satan* (Baltimore: Johns Hopkins University Press, 1999), pp. 81–119.

CHAPTER FOUR

1. The two sequels are *Exorcist II: The Heretic* (1977) and *The Exorcist III* (1990). Other exorcism-related movies of the period include *Abby* (1974), *Night Child* (1975), *Kung Fu Exorcist* (1976), *The Possessed* (1977), *The Child* (1977), *Good Against Evil* (1977), *Beyond the Living* (1977), *The Coming* (1980), *Boogeyman* (1980), *The Evil Dead* (1980), *The Entity* (1982), *Dead of Night* (1987), and *My Demon Lover* (1987). Ed and Lorraine Warren make an appearance in the 1991 Fox television movie *The Haunted*. For an insightful discussion of movies of this genre, see Stanley Rothman, "Is God Really Dead in Beverly Hills?" *American Scholar* (Spring 1996): 272–78.

2. For a balanced overview of the charismatic renewal movement, see Richard Quebedeaux, *The New Charismatics II* (New York: Harper & Row, 1983). For useful sociological accounts of Roman Catholic charismatics, see Meredith B. McGuire, *Pentecostal Catholics* (Philadelphia: Temple University

Press, 1982); and Mary Jo Neitz, *Charisma and Community* (New Brunswick, N.J.: Transaction, 1987).

3. M. Scott Peck, M.D., *The Road Less Traveled* (New York: Simon & Schuster, 1978). For a summary of reviews, see *Current Biography Yearbook* (1991), pp. 441–45.

4. M. Scott Peck, M.D., *People of the Lie: The Hope for Healing Human Evil* (New York: Touchstone, 1983), p. 196.

5. *People of the Lie*, pp. 197, 200–202.

6. See, for example, Judith Rascoe, "Breaking the Self-Help Habit," *New York Times Book Review* (January 1, 1984), p. 10.

7. See "Playboy Interview: M. Scott Peck," *Playboy* (March 1991), pp. 43–62. Peck gets worked over a bit in John Colapinto's "M. Scott Peck at the End of the Road," *Rolling Stone* (October 19, 1995), pp. 80–86, 164.

8. There is a voluminous literature on this subject. See, for example, Debbie Nathan, "Satanism and Child Molestation: Constructing the Ritual Abuse Scare," in James T. Richardson, Joel Best, and David G. Bromley (eds.), *The Satanism Scare* (New York: Aldine de Gruyter, 1991), pp. 75–94; Debbie Nathan, "The Ritual Sex Abuse Hoax," *Village Voice* (June 12, 1990), pp. 36–44; and T. Charlier and S. Downing, "Justice Abused: A 1980s Witchhunt," *Memphis Commercial Appeal* (January 1988, series).

9. For the best of the many books that have been written on this subject, see Richard Ofshe and Ethan Watters, *Making Monsters: False Memories, Psychotherapy, and Sexual Hysteria* (New York: Scribner, 1994); and Debbie Nathan and Michael Snedeker, *Satan's Silence: Ritual Abuse and the Making of a Modern American Witch Hunt* (New York: Basic Books, 1995).

10. See James T. Richardson, "Satanism in the Courts: From Murder to Heavy Metal," in Richardson, Best, and Bromley (eds.), *The Satanism Scare*, pp. 210–13; and William W. Zellner, *Countercultures* (New York: St. Martin's Press, 1995), pp. 87–88. For a different perspective, see Carl Raschke, *Painted Black* (San Francisco: Harper & Row, 1990), p. 171.

11. See Jerry Johnston, *The Edge of Evil: The Rise of Satanism in North America* (Dallas: Word Publishing, 1989), p. 4. For a critical assessment, see David G. Bromley, "Satanism: The New Cult Scare," in Richardson, Best, and Bromley (eds.), *The Satanism Scare*, pp. 56–59.

12. Zellner, *Countercultures*, pp. 77–79.

13. Kenneth Lanning, "Satanic, Occult, Ritualistic Crime: A Law Enforcement Perspective," *The Police Chief* (Fall 1989), p. 82.

14. For a point of view rather different from the one expressed in this paragraph, see Carl Raschke's *Painted Black*.

15. See Zellner, *Countercultures*, pp. 80–81.

CHAPTER FIVE

1. Richard N. Ostling, "No Sympathy for the Devil: A Cardinal Decries Satanic Influence," *Time* (March 19, 1990), pp. 55–56.

2. See Bill Turque, "The Exorcism of Gina," *Newsweek* (April 15, 1991), p. 62; and Thomas H. Stahel, "The Exorcism," *America* (April 27, 1991), pp. 472–73.

3. Father LeBar wouldn't tell me exactly where Father A was based, but he did assure me that it wasn't in the Archdiocese of New York. Contrary to rumors that had been set off by Cardinal O'Connor's "satanism" sermon six years earlier, the New York Archdiocese didn't even have an officially appointed exorcist during the late 1980s and early 1990s—and, in fact, hadn't had one since the post fell vacant in 1965. Nevertheless, it is fairly safe to infer that it was Father A (with Father LeBar serving as assistant) who had presided over the two exorcisms mentioned by Cardinal O'Connor the day of the "satanism" homily.

4. Ed and Lorraine Warren (with William Ramsey and Robert David Chase), *Werewolf: A True Story of Demonic Possession* (New York: St. Martin's Press, 1991). Frank Peretti's best-known book is *This Present Darkness* (Ventura, Calif.: Regal, 1986). For background on Peretti and his work, see Michael G. Maudlin, "Holy Smoke! The Darkness Is Back," *Christianity Today* (December 15, 1989), pp. 58–59.

5. Thomas B. Allen, *Possessed: The True Story of an Exorcism* (New York: Doubleday, 1993), p. 57. For background on Allen's book, see John M. McGuire, "Diary of an Exorcism," *St. Louis Post-Dispatch (Everyday Magazine)* (September 7, 1993). See also Ian Stevenson, "Possession and Exorcism: An Essay Review," *Journal of Parapsychology* 59 (1995): 69–76; and Emily Eakin, "Exorcising 'The Exorcist,'" *Brill's Content* (September 2000), pp. 86–91, 140. A movie based on Allen's book, directed by Steven de Souza and also called *Possessed*, aired on cable television in October 2000.

CHAPTER SIX

1. I have taken every effort here to conceal real-life identities, including the provision of pseudonyms and the alteration of potentially identifying personal details.

CHAPTER SEVEN

1. See "Rector and a Rumpus," *Newsweek* (July 4, 1960), p. 77; and "Speaking in Tongues," *Time* (August 15, 1960), pp. 53, 55. For a fuller account of the St. Mark's episode, see Richard Quebedeaux, *The New Charismatics II* (New York: Harper & Row, 1983), pp. 61–64; and Vinson Synan, *The Holiness-Pentecostal Tradition* (Grand Rapids, Mich.: William B. Eerdmans Publishing, 1997), pp. 227–30.

2. See Harvey Cox, *Fire from Heaven* (Reading, Mass.: Addison-Wesley, 1995), pp. 45–48. It has become something of a convention to date the beginning of the Pentecostal movement from the Azusa Street revival of 1906. The actual reality is somewhat more complicated. For an account of Pentecostal stirrings that preceded Azusa Street, see Synan, *The Holiness-Pentecostal Tradition*, pp. 1–83.

3. See Robert Mapes Anderson, *Vision of the Disinherited: The Making of American Pentecostalism* (New York: Oxford University Press, 1979). Although of humble origins, Pentecostalism would eventually succeed in winning a place for itself in the nation's religious and cultural mainstream. For an account of the challenges currently facing one of the leading Pentecostal denominations in America, see Margaret Poloma, *The Assemblies of God at the Crossroads* (Knoxville: University of Tennessee Press, 1989).

4. On the rapid growth of the charismatic renewal movement, see Synan, *The Holiness-Pentecostal Tradition*, pp. 220–64.

5. *The Cross and the Switchblade* (Old Tappan, N.J.: F. H. Revell, 1964); *They Speak with Other Tongues* (New York: Pyramid Books, 1965). For fuller accounts of the rise of Roman Catholic neo-Pentecostalism, see Terrence Robert Crowe, *Pentecostal Unity* (Chicago: Loyola University Press, 1993), pp. 55–109; and Synan, *The Holiness-Pentecostal Tradition*, pp. 234–52.

6. Anderson, *Vision of the Disinherited*, pp. 16–17.

7. Cox, *Fire from Heaven*, pp. 106–7.

8. Anderson, *Vision of the Disinherited*, p. 96. Anderson (pp. 96–97) astutely observes that the practice of exorcism declined within classical Pentecostalism with the gradual deemphasis of an imminent Second Coming eschatology. Nevertheless, I wouldn't want to stretch the point too far. Exorcism is still practiced within the classical Pentecostal tradition, though not nearly on so grand a scale as was once the case. During my research I observed Pentecostal exorcisms at a number of locations, including Pastor Ernest Angley's church in Akron, Ohio, and the Salvation and Deliverance Temple in Harlem.

9. Vinson Synan (interview: April 22, 1998) is dean of the School of

Divinity at Regent University in Virginia Beach and author of the magisterial *The Holiness-Pentecostal Tradition*. On this matter of exorcism within the classical Pentecostal tradition, I am also indebted to Pentecostal scholar David Moore (interviews: April 27, 1998; April 30, 1998). Moore is senior pastor of New Hope Church in Manteca, California. For helpful overviews, see Jacques Theron, "A Critical Overview of the Church's Ministry of Deliverance from Evil Spirits," *Pneuma: The Journal of the Society for Pentecostal Studies* 18 (1996): 79–92; and L. Grant McClung, Jr., "Pentecostal/Charismatic Understanding of Exorcism," in C. Peter Wagner and F. Douglas Pennoyer (eds.), *Wrestling with Dark Angels* (Ventura, Calif.: Regal Books, 1990), pp. 195–214. McClung (p. 196) rightly points out that "exorcism has been practiced but not formally theologized" within the classical Pentecostal tradition. Most historical accounts of Pentecostalism by Pentecostal scholars, in fact, include very few references to exorcism. See, for example, Edith L. Blumhofer, *The Assemblies of God*, Volume I (Springfield, Miss.: Gospel Publishing House, 1989).

10. Don Basham, *Deliver Us from Evil: The Story of a Man Who Dared to Explore the Censored Fourth of Christ's Ministry* (Grand Rapids, Mich.: Chosen Books, 1972), p. 73.

11. All biblical quotations not taken directly from my field notes are from the Revised Standard Version. See Francis MacNutt, *Deliverance from Evil Spirits: A Practical Manual* (Grand Rapids, Mich.: Chosen Books, 1995), pp. 37–38, for additional Gospel accounts of Jesus' exorcism ministry.

12. This episode is also recounted, in somewhat varied form, in Mark 5:1–20 and Luke 8:26–39. See MacNutt, *Deliverance from Evil Spirits*, p. 38.

13. *Deliver Us from Evil*, p. 55.

14. See McClung, Jr., "Pentecostal/Charismatic Understanding of Exorcism," pp. 206–7; and Gordon Lindsay, *Demon Manifestations and Delusion* (Dallas: Christ for the Nations, 1972), p. 23.

15. Basham, *Deliver Us from Evil*, pp. 101–6. See also Derek Prince, *Expelling Demons: An Introduction into Practical Demonology* (Fort Lauderdale, Fla., pamphlet, no date); and Derek Prince, *Spiritual Warfare* (Springdale, Pa.: Whitaker House, 1987). For autobiographical information on Prince, see Derek Prince, *Blessing or Curse* (Grand Rapids, Mich.: Chosen Books, 1990), pp. 262–63.

16. Basham, *Deliver Us from Evil*, pp. 107–201. H. A. Maxwell Whyte was pastor of a Pentecostal church in Toronto famous for its exuberant exorcism sessions. See his *Demons and Deliverance* (Springdale, Pa.: Whitaker House, 1989). It isn't surprising that Pentecostal pastors such as Derek Prince and Maxwell Whyte should play so prominent a role in helping Don Basham fashion his exorcism ministry. The boundaries between classical Pentecostalism and the charismatic movement were really quite fluid during these early years.

I am indebted to Margaret Poloma (interview: May 2, 1998) for her insights on this matter.

17. I received valuable background information on the early years of charismatic deliverance from Brick Bradford, a Presbyterian minister based in Oklahoma City (interview: May 2, 1998). A colleague of Bradford's, who has requested anonymity, was also helpful. The colleague said that he gave a radio interview on deliverance shortly after *The Exorcist* was released and was subsequently swamped with calls for help. Since then he has taken pains to operate more discreetly.

CHAPTER EIGHT

1. Barbara Shlemon Ryan (interview: April 20, 1998) provided me valuable information on the early days of charismatic deliverance. She is currently part of the leadership team of Beloved Ministry in Brea, California.

2. See Michael Scanlan, T.O.R., and Randall J. Cirner, *Deliverance from Evil Spirits* (Ann Arbor, Mich.: Servant Books, 1980); and Michael Harper, *Spiritual Warfare* (London: Hodder and Stoughton, 1970). Basham and Prince, it seems, visited the Word of God community in March 1970.

3. See Charles M. Irish, *Back to the Upper Room* (Nashville: Thomas Nelson, 1993). For background information on charismatic Episcopal deliverance, I am also indebted to the following people: Father Fred Goodwin (Episcopal Renewal Ministries; Marietta, Georgia), Father Roger Ames (St. Luke's Episcopal Church; Akron, Ohio), and Father Dean Heckle (Burlington, Wisconsin).

4. I am especially grateful to Bob Burmeister of North Heights Lutheran for his frank discussion, over the course of several interviews in 1998, of charismatic Lutheran deliverance ministry.

5. See Don W. Basham, *Can a Christian Have a Demon?* (Kirkwood, Miss.: Impact Books, 1991); and Erwin E. Prange, *Demons: Fact or Fantasy?* (unpublished manuscript, 1998).

6. Frank and Ida Mae Hammond, *Pigs in the Parlor: A Practical Guide to Deliverance* (Kirkwood, Miss.: Impact Books, 1996). See especially pp. 111–21.

7. Francis MacNutt, *Healing* (Altamonte Springs, Fla.: Creation House, 1988), p. 226. See also Francis MacNutt, *The Power to Heal* (Notre Dame, Ind.: Ave Maria Press, 1977). For an insightful, scholarly discussion of charismatic healing techniques, see Meredith B. McGuire, *Pentecostal Catholics* (Philadelphia: Temple University Press, 1982), pp. 131–39.

CHAPTER NINE

1. In my brief presentation of this case I have smudged any potentially identifying details.

2. On the "shepherding" controversy, see Richard Quebedeaux, *The New Charismatics II* (San Francisco: Harper & Row, 1983), pp. 138–42; Vinson Synan, *The Holiness-Pentecostal Tradition* (Grand Rapids, Mich.: William B. Eerdmans Publishing, 1997), pp. 264–66; and Terrence Robert Crowe, *Pentecostal Unity* (Chicago: Loyola University Press, 1993), pp. 44–47. David Moore (interviews: April 27, 1998; April 30, 1998) is currently writing a doctoral dissertation at Regent University on the controversy.

3. See Crowe, *Pentecostal Unity,* pp. 79–84.

4. On this theme, see Mary Jo Neitz, *Charisma and Community* (New Brunswick, N.J.: Transaction Books, 1987), pp. 227–36; and Quebedeaux, *The New Charismatics II,* pp. 229–30. Both Neitz and Quebedeaux broach the theme in more general terms, without specific reference to deliverance. See also Roy Wallis, "Varieties of Psychosalvation," *New Society* 20 (December 27, 1979), pp. 649–51.

5. For additional textual evidence on this point, see Michael Scanlan, T.O.R., and Randall J. Cirner, *Deliverance from Evil Spirits* (Ann Arbor, Mich.: Servant Books, 1980), pp. 37–52. See also the advertisements for books on deliverance in Frank and Ida Mae Hammond, *Pigs in the Parlor: A Practical Guide to Deliverance* (Kirkwood, Miss.: Impact Books, 1996), pp. 154–56.

6. "The Christian Ministry of Deliverance and Healing," An Interim Report to the Lord Archbishop of York (March 1974).

CHAPTER TEN

1. Cited in Richard Quebedeaux, *The New Charismatics II* (San Francisco: Harper & Row, 1983), p. 221.

2. See Michael Perry (ed.), *Deliverance: Psychic Disturbances and Occult Involvement* (London: SPCK, 1987), pp. 110–14. This book is produced by an Anglican organization called the Christian Exorcism Study Group. The Roman Catholic position is clearly laid out in Corrado Balducci, *The Devil,* translated by Jordan Aumann (New York: Alba House, 1990), pp. 166–71.

3. See Perry (ed.), *Deliverance,* pp. 110–14; and Balducci, *The Devil,* p. 162. Barbara Shlemon Ryan (interview: April 20, 1998) helped get me on track in the writing of this section.

4. *New Covenant*, a monthly magazine and the major publication of the Roman Catholic wing of the renewal, contained relatively few references to deliverance ministry throughout the 1980s.

5. Matthew 12:29 ("Or how can one enter a strong man's house and plunder his property, without first tying up the strong man? Then indeed the house can be plundered") is the scriptural passage most often invoked by charismatics as support for the practice of binding spirits. See Richard McAlear, O.M.I., and Elizabeth Brennan, "Deliverance: A Perspective from Experience," in Matthew Linn and Dennis Linn (eds.), *Deliverance Prayer: Experiential, Psychological and Theological Approaches* (New York: Paulist Press, 1981), pp. 160–73. For a scholarly assessment of "binding" see Thomas J. Csordas, *The Sacred Self* (Berkeley: University of California Press, 1994), pp. 175, 259–60.

6. Brennan still occasionally performs deliverance. McAlear, claiming burnout, left the ministry in 1990 and is now stationed in Washington, D.C., where he is vocation director of the Oblates for the Eastern U.S.A.

7. On this and other aspects of Roman Catholic deliverance ministry, I have also been helped by interviews with the following people: Abbot David Geraets (San Luis Obispo, California); Father Chris Aridas, Steve Benthel, and Felipe Sin (Long Island, New York); Dr. Bernard Klamecki and Dr. Margaret Schlientz (Milwaukee); Father Kenneth Metz (Kenosha, Wisconsin); Father Robert DeGrandis (Galveston, Texas); Father Hal Cohen, Rosemary Breaux, Sister Olga Rushing, and Edwin Besson (New Orleans); and Michele Needham-Greischar and Father Bob Sears (Chicago). For an impressively balanced approach to deliverance, see Michele Needham-Greischar's "And Deliver Us from Evil: Steps for Discernment and Deliverance Prayer," *Chariscenter USA* (October 1994), pp. 3–5; and "Psychotherapy and Christian Spiritual Healing: Case Studies Revealing God's Transforming Love," *Journal of Christian Healing* 13, 4 (1991): 12–27.

8. See Michael Scanlan, T.O.R., and Randall J. Cirner, *Deliverance from Evil Spirits* (Ann Arbor, Mich.: Servant Books, 1980), pp. 63–69; John B. Healey, S.T.L., "The Tradition for Charismatic Deliverance Prayer," in Linn and Linn (eds.), *Deliverance Prayer*, pp. 102–4; and Balducci, *The Devil*, pp. 166–71.

9. Cardinal Léon-Joseph Suenens, *Renewal and the Powers of Darkness*, translated by Olga Prendergast (Ann Arbor, Mich.: Servant Books, 1983), pp. 73–74, 96–103. On September 29, 1985, the Vatican's Congregation for the Doctrine of the Faith issued a letter to Catholic bishops throughout the world on the same subject. See Balducci, *The Devil*, p. 170.

10. See William P. Wilson, "Hysteria and Demons, Depression and Oppression, Good and Evil," in J. W. Montgomery (ed.), *Demon Possession* (Minneapolis: Bethany House, 1976), pp. 223–30.

11. See Aloysius Balawyder, *The History of ACT: Toward Wholeness and*

Holiness in the Healing Professions (Laurel, Md.: Association of Christian Therapists, 1995).

12. Meg Jones, "Woman Strives to Resume Life after Multiple Personality Ordeal," *Milwaukee Journal Sentinel* (November 29, 1997).

13. From the extensive charismatic literature on intergenerational healing and deliverance, see especially Kenneth McAll, *Healing the Family Tree* (London: Sheldon Press, 1984); and John H. Hampsch, *Healing Your Family Tree* (Everett, Wash.: Performance Press, 1986). For a sharply critical appraisal see David Powlison, *Power Encounters* (Grand Rapids, Mich.: Baker Books, 1995), pp. 126–27.

14. Not long after this encounter I had an opportunity to view an exorcism that was performed by Prange and televised on KARE-TV in Minneapolis on November 30, 1994. The subject of the exorcism was a clean-cut young man who had presumably fallen victim to demonic possession after watching the movie version of *Damn Yankees* on an oldies channel. He screamed and wailed and wept, while Prange, loudly commanding "Satan—begone! Satan—begone!" went about his business with grim determination.

15. See MacNutt's *Deliverance from Evil Spirits* (Grand Rapids, Mich.: Chosen Books, 1995), which is now the state-of-the-art charismatic work on deliverance.

16. Jerome D. Frank, *Persuasion and Healing: A Comparative Study of Psychotherapy* (New York: Schocken Books, 1974), pp. 325–30. See also M. J. Lambert, "The Individual Therapist's Contribution to Psychotherapy Process and Outcome," *Clinical Psychology Review* 9 (1989): 469–86; and L. Grencavage and J. C. Norcross, "Where are the Commonalities among the Therapeutic Common Factors?" *Professional Psychology* 21 (1991): 372–78. Sociologists have tended to argue that charismatic deliverance may be positively functional in terms of both integrating individuals into their prayer groups and maintaining group boundaries. See, for example, Stephen Hunt, "Managing the Demonic: Some Aspects of the Neo-Pentecostal Deliverance Ministry," *Journal of Contemporary Religion* 13, 2 (1998): 215–30; and Meredith B. McGuire, *Pentecostal Catholics* (Philadelphia: Temple University Press, 1982), pp. 133–35. For a phenomenological assessment of deliverance, see Csordas, *The Sacred Self,* pp. 165–227.

17. I received valuable input in the writing of this section from Dr. Marvin Reznikoff of the department of psychology at Fordham University. Most practitioners of deliverance, it should be noted, would reject the idea that a psychiatric diagnosis necessarily rules out a demonic one. The psychiatric versus the demonic, in their view, is a false dichotomy. An individual may be psychologically sick *and* demonically afflicted at one and the same time. Indeed, they

would argue that the former condition may sometimes set the stage for the latter. This point is made frequently by MacNutt in *Deliverance from Evil Spirits.*

CHAPTER ELEVEN

1. I have employed pseudonyms for several of the subjects in this section.

2. Some of the more popular titles at the Hegewisch bookstore include the following: Win Worley, *Battling the Hosts of Hell—Diary of an Exorcist* (Lansing, Ill.: H.B.C., 1980); Win Worley, *Harassing the Hosts of Hell—Attack! Attack! Attack!* (Lansing, Ill.: H.B.C., 1993); Win Worley, *Holding Your Deliverance* (Lansing, Ill.: WRW Publications, 1992); Joan Hake Robie, *Reverse the Curse in Your Life* (Lancaster, Pa.: Starburst, 1991); John Eckhardt, *Deliverance Thesaurus: Demon Hit List* (Chicago: Crusaders Ministries, 1995); and *Blumhardt's Battle: A Conflict with Satan,* translated by Frank S. Boshold (New York: Thomas E. Lowe, 1970). The last title, a first-person account of a marathon exorcism performed by a German Lutheran pastor named Johann Christoph Blumhardt in the 1840s, has been enormously influential within certain exorcism circles in the United States.

CHAPTER TWELVE

1. Mark Wrolstad, "Tilton Uses New Style in Ministry," *Dallas Morning News* (February 28, 1995); Wister Jackson, "Former Members, Others Level Charges, Criticisms at Church," *Daily Courier,* Forest City, N.C. (February 28, 1995); " 'I Just Had to Get Out, Even if It Was Without My Daughter,' " *Daily Courier,* Forest City, N.C. (February 28, 1995); Gary Henderson, "Former Word of Faith Members Say Church Controlled Their Lives," *Spartanburg Herald-Journal* (March 19, 1995); and Marketta Gregory, "Exodus Crippled Small Fellowship," *Muskogee Daily and Times-Democrat* (September 29, 1997). I was provided additional information on the Spindale controversy by Ole Anthony of the Trinity Foundation in Dallas (interview: July 18, 1999); John Morehead of the TruthQuest Institute in Loomis, California (interview: May 20, 1999); and Craig Branch and Clete Hux of the Watchman Fellowship in Birmingham (interviews: May 8, 1998). See especially Clete Hux, "Spindale Word of Faith Fellowship," *Watchman Expositor* 12, 3 (1995), pp. 18, 21.

2. On the Faith Movement, see Hank Hanegraaff, *Christianity in Crisis* (Eugene, Oreg.: Harvest House, 1993); and D. R. McConnell, *A Different Gospel* (Peabody, Mass.: Hendrickson Publishers, 1995).

3. Marketta Gregory, "Shout at the Devil," *Muskogee Daily and Times-Democrat* (September 28, 1997), p. 7A.

CHAPTER THIRTEEN

1. I have disguised Hannah's real-life identity.

2. A brief word on terminology seems in order. I refer to the subjects of this and the following chapter as "Protestant evangelicals" because this is their own preferred self-designation. They do not, by and large, refer to themselves as "fundamentalists," and they take special pains to distinguish themselves from Pentecostals or charismatics. In a broader context, of course, it has become increasingly difficult of late to tell evangelicals and Pentecostals apart. Over the past twenty years the boundaries between evangelicalism and Pentecostalism, evangelicalism and the charismatic movement, have become increasingly fluid and porous.

3. See David Powlison, *Power Encounters* (Grand Rapids, Mich.: Baker Books, 1995).

4. I also attended, in November 1997, an evangelical exorcism and spiritual warfare conference that is held biannually in Gettysburg, Pennsylvania, and is sponsored by the Susek Evangelistic Association. The Sioux City and Gettysburg conferences are the two largest of their kind in the United States.

5. For a highly selective reading of recent evangelical books on exorcism and spiritual warfare, see the following: Mark I. Bubeck, *Overcoming the Adversary* (Chicago: Moody Bible Institute, 1984); Mark I. Bubeck, *Raising Lambs Among Wolves* (Chicago: Moody Press, 1997); C. Fred Dickason, *Demon Possession and the Christian* (Wheaton, Ill.: Crossway Books, 1987); Thomas B. White, *The Believer's Guide to Spiritual Warfare* (Ann Arbor, Mich.: Servant Publications, 1990); Timothy M. Warner, *Spiritual Warfare* (Wheaton, Ill.: Crossway Books, 1991); and Richard Ing, *Spiritual Warfare* (Springdale, Pa.: Whitaker House, 1996). Don Rogers, John Restea, and Dr. John D. Ellenberger helped clarify my thinking for the earlier sections of this chapter.

6. On the enormous suggestive powers of *The Exorcist*, even among evangelicals, see Mark I. Bubeck, *Overcoming the Adversary*, p. 13. For Merrill F. Unger's altered position on the issue of demonization, see his *Demons in the World Today* (Wheaton, Ill.: Tyndale House, 1971); and *What Demons Can Do to Saints* (Chicago: Moody Bible Institute, 1977). For an introduction to Kurt E. Koch's writings, see *Between Christ and Satan* (1965), *The Devil's Alphabet* (1971), and *Occult ABC* (1981), all of which were published by Kregel in Grand Rapids, Michigan.

7. See Mark I. Bubeck, *The Adversary* (Chicago: Moody Bible Institute,

1975). Ernest Rockstad operated Faith and Life Ministries out of Andover, Kansas. Two of his more popular teaching tapes were "Exposing and Dispatching Demons" and "Symptoms of Demonic Invasion." On Dean Hochstetler see "Hochstetler Ordained to Deliverance Ministry," *Gospel Evangel* (July/August 1986), p. 9. (*Gospel Evangel* is a publication of the Indiana/Michigan Conference of the Mennonite Church.) Yet another evangelical pioneer in this area was Victor Matthews, who taught at Grand Rapids Baptist Seminary during the 1960s. Several of my informants told me that Jessie Penn-Lewis's *War on the Saints* was an especially influential book during the formative years of evangelical deliverance. (It was republished in abridged form by Whitaker House in 1996.) On the popular appeal of Frank Peretti's novels (especially *This Present Darkness*, published in 1986 by Regal of Ventura, California), see Harvey Cox, *Fire from Heaven* (Reading, Mass.: Addison-Wesley, 1995), pp. 281–84. I owe a special word of thanks to Dr. Timothy M. Warner for helping me sort out these early influences.

8. The "dispensationalist" or "cessationist" theology that obtains within certain sectors of conservative Protestantism holds that spiritual gifts and miraculous signs were intended for the apostolic age—but not afterward.

9. The course was actually taught at a division of Fuller Theological Seminary—the School of World Mission. Opposition to it came mostly from theology professors connected with the seminary proper. For most of these historical details I am indebted to Chuck Kraft (interview: June 11, 1999). Wimber assumed de facto leadership of the Vineyard in 1982. For useful accounts of the Vineyard, see Donald E. Miller, *Reinventing American Protestantism* (Berkeley: University of California Press, 1997), pp. 44–51; and Mark A. Shibley, *Resurgent Evangelicalism in the United States* (Columbia: University of South Carolina Press, 1996), pp. 83–92. On Wimber's influence within evangelical exorcism circles, see C. Peter Wagner, "Introduction," in C. Peter Wagner and F. Douglas Pennoyer (eds.), *Wrestling with Dark Angels* (Ventura, Calif.: Regal Books, 1990), pp. 6–9. (In the same volume, see also John Wimber's "Power Evangelism: Definitions and Directions," pp. 13–42.)

10. See C. Peter Wagner, *The Third Wave of the Holy Spirit* (Ann Arbor, Mich.: Servant Publications, 1988). For the writing of this section I have benefited from conversations with Doris Wagner, Chuck Kraft, Clinton Arnold, and Mark Bubeck.

11. David Powlison, author of *Power Encounters*, claims that there was an "explosion of interest in the therapeutic" among evangelicals in the United States during the early 1980s (interview: August 25, 1999). Much like the population at large, if not quite to the same excess, evangelicals were developing a preoccupation with the self and an expectation of unfettered personal fulfillment. James Davison Hunter (interview: August 27, 1999) likewise claims that

evangelicals on the whole tuned in to the "therapeutic ethos" of the broader culture during the late 1970s and early 1980s. On the "psychologization of morality" among American evangelicals during this period, see Hunter's *American Evangelicalism* (New Brunswick, N.J.: Rutgers University Press, 1983), pp. 97–99; and *Evangelicalism: The Coming Generation* (Chicago: University of Chicago Press, 1987), pp. 64–71.

12. For more extensive discussions of this process, see Richard Ofshe and Ethan Watters, *Making Monsters: False Memories, Psychotherapy, and Sexual Hysteria* (New York: Scribner, 1994); Debbie Nathan and Michael Snedeker, *Satan's Silence: Ritual Abuse and the Making of a Modern American Witch Hunt* (New York: Basic Books, 1995); and Mark Pendergrast, *Victims of Memory: Incest Accusations and Shattered Lives* (Hinesburg, Vt.: Upper Access, 1995).

13. See E. S. Rose, "Surviving the Unbelievable," *Ms.* (January/February 1993), pp. 40–45.

14. Hammond laid out this scenario at the Fourth Annual Eastern Regional Meeting on Abuse and Multiple Personality (June 25–29, 1992). For a fuller discussion of the conspiracy theories of these leading MPD therapists, see Mark Pendergrast, *Victims of Memory*, pp. 191–93; Richard Ofshe and Ethan Watters, *Making Monsters*, pp. 187–93, 237–40; and Jeffrey S. Victor, *Satanic Panic: The Creation of a Contemporary Legend* (Chicago: Open Court, 1993), pp. 294–95. The CIA did in fact undertake experiments in mind control during the Cold War, but these experiments seem to have been wildly unsuccessful. See John Marks, *The Search for the Manchurian Candidate* (New York: Times Books, 1979).

15. Lauren Stratford, *Satan's Underground* (Eugene, Oreg.: Harvest House, 1988); Gretchen Passantino, Bob Passantino, and Jon Trott, "Satan's Sideshow," *Cornerstone* 18, 90 (1990): 24–28; "Statement Regarding *Satan's Underground,*" letter from the publisher, Harvest House, January 26, 1990. See also Jeffrey Victor, *Satanic Panic*, pp. 99–100.

16. Frederick Crews, *The Memory Wars: Freud's Legacy in Dispute* (New York: NYREV, 1995); Elizabeth Loftus and Katherine Ketcham, *The Myth of Repressed Memory* (New York: St. Martin's Griffin, 1994); and Lawrence Wright, *Remembering Satan* (New York: Knopf, 1994). On the False Memory Syndrome Foundation, see Debbie Nathan and Michael Snedeker, *Satan's Silence*, pp. 237–39. Jeffrey Victor *(Satanic Panic*, pp. 7–24) argues that the satanism scares of the 1980s and 1990s fit the pattern of what folklorists call a contemporary (or urban) legend. On the phenomenon of urban legends more generally, see Jan Harold Brunvand, *The Vanishing Hitchhiker* (New York: Norton, 1981).

17. On "spiritual warfare," see C. Peter Wagner, *Warfare Prayer* (Ventura, Calif.: Regal, 1992); C. Peter Wagner (ed.), *Breaking Strongholds in Your City* (Ventura, Calif.: Regal, 1993); C. Peter Wagner, *Confronting the Powers*

(Ventura, Calif.: Regal, 1996); and C. Peter Wagner and F. Douglas Pennoyer (eds.), *Wrestling with Dark Angels*. For a highly critical assessment of the "spiritual warfare" movement, see Robert J. Priest, Thomas Campbell, and Bradford A. Mullen, "Missiological Syncretism: The New Animistic Paradigm," in Edward Rommen (ed.), *Spiritual Power and Missions* (Pasadena, Calif.: William Carey Library, 1995), pp. 143–68. For a general discussion, see Harvey Cox, *Fire from Heaven,* pp. 281–97.

18. For an impressively balanced and sophisticated treatment of issues raised in this chapter, see Clinton E. Arnold, *3 Crucial Questions About Spiritual Warfare* (Grand Rapids, Mich.: Baker Books, 1997). I am also indebted to Doug Hayward, a colleague of Arnold and Kelley at Biola University, for his insightful comments. James G. Friesen's writings on multiple personality/dissociative identity disorder have been enormously influential within both evangelical and charismatic exorcism circles. See his *Uncovering the Mystery of MPD* (Nashville: Thomas Nelson, 1991); and *More than Survivors* (Nashville: Thomas Nelson, 1992). In recent years a number of psychologists, evangelical and otherwise, have attempted to assess the therapeutic benefits of treating cases of MPD/DID with exorcism. See, for example, Christopher H. Rosik, "When Discernment Fails: The Case for Outcome Studies on Exorcism," *Journal of Psychology and Theology* 25, 3 (1997): 354–63; and Dennis L. Bull, Joan W. Ellason, and Colin A. Ross, "Exorcism Revisited: Positive Outcomes with Dissociative Identity Disorder," *Journal of Psychology and Theology* 26, 2 (1998): 188–96.

19. Neil T. Anderson, *The Bondage Breaker* (Eugene, Oreg.: Harvest House, 1993), pp. 55, 77, 101–8, 169, 188–212, 234. See also Anderson's *Released from Bondage* (Nashville, Thomas Nelson, 1993); and *Freedom in Christ* (Ventura, Calif.: Regal, 1995). For a hard-hitting evangelical critique of Anderson's theology and approach, see Elliot Miller, "The Bondage Maker," *Christian Research Journal* (July–September 1998), pp. 17–22, 26, 43–44; and Elliot Miller, "Spiritual Warfare and the 'Truth Encounter,' " *Christian Research Journal* 21, 2 (1998), pp. 10–20. I am using *The Bondage Breaker* as my principal exhibit not because it makes an especially easy target. It's actually near the head of the class in current evangelical deliverance literature. Despite my criticisms, it's more balanced than many of its competitors, and it's occasionally blessed with significant psychological insight. For a wry take on the recovery movement in general, see Wendy Kaminer, *I'm Dysfunctional, You're Dysfunctional* (Reading, Mass.: Addison-Wesley, 1992).

CHAPTER FOURTEEN

1. Here again I have disguised real-life identities.

2. Leanne Payne, *Restoring the Christian Soul* (Grand Rapids, Mich.: Baker Books, 1991), pp. 175, 180. See also her *Healing Homosexuality* and *The Broken Image*, both published by Baker Books in 1996. For a general discussion of ministries of this sort, see John Leland and Mark Miller, "Can Gays 'Convert'?" *Newsweek* (August 17, 1998), pp. 47–52.

3. I spoke with Mario Bergner by phone several months afterward. He struck me (in every respect) as a gracious and compassionate man.

4. In Matthew 23, Jesus delivers a speech denouncing the scribes and Pharisees. The verses in question (29–33) read as follows: "Woe to you, scribes and Pharisees, hypocrites! For you build the tombs of the prophets and decorate the graves of the righteous, and you say, 'If we had lived in the days of our ancestors, we would not have taken part with them in shedding the blood of the prophets.' Thus you testify against yourselves that you are descendants of those who murdered the prophets. Fill up, then, the measure of your ancestors. You snakes, you brood of vipers! How can you escape being sentenced to hell?"

5. Quite a few evangelical deliverance ministers are former missionaries. Some claim to have received their first exposure to demons and demonization while in the mission field.

6. For lucid discussion of these issues, see David Powlison, *Power Encounters* (Grand Rapids, Mich.: Baker Books, 1995); and Clinton E. Arnold, *3 Crucial Questions about Spiritual Warfare* (Grand Rapids, Mich.: Baker Books, 1997), pp. 32–37.

CHAPTER FIFTEEN

1. I have taken special effort throughout this chapter to disguise real-life identities. For the English-language version of the Roman Catholic exorcism ritual that was officially in use throughout most of my research, see Philip T. Weller, *The Roman Ritual, Volume 2* (Milwaukee: Bruce Publishing, 1952), pp. 160–229. A slightly different version (which is the one employed here) may be found in Malachi Martin's *Hostage to the Devil* (New York: Reader's Digest Press/Thomas Y. Crowell Company, 1976), pp. 459–72.

CHAPTER SIXTEEN

1. Much of my information in this chapter is drawn from confidential sources.

2. See John J. Nicola, *Diabolical Possession and Exorcism* (Rockford, Ill.: Tan Books, 1974); and Corrado Balducci, *The Devil,* translated by Jordan Aumann, O.P. (New York: Alba House, 1990), pp. 123–51. For more general discussions, see Richard J. Woods, O.P., "The Possession Problem," *Catholic Mind* (September 1973): 38–50; Patrick Dondelinger, "The Practice of Exorcism in the Church," *Concilium* 5 (1998): 58–67; Juan B. Cortés, S.J., and Florence M. Gatti, *The Case Against Possessions and Exorcisms* (New York: Vantage Press, 1975); T. K. Oesterreich, *Possession: Demoniacal and Other* (New York: University Books, 1966); and Herbert Thurston, *Ghosts and Poltergeists* (Chicago: J. H. Crehan, 1954).

3. On the new rite, see John Tagliabue, "Vatican's Revised Exorcism Rite Affirms Existence of Devil," *New York Times* (January 27, 1999), p. A16.

4. Many of the Catholic exorcists I met hold something in common with evangelical deliverance ministers. They, too, believe that there has been an alarming rise of late in satanic and occult activity throughout the Western world, and that this has resulted in increasing numbers of people falling prey to demonic influence. For an interview with Father Gabriele Amorth, the exorcist of the Diocese of Rome, on this topic, see Stefano M. Paci, "The Devil of Fashion," *30 Days* (January 1996), pp. 18–21. See also Rossana Ansuini, "Turin Triples Its Exorcists," *30 Days* (January 1989), p. 61. (The January 1989 issue of *30 Days* features several additional articles on satanism and the occult.) For an American Catholic view, see Father Joseph F. Brennan, *The Kingdom of Darkness* (Lafayette, La.: St. Genevieve Church, 1993). Father Brennan, who is based in Lafayette, and several confidential New Orleans–based informants helped clarify my thinking in this area. See also John L. Allen, Jr., "Exorcism: Ancient Ministry Attracts New Practitioners," *National Catholic Reporter* (September 1, 2000), pp. 5–7.

CONCLUSION

1. See, for example, Andrew Delbanco, *The Death of Satan* (New York: Farrar Straus & Giroux, 1995).

2. See Margaret Talbot, "The Placebo Prescription," *New York Times Magazine* (January 9, 2000), pp. 34–39, 44, 58–60.

3. See Henry K. Lee, "Five Women Accused of Murder in East Bay Ritual Death," *San Francisco Chronicle* (March 17, 1995); Ann W. O'Neill, "Two Men Get Prison Time in Exorcism Death," *Los Angeles Times* (April 25, 1997); and Michael Cooper, "Mother and Grandmother Charged with Fatally Poisoning Girl," *New York Times* (May 19, 1997). Roman Catholic exorcisms have also sometimes resulted in tragedy. In 1976 a German court of law charged two priest-exorcists with negligent homicide after the death of a university student they had been exorcising. See Felicitas D. Goodman, *The Exorcism of Anneliese Michel* (New York: Doubleday, 1981).

4. See Jessica Kowal, "They Tried to 'Rid Her of Demons,' " *New York Newsday* (January 22, 1998); John T. McQuiston, "Sister of Dead Long Island Teenager Offers Account of Killing in Exorcism," *New York Times* (January 21, 1998); and Andrew Metz and Chau Lam, "Sister Describes Last Hours of Girl They Believed Was Possessed," *New York Newsday* (January 21, 1998). I am grateful to James Dobson for his input on this case.

5. Belief in demons and demonic possession is widespread throughout the world. Such belief, even in the United States, isn't always dependent upon the popular culture industry or some functional equivalent thereof. My central point here is that exorcism-related beliefs took hold within certain sectors of (mainly white) middle-class America only when Hollywood and its allies began spreading the message. Again, there is nothing (to my mind) surprising about this. There seems no limit to the effects of suggestibility on human thought and behavior. We know, for example, that people in general complain of being afflicted by certain physical maladies (such as repetitive-motion disorder) only when these maladies have been publicized by the media. And we also know (on an entirely different front) that people in thirteenth-century Europe claimed to be stigmatized only after popular accounts of the stigmata of St. Francis were published. See Atul Gawande, "The Pain Perplex," *New Yorker* (September 21, 1998), pp. 86–94; and Herbert Thurston, S.J., *The Physical Phenomenon of Mysticism* (Chicago: Henry Regnery, 1952), pp. 120–29. Psychologists Elizabeth Loftus, Giuliana Mazzoni, and Irving Kirsch have recently performed experimental research that directly supports my thesis concerning the power of the media to induce belief in diabolical possession. For a good account of their study, see Ray Rivera, "Demons Usually in the Mind not Body of Victim, Experts Say," *Seattle Times* (October 28, 2000). For a good introduction to the vast literature on exorcism-related belief and practice throughout the world, see Felicitas D. Goodman, *How About Demons?* (Bloomington: Indiana University Press, 1988). For a more extensive treatment of some of these issues, see Michael W. Cuneo, "Of Demons and Hollywood: Exorcism in American Culture," *Studies in Religion/Sciences Religieuses* 27, 4 (1998): 455–65.

index

Abby (film), 285 *n. 1*

Adversary, The (Bubeck), 201–2, 295–96 *n. 7*

Akron Beacon Journal, 105

Alcoholism, 93, 95

Alexian Brothers Hospital, St. Louis, 68–69

Allen, Thomas, 68–69, 70, 287 *n. 5*

Amantini, Candido, 263

America magazine, 11

American culture
  books on or by charismatics, 107–9
  books on exorcism and satanism, xii–xiii, 8–11, 13, 15–20, 41, 50–51, 55, 60, 68–69, 127, 295 *n. 6*
  commercialism and exorcism, 49–50
  ethos of, xiii–xiv
  exorcism and demonology, rise of, and, xi, 13, 15, 16, 49–50, 57–58, 127–28, 138–39, 247, 271–72, 295 *n. 6*, 300 *n. 4*, 301 *n. 5*
  Faith Movement and, 184–86
  film (TV and Hollywood) and exorcism, xii–xiii, 11–12, 13, 41, 49–51, 60, 68, 127, 271, 280–81, 285 *n. 1*, 290 *n. 17*
  as media driven, 55–58, 206–7, 272–73
  pop, xiii, xiv, 49–51, 68–70, 271–72

priest-exorcist as hero in, 5, 59–70

satanic panics of the 1980s, 51–58, 203–9

Satanic Ritual Abuse (SRA), media hype and recovered memories, 206–9

sexual revolution, 4, 119

shopping malls, 184–85

therapeutic ethic and recovery programs, rise of, 125–26, 213, 214, 216

volatility of 1960s and 1970s, 4, 119, 125

Ames, Father Roger, 290 *n. 3*

Amityville Horror, The (Anson), 29

Amityville Horror, The (film), 29

Amorth, Father Gabriele, 266, 300 *n. 4*

Anderson, Neil, 209, 213–14, 215–16, 235, 298 *n. 19*

Anderson, Robert Mapes, 87, 88

Angley, Ernest, 288 *n. 8*

Anson, Jay, 29

Anthony, Ole, 294 *n. 1*

Arnold, Clinton, 210, 296 *n. 10*, 298 *n. 18*

Assembly of God, 89

Association of Christian Therapists (ACT), 144–64

Balducci, Corrado, 291 *n. 2*

Banever, Jennifer, 258–59

Baptist Church, charismatics in, 179. *See also* Hegewisch Baptist Church, IN

Basham, Don, 89–95, 96, 98, 99–100, 104, 105, 107, 289–90 *n. 16*, 290 *n. 2*
  exorcisms performed by, 92–94
  shepherding or social control and, 121–22, 291 *n. 2*

Beattie, Melodie, 223

Bed by the Window, A (Peck), 46

Beloved Ministry, Brea, CA, 290 *n. 1*

Bennett, Dennis, 83, 85, 94

Bergner, Mario, 224–26, 299 *n. 3*

Bermingham, Father Thomas, 6–7, 12, 20, 284 *n. 9*

Beyond the Living (film), 285 *n. 1*

Binding or boxing of demons, 132–37, 170, 235, 292 *n. 5*

Biola University, Talbot School of Theology, 210–11, 298 *n. 18*

Blair, Linda, 10

Blatty, William Peter, xii, 60
  background, 5–6
  The Exorcist (book), 7–10, 60
  The Exorcist (film), xii, 10–15, 20, 47, 60, 127, 139, 146, 201, 280–81, 283 *n. 3*, 283 *n. 4*, 284 *n. 9*, 290 *n. 17*
  research for *The Exorcist*, 6–7, 69

Blessed Trinity Society, 85

Bloy, Francis, 83

Blumhardt, Johann Christoph, 294 *n. 2*

Blumhardt's Battle (Boshold, trans.), 228, 294 *n. 2*

Bondage Breaker, The (Anderson), 213–14, 215–16, 298 *n. 19*

Boogeyman (film), 13, 285 *n. 1*

Boston, physician exorcism, xi

Bowdern, Father William, 69

Bradford, Brick, 105, 290 *n. 17*

Branch, Craig, 294 *n. 1*

Braun, Bennett, 207

Brennan, Betty, 133–37, 292 *n. 6*

Brennan, Father Joseph F., 300 *n. 4*

Brolin, James, 29

Brown, Jim, 94

Bubeck, Mark, 201–2, 231, 295–96 *n. 7*, 296 *n. 10*

Burmeister, Bob, 154–55, 162, 290 *n. 4*

Campion, Father Donald, 11

Can a Christian Have a Demon? (Basham), 107

Case Against Possessions and Exorcisms, The, 13

Catholic News, 11

Chardin, Teilhard de, 18, 283 *n. 4*

Charismatics, 84–86, 88–110, 112–28, 129, 285–86 *n. 2*, 289–90 *n. 16*, 295 *n. 2*. *See also* Deliverance ministries; Pentecostalism
  ACT and, 144
  cults and, 122–23
  discerning demons, 118–28, 156, 159
  Faith Movement and, 186
  style of prayer groups, 114–15
  therapy and, 144–64, 290 *n. 7*

Child, The (film), 285 *n. 1*

Chitwood, Helen, 56

Christian Exorcism Study Group, 291 *n. 2*

Christian Growth Ministries, 122–23

Christian Healing Ministries (CHM), 158–60

Church of Satan, 54, 55

Cirner, Randall, 99

Clark, Eugene, 33

Codependent No More (Beattie), 223

Collins, David and Virginia, 103–4

Coming, The (film), 285 *n. 1*

Commonweal, 20

Cool, Nadean, 144–45

Copeland, Kenneth, 186

Cornerstone magazine, 208

Courage to Heal, The (Bass & Davis), 153, 206

Cox, Harvey, 87

Crews, Frederick, 208

Cross and the Switchblade, The (Wilkerson), 85

Cuneo, Michael W.
  academic study (at Jesuit University), xv

ACT members, meeting with, 144–64
Biola University meetings, 210–12
charismatic groups, experience with, 115–19
deliverance meetings, attendance, 160–62, 167–76
evangelical deliverance ministers interviewed, 227–35
evangelical exorcism attended, 217–22, 295 n. 4
The Exorcist (film), and, xv
LeBar, Father James, meetings, 64–68, 258
MacNutt and Prange meetings, 154–60
Martin, Malachi, interview, 23–24
McAlear and Brennan meetings, 133–37
McKenna, Father Robert, interview, 37–40
observer at deliverance ministry, case of Paul, 73–82, 163–64
observer of Prange's televised exorcism, 293 n. 14
Peck, M. Scott, phone interview, 47–49
Pentecostal exorcisms observed, 288 n. 8
research strategy, xv
Roman Catholic exorcisms observed, 239–56, 257–61, 264–65, 273–76
Scanlan, Michael, interview, 100–101
Sioux City, IA, conference and, 195–200
Spindale visit, and Whaleys, 186–92
Warrens' meeting with, 33–36
Wheaton College conference and healing session, 222–27
Curran, Robert, 31, 32
Curses, 220. *See also* Intergenerational evil or demonism

Dead of Night (film), 285 n. 1
DeFeo, Ronald, 29
Deliver Us from Evil (Basham), 90, 92, 107
Deliverance ministries, 41–42, 48, 57

anti-Catholic positions by, 170–71, 172, 173, 179, 180, 181, 183
approaches taken by, 111, 132
atrocity stories, 184
Basham and Prince, 92–94, 96, 98, 99–100, 105
binding of demons and, 132–37, 170, 292 n. 5
Brennan, Betty, and, 133–37, 292 n. 6
case of Carol, 119–21
case of Paul, 73–82, 163–64
charismatics, demons among, 112–28
charismatics, style of meetings, 114–15
Collins, David and Virginia, and, 103–4
discerning demons and, 118–28, 159
emotional manipulation and, 114–18
Episcopal, 103–5, 129–32
evangelical Protestants and, 198–200, 209–16
group deliverance, xi, 93–94, 167–76, 224–26
healing sessions, examples, 160–62
Hegewisch Baptist Church and, 177–83, 192
Irish, Charles, and, 104–5
Lutheran, 105–6
MacNutt, Francis, and, 96–99, 121
McAlear, Father Richard and, 133–39, 292 n. 6
physical manifestations of demons leaving, 100, 104, 132, 135, 138, 167–76
psychotherapists, use of and, 144–64, 293–94 n. 17
as reflection of cultural hype concerning demons, 1970s, 127–28
rise of, 88–95, 111–12
rite of deliverance, 79–81
Roman Catholic, 100–103, 129–32, 139–42, 292 n. 7, 292 n. 9
"rough-and-ready" school of, 183
Scanlan, Michael, and, 100–101
Shlemon, Barbara, and, 98–99, 132
social control (shepherding) and, 121–25, 291 n. 2
sociological view of, 293 n. 16

Thierer, Mike, and, 167–81
Thomas, Richard, and, 101–3
Vaagenes, Morris, and, 105–6
various ministers, and, 94, 105
Whittaker, Bob, and, 94–95
Wilson, William P., and, 143–44
women in, 121, 124
Word of Faith Fellowship, 183–92
workshop, Buffalo, NY, 167–76
Demonologist, The (Brittle), 30
Demonology and demonic possession
Amityville, Long Island, NY, Lutz
family and, 29–30, 285 *n. 1*
Anderson's levels of demonic bondage,
215
case of "Tom," 147–48
Catholic Church response, belated,
66–68
Catholic Church unresponsive to
increased demands for exorcism, 30,
33, 34, 48, 49, 57, 66–67
charismatics and, 111–28
complete or perfect possession, 20, 38,
93, 102, 107, 157, 161, 255
demonic affliction, 38, 41, 93, 102, 112,
134, 145, 161
demonic infestation, 255
demonic obsession, 255
demonic oppression, 22, 255
deliverance weekend of casting out
demons, Buffalo, NY, 167–76
devil and, 38–39
"Eileen," 38–39
evangelical Protestants and, 198–200,
209–16, 217–26
evidence of existence of, 273–76
in *The Exorcist*, 10
in *Hostage to the Devil*, 17–20
Leopard Man, 40
levitation and, 7, 138, 233, 246,
263–64, 274, 275, 283 *n. 1*
Martin, Malachi, on frequency of
phenomenon, 56
McAlear, cases of and, 137–38
middle class concern with, 41–42,
46–47, 82, 301 *n. 5*

Mount Rainier case, 5–6, 7, 68–69, 283
n. 1
Mueller's experience with, 233–34
Multiple Personality Disorder and, 48,
205, 212, 234, 297 *n. 14*, 298 *n. 18*
Nicola as advisor on, 21, 263
occult and, 229, 249, 261
Ouija boards and, 31
Peck's experience with, 45
personal demons and, 42, 93, 104, 105,
106, 109, 114–15, 167–81, 212–16
poltergeist, 233
in pop culture, xi, xiii, 13, 15, 16,
49–50, 57–58, 127–28, 138–39, 247,
271–72, 301 *n. 5*
public reactions to *The Exorcist* and,
12–13
psychotherapy and, 144–64, 195–216,
217–21
rarity of, 12, 16, 46, 48, 60, 101, 107
"rough-and-ready" school of demon
expulsion, 183
Smurl family, West Pittson, PA, 31–33,
36, 38
stages of possession, Martin's (entry,
erroneous judgments, voluntary
yielding of control, complete or
perfect), 19–20, 283 *n. 4*
symptoms of possession, 154–55
Thomas, Richard, cases witnessed,
101–3
transgenerational or intergenerational,
149–54, 229, 293 *n. 13*
20/20 televised, sanctioned exorcism of
"Gina," 61–63, 65–66, 160, 243
world-wide belief in, 301 *n. 5*
Depression, healing for, 98, 114–15
Devil. *See* Demonology and demonic
possession; Satan
Devil, The (Balducci), 291 *n. 2*
Devil Times Five (film), 13
Devil's Bride, The, 13
Diabolical Possession and Exorcism, 13
Different Drum, The (Peck), 46
Dobson, James, 301 *n. 4*
Dodge, Florence, 85

Dominicans, 96, 99
Downs, Hugh, 61, 62
Driving Out the Devils, 13
Duquesne University, 85

Ellenberger, John D., 295 *n. 5*
Entity, The (film), 285 *n. 1*
Epilepsy, 93, 143
Episcopal Charismatic Fellowship
   (ECF), 105
Episcopal Church
   charismatics in, 84–85, 103, 116–18,
      290 *n. 3*
   deliverance ministries, 103–5, 131–32
   exorcisms, xii
   sacramental life and exorcism, 130
   St. Mark's, Van Nuys, CA, 83
Evangelicalism. *See* Protestant
   denominations
Evans, Leonard, 94
Evans, Pete, 187
Evil, 10, 43, 44–45, 47, 49, 63, 148,
      254–55, 268, 274
   intergenerational, 149–54, 229, 293 *n. 13*
Evil Dead, The (film), 285 *n. 1*
Exodus 20:5, 150
Exorcism. *See also* Deliverance ministries
   Archdiocese of Chicago, 259–60
   Archdiocese of New York, 21, 22, 23,
      60–61, 258
   availability of, 270
   Basham's, 92–94
   Blatty's *The Exorcist,* influence of, 27,
      60, 127, 139, 146, 201, 272
   benefits of, xiii–xiv, 144–64, 195–98,
      273, 277–78
   Burmeister's, 154–55
   charismatics and, 111–28, 155. *See also*
      Deliverance ministries
   contacting exorcists, 28
   deliverance ministry, case of Paul,
      73–82
   fatalities and, 279–80, 301 *n. 3,* 301 *n. 4*
   "fireworks," 248–49, 273
   increase in number of, 27, 270–71
   Graves's, 217–22

Italian, 265
Jesus and, 90, 271, 289 *n. 11,* 289 *n. 12,*
      299 *n. 4*
Martin's *Hostage to the Devil* and
      demand for, xiii, 15–25, 56, 63, 78,
      127, 139, 159, 231, 272
   maverick priests and clandestine, 28,
      30–31
   McAlear's, of woman, 138
   McKenna's, of "Eileen," 38–39
   McKenna's, of farmer, Warren, MA,
      35
   McKenna's, of Leopard Man, 40
   McKenna's, *PrimeTime Live,* 258–59
   Pentecostal and, 88, 288 *n. 8,* 288–89
      n. 9, 289 *n. 16*
   physical manifestations of demons
      leaving, 100, 104, 132, 135, 138,
      167–76
   Prange's, 156–57, 293 *n. 14*
   PrimeTime Live televised, 258–59
   Prince's, 92–94
   Protestant, xi–xii, xiv–xv, 178–83, 201,
      217–26, 234–35, 294 *n. 2*
   Roman Catholic, xi, xii, xiv, 61–63, 65,
      138, 140–41, 239–56, 257–61,
      265–66, 273–76, 291 *n. 2,* 301 *n. 3*
   Roman Catholic, rite of, 12, 16, 63–64,
      66, 130, 140–41, 243–45, 248, 256,
      265, 271, 299 *n. 1*
   Rome, chief exorcist and meeting of
      International Association of
      Exorcists, 266, 300 *n. 4*
   "rough-and-ready" school of demon
      expulsion, 183
   Satanism scares and revitalizing of, 57
   stages of exorcism, Martin's (pretense,
      breakpoint, clash, expulsion), 19–20,
      283 *n. 4*
   success of, 273
   teaching tapes on, 201, 295–96 *n. 7*
   therapeutic use of, xiii–xiv, 144–64,
      195–98
   Thomas's, 102–3
   20/20 televised, of "Gina," 61–63, 65, 243
   Wilson's, 143–44

Exorcism: Fact, Not Fiction, 13

Exorcist, The (Blatty), 7–8, 47, 60, 295 *n. 6*
  Karras, Damien, as hero-priest, 8–10,
    264, 268–69
  Merrin, Father Lancaster, as hero-
    priest, 9–10, 283 *n. 4*
  levitation scene, source for, 263
  reviews, 11
  source of, Mount Rainier possession
    case, 6–7, 16, 283 *n. 1*
  story line, 8–10
  success of, 8

Exorcist, The (film), xii, 10, 20, 47, 60,
    127, 139, 146, 201, 280–81, 283 *n. 3,*
    283 *n. 4,* 284 *n. 9,* 290 *n. 17*
  sequels, 41, 285 *n. 1*

Faith Movement, 184–86, 294 *n. 2*
False Memory Syndrome Foundation,
    208
Farmer, Joshua, 188, 189–91
Farmer, Ray, 188, 189–91
Fenton, Father Francis, 36–37
Final Conclave, The (Martin), 17
Fort Wayne Bible College, 230
Foundation for Community
    Encouragement, 46
Franciscan University, 100
Frank, Jerome, 162
Freedom in Christ Ministries, 209
Friedkin, William, 10
Friesen, James G., 298 *n. 18*
Fuller Theological Seminary, course on
    "Signs, Wonders, and Church
    Growth," 202–3, 296 *n. 9*

Gettysburg, PA, Susek Evangelistic
    Association, spiritual warfare
    conference, 295 *n. 4*
Ghost Hunters (Warren), 31, 33
Good Against Evil (film), 13, 285 *n. 1*
Goodwin, Father Fred, 290 *n. 3*
Gospel Evangel, 295–96 *n. 7*
Grand Rapids Baptist Seminary, 231,
    295–96 *n. 7*
Graves, Donald, 217–22

Greenfield, Jeff, 62
Groeschel, Father Benedict, 21–23, 48,
    133, 137

Hagin, Kenneth, 184, 185–86
Halloran, Rev. Walter, 68–69
Hammond, Cory, 207, 297 *n. 14*
Hammond, Frank and Ida Mae, 107–9
Harper, Michael, 99
Haunted, The (Curran), 31
Haunted, The (TV movie), 31, 285 *n. 1*
Hayward, Doug, 298 *n. 18*
Healing (MacNutt), 109–10, 143
Healing, faith and miraculous, 88, 97–99,
    109–10, 146–54, 290 *n. 7*
  cultural anthropology and, 152, 293
    n. 16
  evangelical, 217–26
  Faith Movement and, 185–86
  harm of patient and, 163–64, 279–80
  placebo effect, 277–78
  therapy and therapeutic benefits,
    155–62, 277, 279. *See also* Therapy,
    exorcism and deliverance ministries
  transgenerational, 149–54
Healing the Family Tree (McAll), 149
Heckle, Father Dean, 290 *n. 3*
Hegewisch Baptist Church, IN, 177–83,
    192, 201, 294 *n. 2*
Higgins, Monsignor George, 15
Hinn, Benny, 186
Hochstetler, Dean, 201, 227–30, 233–34,
    235, 236, 295–96 *n. 7*
Holiness-Pentecostal Tradition, The (Synan),
    288–89 *n. 9*
Homosexuality, 224–26
Hostage to the Devil (Martin), xiii, 15–25,
    56, 63, 78, 127, 139, 159, 231, 272
  author's caveat in, 16
  cases of demonic possession reported
    in, 17–20
  Peck, M. Scott, and, 43, 47–48, 231
Hudson River State Hospital for the
    Insane, 64, 258
Hunter, James Davison, 296–97 *n. 11*
Hux, Clete, 294 *n. 1*

In a Different Voice (Gilligan), 153
Insanity, demons and, 93
Inside Edition, 68–69, 183, 186
Intergenerational evil or demonism,
    149–54, 229, 293 *n. 13*
International Association of Exorcists,
    266
International Center for Biblical
    Counseling (ICBC), 198–200, 209,
    231
International Church of the Foursquare
    Gospel, 89
International Society for the Study of
    Multiple Personality Disorder, 207
Irish, Charles, 104
Italy, exorcisms in, 265

Jarriel, Tom, 61, 62
Jesuits
    America magazine, review of *The
        Exorcist*, 11
    Blatty and, 6
    demon possession and, 146
    exorcism, Washington, DC, and, 6–7,
        68–69
    Malachi Martin and, 14–15
    Thomas, Richard, and, 101, 102
Jesuits, The (Martin), 17, 283 *n. 3*
Jesus, exorcisms and demon-expulsion
    by, 90, 271, 289 *n. 11*, 289 *n. 12*, 299
    n. 4
John XXIII, 14
Judas Priest band, 55

Kael, Pauline, 11
Kaiser, Robert Blair, 15
Kaplan, Stephen, 29, 285 *n. 1*
Keifer, Ralph, 85
Kelley, John, 210–12
Keys of This Blood, The (Martin), 17
Kidder, Margot, 29
Klimek, Joseph, 258–59
Koch, Kurt, 201, 211, 228, 231, 295 *n. 6*
Koppel, Ted, 63
Kraft, Charles "Chuck," 202, 231, 296
    n. 9, 296 *n. 10*

Kuhlman, Kathryn, 99
Kung Fu Exorcist (film), 13, 285 *n. 1*
Landau, Jon, 11
LeBar, Father James, 61, 63, 259, 287
    n. 3
    author's meetings with, 64–68, 258
LeFranz, Father Emile, 260
Leo XIII, 130
Leopard Man, 40
Levitation, 7, 138, 233, 246, 263–64, 274,
    275, 283 *n. 1*
Lindsey, Hal, 201
Loftus, Elizabeth, 208
Loyola University, 15
Luke
    4:31–37, 90
    8:26–39, 289 *n. 12*
    9:1–2, 98
    10:17–19, 80, 91
    13:10–17, 90
Lussier, Lou, 139–40
Lutheran Church, 99, 105, 290 *n. 4*, 294
    n. 2. See also Prange, Erwin;
    Vaagenes, Morris
Lutz, George and Kathleen, 29–30

MacLaine, Shirley, 283 *n. 3*
MacNutt, Francis, 96–99, 109–10, 131,
    132, 139, 141, 144, 154, 158–60, 228
Making Monsters (Ofshe & Watters), 286
    n. 9, 297 *n. 12*
Mark
    1:21–28, 90
    5:1–20, 289 *n. 12*
    7:24–30, 90
    16:15–18, 91
Martin, Malachi, xiii, 70, 139, 181, 228,
    231, 284 *n. 6*
    author's interview with, 23–24
    background, 14–15, 17
    exorcisms attended, 24, 57
    fact and fiction blended in writings of,
        17, 21, 283 *n. 3*
    Groeschel's evaluation of, 23
    Hostage to the Devil and, 15–16, 17–20,
        23–24, 139, 159–60

lifestyle, 23
  on *Oprah,* 55–57, 157
  Peck, M. Scott, and, 47–48
  Prange, Erwin, and, 157
  stages of possession and exorcism,
    19–20, 283 *n. 4*
Matthew
  8:16, 90
  8:28–32, 90–91
  12:29, 292 *n. 5*
  15:21–28, 90
  23:29–33, 229, 299 *n. 2*
Matthews, Victor, 231, 295–96 *n. 7*
McAlear, Father Richard, 133–39, 292 *n. 6*
McAll, Kenneth, 149
McBrien, Father Richard, 60, 63
McClung, L. Grant, Jr., 288–89 *n. 9*
McFadden, Cynthia, 259
McKenna, Father Robert, 32, 35, 36–40
  author's interview with, 37–40
  case of Eileen and, 38–39
  exorcisms by, 37–38
  Leopard Man and, 40
  ORCM and, 36–37, 39
  PrimeTime Live televised exorcism,
    258–59
  Warrens and, 39, 68
Mennonite Church, 295–96 *n. 7*
  exorcist, 227–30
Michelle Remembers (Smith & Pazder), 55,
    204–5, 206
Miranda, Charity, 279–80, 301 *n. 4*
Moore, David, 288–89 *n. 9*
Morehead, John, 294 *n. 1*
Mount Rainier possession case, 5–6, 7,
    68–69, 283 *n. 1*
Mueller, Barbara, 232
Mueller, Bob, 232–35
Multiple Personality Disorder (MPD),
    48, 205, 212, 234, 297 *n. 14,* 298 *n. 18*
Murray, John Courtney, 15
My Demon Lover (film), 285 *n. 1*

Nathan, Debbie, 208, 286 *n. 9,* 297 *n. 12*
National Review, 20
Neo-Pentecostalism. *See* Charismatics

New Covenant magazine, 158, 292 *n. 4*
New York Times, 20, 44
New Yorker, 11
Newsweek, 20, 83, 84
Nicola, Father John, 20–21, 66, 263–64,
    268
Night Child (film), 285 *n. 1*
Nightline, 62–63
North Heights Lutheran Church, St.
    Paul, MN, 106
Northern Ohio Christian Conference, 104

O'Connor, John Cardinal, 60–61, 287
    n. 3
O'Malley, Father William, 12–13, 20
"Of Demons and Hollywood: Exorcism
    in American Culture" (Cuneo), 301
Ofshe, Richard, 208, 286 *n. 9,* 297 *n. 12*
Olson, Kenneth C., 145
Oprah Winfrey Show, The, Malachi Martin,
    Chitwood, and Prange on, 55–57,
    157
Orthodox Roman Catholic Movement
    (ORCM), 36–37
Osbourne, Ozzy, 53, 60
Ouija boards, 30, 31
Our Lady of the Rosary Chapel,
    Monroe, CT, 37, 39

Painted Black (Raschke), 286 *n. 14*
Pastoral Care Ministries, 223
Paul VI, 15
Payne, Leanne, 223–24, 299 *n. 2*
Pazder, Lawrence, 204
Peck, M. Scott, 42–49
  author phone interview with, 47–49
  background, 43
  demonic possession and exorcism,
    personal experiences with, 45, 48
  exorcist as hero and, 45–46
  marriage to Lily Ho, 43
  Martin, Malachi, and, 43, 47–48, 231
  People of the Lie and, 42–43, 44–45, 46,
    47, 48, 142–43
  proposed institute to study exorcism,
    49

Penn-Lewis, Jessie, 228, 295–96 *n. 7*
Pentecostalism, 41–42, 83–95, 129, 288
    n. 3
  "baptism in the Holy Spirit," 42, 83,
    86, 115
  Camp Farthest Out, 97
  charismatics in, 84–86, 89–110, 129,
    289–90 *n. 16*
  cultural acceptance of, 129
  deliverance ministries, 41–42, 48, 57,
    73–82, 88–95, 129–30
  demonism and, 88–89, 92
  exorcisms and, 88, 288 *n. 8,* 288–89
    n. 9, 289 *n. 16*
  mainline, middle-class and, 85–88, 288
    n. 3
  origin of, 84, 86, 88, 288 *n. 2*
  Roman Catholic Neo-, 85–86, 288 *n. 5*
People of the Lie (Peck), 42–43, 44–45, 46,
  47, 48, 142–43, 153, 223
People of Praise prayer community,
  South Bend, IN, 99
Peretti, Frank, 68, 202, 287 *n. 4,* 295–96
  n. 7
Pigs in the Parlor (Hammond), 107–9, 126,
  291 *n. 5*
Plessix Gray, Francine du, 20
Poloma, Margaret, 289–90 *n. 16*
Poltergeist, 233
Pontifical Biblical Institute, 14
Possessed (Allen), 68–69, 287 *n. 5*
Possessed (TV movie), 287 *n. 5*
Possessed, The (film), 13, 285 *n. 1*
Possession. *See* Demonology and
  demonic possession
Power of Penance (Scanlan), 100
Powlison, David, 199, 296–97 *n. 11*
Prange, Erwin, 55–56, 94, 99, 106, 107,
  154–58, 293 *n. 14*
  Martin, Malachi, and, 157
Prayer of deliverance, 22
Presbyterian Church (U.S.A.), 94–95, 105
Prescott, Peter, 20
PrimeTime Live televised exorcism, 258–59
Prince, Derek, 92–93, 96, 98, 99–100,
  104, 105, 289–90 *n. 16,* 290 *n. 2*

shepherding or social control and,
  121–22, 291 *n. 2*
Proctor & Gamble, 54
Protestant denominations. *See also*
  Charismatics; Neo-Pentecostalism;
  specific denominations
  Christian psychotherapists and,
    195–200
  deliverance ministries, 41–42, 48, 57,
    73–83, 88–95
  evangelical deliverance ministers,
    227–35, 299 *n. 5*
  evangelical deliverance ministries and
    exorcism, 57–58, 178–83, 200–4,
    209–16, 217–22
  evangelical strategies against
    supernatural evil, 209
  evangelicals, 295 *n. 2*
  exorcisms by, xi–xii, xiv–xv, 178–83,
    201, 217–26, 234–35, 295 *n. 4*
  ICBC and, 198–200
  number of evangelical exorcism
    ministries, 209
  opposition to evangelical deliverance
    ministries, 235–36, 296 *n. 8*
  popular culture, influence of, 58, 201–4
  Wheaton College conference and
    healing session on sexual perversity,
    222–27
Psalm 34:17, 80

Raphaël, Sally Jessy, 55, 160
Raschke, Carl, 286 *n. 14*
Recovered memory cases, 52, 54, 204–9,
  211
Renewal and the Powers of Darkness
  (Suenens), 140
Restea, John, 295 *n. 5*
Restoring the Christian Soul (Payne), 224
Reznikoff, Marvin, 293–94 *n. 17*
Rhema Bible Training Center, 184
Rhine, Joseph B., 263
Rivera, Geraldo, 55
Road Less Traveled, The (Peck), 43–44
Rockstad, Ernest, 201, 230, 295–96 *n. 7*
Rogers, Don, 295 *n. 5*

Rolling Stone, 11

Roman Catholic Church
  America, number of members, 258
  appointment of exorcists, 1990s, 258
  Archdiocese of Chicago and exorcisms, 259–60
  Archdiocese of New York and exorcisms, 21, 22, 23, 60–61, 258, 287 *n. 3*
  Blatty's impact on perception of, 5
  Cardinal O'Connor's sermon on Satanism, 60–61, 287 *n. 3*
  charismatics in, 85–86, 99–103, 123, 129–30, 131–32, 139–42. *See also* MacNutt, Francis,
  deliverance ministries in, 100–103, 131–32, 139–42, 292 *n. 7,* 292 *n. 9*
  evaluation of cases of possession, xii, 21, 33, 65, 240, 253–54, 261–64
  exorcisms by, xi, xii, xiv, 61–63, 65, 138, 140–41, 239–56, 257–61, 273–76, 291 *n. 2,* 301 *n. 3*
  exorcist association formed, 266
  exorcists, official, 27, 59, 66, 67–68, 239–56, 257–59, 260–61, 265–66, 300 *n. 4*
  exorcists, quasi-official, 259–61
  New Orleans, exorcist-without-portfolio, 260
  Nicola, Father John, as investigator, 263–64
  Pentecostals, 85–86, 288 *n. 5*
  psychiatrists as consultants to, 240–53, 262–64
  reactions to *The Exorcist* and, 11–12
  relevance of, and exorcisms, 6, 10
  right-wing fringes of, 27–28
  rite of exorcism (Roman Ritual of Exorcism), 12, 16, 63–64, 66, 130, 140–41, 231, 243–45, 248, 256, 261–62, 271, 299 *n. 1*
  rite of exorcism, revised 1999, 265, 300 *n. 3*
  Rome, chief exorcist of, 266
  sacramental life and exorcism, 130
  Second Vatican Council and, 4, 5, 37, 60

  training program for exorcists proposed, 267
  20/20 televised, sanctioned exorcism of "Gina," 61–63, 65, 160, 243
  traditionalist movement, 37, 285 *n. 6*
  unresponsive to increased demands for exorcism, 30, 33, 34, 48, 49, 57, 66–67

Roman Catholic priesthood
  American negative view of priest-exorcist, 267–68
  contemporary problems of, 3
  demonic affliction and, 134
  exorcist guild formed, 266–67
  exorcist as hero, 5–6, 8, 10, 19, 45–46, 59–70, 247, 267, 268–69
  exorcists, official, 67–68, 239–56, 257–61, 266
  mavericks as exorcists, 27, 28, 35, 259
  Father Robert McKenna as, 32
  source of problems in, 4

Rosemary's Baby (film), 51
Ross, Colin, 207
Rush Presbyterian-St. Luke's Medical Center, Chicago, 207

St. Francis Seminary, Loretto, PA, 100
St. Luke's Episcopal Church, Akron, OH, 104
St. Mark's Episcopal Church, Van Nuys, CA, 83, 84
St. Philip's Cathedral, Atlanta, 103
St. Xavier Church, St. Louis University, 69
Salvation and Deliverance Temple, Harlem, NY, 288 *n. 8*
Sanford, Agnes, 97
Satan
  belief in, unexpected, 270–71
  charismatics and, 113
  new Mass and, 39
  possession and, 93, 157
  possession of "Eileen" and, 38–39
  possession witnessed by F. Scott Peck and, 45
Satan Is Alive and Well on Planet Earth (Lindsey), 201

Satanism, 51–58
  Cardinal O'Connor's sermon on,
    60–61, 287 *n. 3*
  conspiracies, 195–216, 231–32
  exaggerated claims of, 54, 286 *n. 14*
  fraud and, 207–9, 231
  heavy metal rock music and, 53, 60
  McMartin Preschool, 52
  panics of the 1980s, 51–58, 203–9, 297
    n. 16
  Proctor & Gamble and, 54
  "recovered memory" cases, 52, 54,
    204–9, 211
  SRA (Satanic Ritual Abuse), 151,
    195–200, 203–9, 232
Satan's Silence (Nathan & Snedeker), 286
  n. 9, 297 *n. 12*
Satan's Underground (Willson), 55, 206, 208
Savelle, Jerry, 186
Sawyer, Diane, 258
Scanlan, Father Michael, 100–101,
  141–42
Second Vatican Council, 4, 22, 37, 60
Selby, Morris, 128
Sewell, Judith, 139, 158
Seymour, William, 84
Sherrill, John, 85
Shlemon, Barbara (Ryan), 98, 132, 290
  n. 1, 291 *n. 3*
Sioux City, International Center for
  Biblical Counseling, conference,
  195–200, 231, 295 *n. 4*
Smith, Ed, 200
Smith, Joan, 240–53, 262
Smith, Michelle, 204–5
Smoke of Satan, The (Cuneo), 285 *n. 6*
Smurl family, 31–33, 36, 38
Snedeker, Michael, 286 *n. 9*, 297 *n. 12*
Social class
  deliverance ministry and, 42, 81–82,
    112, 167–76
  exorcism as middle class phenomenon,
    xii, 41–42
  middle class consumerism, 126
  Neo-Pentecostal movement and,
    41–42, 83–95

Peck and exorcism, respectability of,
  46–47, 142–43
therapeutic ethic and, 125–26, 296–97
  n. 11
upper-middle, baptism in the Holy
  Spirit and St. Mark's Episcopal
  Church, 83
Speaking in tongues (glossolalia), 42, 83,
  84, 85–86, 179, 186, 224–26, 231
Spindale, NC, 188–92
Spiritual warfare, 195, 209–16, 295 *n. 4*,
  295 *n. 5*, 297–98 *n. 17*, 298 *n. 18*
Stone, Jean, 85
Storey, William, 85
Story Behind 'The Exorcist,' The, 13
Suenens, Cardinal Léon-Joseph, 140–42,
  292 *n. 9*
Synan, Vinson, 88, 89, 288–89 *n. 9*

Television
  Amityville haunting, Warrens and, 285
    n. 1
  Fox TV movie, *The Haunted*, 285 *n. 1*
  Inside Edition and *Unsolved Mysteries* on
    Mount Rainier case, 68–69
  Inside Edition on Word of Faith
    Fellowship, 183, 186
  Nightline, 62–63
  pop culture and, 70
  Prange's televised exorcism, WARE-
    TV, 293 *n. 14*
  PrimeTime Live televised exorcism,
    258–59
  talk shows, Satanism discussed on,
    55–58
  20/20, Church sanctioned exorcism of
    "Gina," 61–63, 65, 160, 243
ten Boom, Corrie, 94–95
Therapy, exorcism and deliverance
  ministries
  abreactions, 205
  Arnold, Clinton, and, 210
  benefits of, 161–62, 178, 277–79
  Christian psychotherapists and,
    195–200, 203, 209–16, 293–94 *n. 17*

deliverance ministry group weekend
session, 167–76
healing practitioners and sessions,
147–64, 217–22
Kelley, John, 210–12
MacNutt and, 158–60
Multiple Personality Disorder (MPD)
and, 48, 205, 212, 234, 297 *n. 14,* 298
n. 18
Peck's book and, 142–43
placebo effect, 277–78
Prange and, 154–58
"recovered memory" cases, 52, 54,
204–9, 211
rise parallel with twelve step, recovery,
and codependency programs,
212–16, 298 *n. 19*
Satanism scares and, 203–9
switching behavior, 205
transgenerational or intergenerational
healing, 149–54, 229, 293 *n. 13*
Wilson's use of, 143–44
Therapeutic ethic, rise of, 125–26, 213,
214, 216, 296–97 *n. 11*
They Speak with Other Tongues (Sherrill),
85
Thierer, Mike, 167–81
This Present Darkness (Peretti), 295–96 *n. 7*
Thomas, Father Richard, 101–3, 107, 143
Tilton, Robert, 183, 186
Time, 83, 84
Trinity Foundation, 187
Trinity International University, 230
Tyson, Tommy, 97

Unger, Merrill, 201, 211, 295 *n. 6*
U.S. Catholic Conference, Division of
Film and Broadcasting, 11

Vaagenes, Morris, 105–6, 122–23
Vineyard Christian Fellowship, 202, 296
n. 9

Wagner, C. Peter, 202, 209, 236
"third wave of the Holy Spirit" and, 203
Wagner, Doris, 296 *n. 10*

Wallace, Rob, 62–63
Walters, Barbara, 61, 62
War on the Saints (Penn-Lewis), 228,
295–96 *n. 7*
Warner, Eleanor, 230–32
Warner, Timothy, 229–32, 236, 295–96 *n. 7*
Warren, Ed and Lorraine, 28–36
Amityville case and fame of, 29–30,
285 *n. 1*
author's meeting with, 33–36
exorcism of Leopard Man, 40
as exorcism brokers, 30–31, 35, 36, 37,
39
Fox TV movie, *The Haunted,* and, 285 *n. 1*
Smurl family and, 31–33
Werewolf, 68
Washington Post, 5–6, 7, 44
Watters, Ethan, 286 *n. 9,* 297 *n. 12*
Weakland, Bishop Rembert, 139
Werewolf (Warren), 68
Whaley, Jane and Sam, 183–84, 189,
191–92
Wheaton College conference and healing
session on sexual perversity, 222–27
Whittaker, Bob, 94–95, 96
Whyte, H. A. Maxwell, 93, 104, 289 *n. 16*
Wilkerson, David, 85
Willson, Laurel, 208
Wilson, William P., 143–44
Wimber, John, 202–3, 231, 296 *n. 9*
Winfrey, Oprah, 55–57
Women
charismatic, 153
deliverance movement and, 121, 124
exorcisms of, 234
"intergenerational" evil and, 153
Word of Faith Fellowship, Spindale, NC,
183–92, 294 *n. 1*
waiver, releasing church from liability,
187–88
Word of God prayer community, Ann
Arbor, MI, 99, 290 *n. 2*
Worley, Joy, 178
Worley, Win, 178–83, 201, 228

Zion Lutheran Church, IN, 232

MICHAEL CUNEO teaches sociology and anthropology at Fordham University in New York City. His previous books include the highly praised *The Smoke of Satan,* and he has been featured in such publications as the *New York Times* and *Los Angeles Times* as the foremost authority on exorcism in America. He divides his time between New York and Toronto and is currently at work on a true-crime book about a triple homicide in Missouri's Ozarks.